The Global Economy, 1944–2000
The Limits of Ideology

Scott Newton
Senior Lecturer in Modern British and International History,
Cardiff University

A member of the Hodder Headline Group
LONDON
Distributed in the United States of America by
Oxford University Press Inc., New York

First published in Great Britain in 2004 by
Arnold, a member of the Hodder Headline Group,
338 Euston Road, London NW1 3BH

http://www.arnoldpublishers.com

Distributed in the United States of America by
Oxford University Press Inc.
198 Madison Avenue, New York, NY 10016

British Library Cataloguing in Publication Data
A catalogue record for this book is available from the British Library

Library of Congress Cataloging-in-Publication Data
A catalog record for this book is available from the Library of Congress

ISBN 0 340 76137 7 (hb)
ISBN 0 340 76138 5 (pb)

1 2 3 4 5 6 7 8 9 10

Typeset in 10/12, Sabon by Charon Tec Pvt. Ltd, Chennai, India
Printed and bound in Malta

What do you think about this book? Or any other Arnold title?
Please send your comments to feedback.arnold@hodder.co.uk

No man is an island, entire of itself; every man is a piece of the continent, a part of the main. If a clod be washed away by the sea, Europe is the less, as well as if a promontory were, as well as if a manor of thy friend's or of thine own were: any man's death diminishes me, because I am involved in mankind, and therefore never send to know for whom the bells tolls; it tolls for thee.

John Donne (1573–1632), *Meditation XVII*

CONTENTS

ACKNOWLEDGEMENTS

I would like to thank the School of History and Archaeology at Cardiff University for its financial assistance during the time I worked on *The Global Economy*, and the Arts and Humanities Research Board whose grant enabled me to take research leave in 2002–3 so that I could write it. Emilia Goldoni helped with the collation of documentary and newspaper material. I owe so much to my parents, Charles and Margaret Newton, who brought me up to try and understand the world around me. Above all, thanks are due to my wife, Maria, for her enduring love, encouragement and support. This book is for her.

LIST OF TABLES AND FIGURES

INTRODUCTION

At the end of the twentieth century it was fashionable to talk about the development of 'globalization' – the tendency of capital, whether in the form of multinational manufacturing corporations such as Microsoft, IBM or General Motors, or international banks such as HSBC, to operate across national boundaries. Investors searching for a healthy rate of return moved assets from China to Latin America, while companies produced parts for cars, televisions and computers in a variety of different locations before bringing them all together in one assembly plant. In the world of shipping, in the words of one well-informed commentator, a single vessel could 'be financed, mortgaged, built, registered, owned, managed and insured all in different countries'.[1] Investment became increasingly international: British banks bought property and companies in the United States while firms from Japan (Panasonic and Sony), South Korea (Goldstar) and the USA (Ford) established themselves in regions of the United Kingdom such as South Wales. The revolution in information technology and, above all, the rise of the World Wide Web, encouraged the development of a worldwide market place. A jazz aficionado in London, for example, could not only use a personal computer to browse CD and record catalogues published on the Internet by companies in the USA; he or she could also order and pay for a selection from the other side of the Atlantic simply by pressing a few buttons and entering a credit card number. Such a transaction would bypass all local suppliers and could be effected at any time of the day or night.

If the era of globalization was good for consumers and investors, its benefits were less obvious to governments and producers. In 1992, Britain had been forced out of the European Monetary System by a surge of international financial speculation against sterling: the Conservative government of John Major vainly spent over £4 billion trying to resist the markets. In 1997, a currency crisis started in Thailand and spread to South Korea, Malaysia and Indonesia; capital flight precipitated a Russian default and devaluations in Brazil and Mexico during the course of 1998. Meanwhile, in 1999–2000, the British textile industry faced significant redundancies because Marks & Spencer, hit by falling profitability and demanding shareholders, sought to cut costs by searching for cheaper supplies, many of which came from the Far East.

For many workers the global market meant competing with industries whose prices were so low that the stark alternatives were take less in wages and work longer hours (what a Marxist would call an increase in the rate of exploitation) or become unemployed. It was a fate that had already overtaken hundreds of thousands in British steel manufacturing, coal mining and vehicle production during the previous decade and a half.

Despite the salience of international economic matters, most discussions of them tend to be written for the specialist. Thus Eugene Versluysen's *The Political Economy of International Finance* (1981) discusses multinational banking and the Eurodollar in terms a non-economist would struggle to understand, while the activities of the World Bank and the International Monetary Fund (IMF) feature in Stephen Gill's *American Hegemony and the Trilateral Commission* (1990) – a book more easily appreciated by readers with some background in political science. Few commentators have taken a historical approach; examples are A.L. Kenwood and A.L. Lougheed's *The Growth of the International Economy 1820–2000* (1999), Herman Van der Wee's *Prosperity and Upheaval: the World Economy 1945–1980 (*1987), James Foreman-Peck's *A History of the World Economy: International Economic Relations since 1850* (1983), Sidney Pollard's *The International Economy since 1945* (1997) and Robert Brenner's The economics of global turbulence (1998). Of these, the two most thoughtful and scholarly are the studies by Van der Wee and Brenner. The former, however, has been overtaken by the debt crisis of the 1980s, and by the globalization and financial instability of the 1990s. Brenner's study locates the dynamics of international economic history since 1945 in competition between the advanced capitalist powers. The argument is cogent and supported by numerous statistics. However, its very density, its relative neglect of the political dimension behind the establishment of the postwar international monetary system as well as of themes such as the development of transatlantic economic relations or the struggle for a new international economic order in the 1970s and 1980s, restricts its accessibility to non-economists. Foreman-Peck's account of Bretton Woods and its aftermath runs in parallel with the work of Kenwood and Lougheed. Both books approach the subject largely in terms of institutional development (for example, of the IMF and arrangements for the expansion of international liquidity); they do not dwell on the connection between ideology, politics and the changing policies of international organizations such as the IMF and the World Bank. Meanwhile Brian Tew's *The Evolution of the International Monetary System 1945–88* (1988), is fundamentally a tale of institutional development, which presupposes a state of convertibility and non-discrimination to be natural rather than the product of a specific historical situation – namely the worldwide power of the United States after 1945. Sidney Pollard does root his analysis in the realities of the balance of power, but his coverage amounts to little more than a useful potted history for beginners in the subject.

One of the few texts that not only draws together history, politics and economics but is also accessible to non-specialists is Fred Block's *The Origins of International Monetary Disorder: A Study of United States International Monetary Policy from World War Two to the Present Day* (1977). However, Block covers only the 1945–75 era and focuses on relations between the United States and Europe. Writing from the assumption that the international influence of the United States in the 1970s – buffeted by failure in Vietnam, trade deficits and the rise of alternative power blocs in western Europe and Japan – was shrinking, he assumed the collapse of the postwar order. As we now know, though, the last two decades of the twentieth century witnessed a revival of American power as well as of the liberal capitalism it promoted.

Indeed the liberal tide after 1989 was so strong that it became fashionable to argue, even on the part of one-time Marxists such as Anthony Giddens during his 1998 Reith lectures, that history was tending inexorably in the direction of a world without economic frontiers (globalization) and that the most productive use of capital and labour could only be generated by the complete mobility of these factors.[2] Such projections, although popular among contemporary sociologists and economists, ignore the resilience, even today, of nationalist and radical traditions in Asia, Europe and Latin America, linked to organized labour and peasant movements as well as to local capitalist interests. Neglecting the historical background, these scholars, taking snapshots of the international economy today and using them as the building blocks of theories concerning its long-term future, risk oversimplification and false prophesy. But their version of reality has captured the mind of the public, in part because historians have failed to produce an alternative to existing literature covering the period from the 1940s to the end of the century that is accessible without being oversimplified.

The Global Economy is intended to help make good this deficiency. In doing so it follows a chronological rather than thematic approach to the history of the world economy from the 1940s, and focuses on its evolution from the post-Second World War era of trade and exchange controls to the turn of the century epoch of free capital flows and trade liberalization. It argues that the process was not uncontested but one whose speed altered in response to the balance of forces within and between nation states. Given this concern with how politics, ideology and economic institutions interacted over time to create a global market, this book does not aim to provide an all-inclusive account of how the different regions of the world developed during the second half of the twentieth century. The developing countries and the former Soviet bloc are discussed, but in the context of how and with what results they became integrated into the world economy.

Yet *The Global Economy* does not accept the view that the world is destined to remain locked indefinitely into a free market globalization in which all trade and capital flows are unrestricted: there is an abundance of evidence to demonstrate the impact of national policy choices on international economic development throughout the post-1945 era. These choices determined the shape of European reconstruction after 1945; they influenced the move to neo-liberalism in the 1980s; and they were responsible for helping to plunge globalization into crisis at the end of the twentieth century. If readers finish this book persuaded that humanity is not necessarily destined to be the victim of large impersonal forces and organizations, that people can exercise a degree of control over their own future, it will have succeeded.

◆ New Eras and the Open Door

Globalization reflected the apparent triumph of free market capitalism after a long contest with other forms of political economy. After 1945 one alternative had been characterized by state-led economic planning designed to deliver growth, modernization and flourishing public services. First, the Soviet Union and the eastern European countries within its sphere of influence, then China and developing states anxious to attain independence from former colonial masters in the West, termed their variety of dirigisme 'socialism' and throughout the long years of the Cold War (1947–89) sought to contain the US-led campaign to preserve and extend capitalism. By the start of the 1990s their failure to sustain rising living standards had, however, led these regimes to embrace the free market.

The conversion of the 'socialist' regimes found an echo among social democratic and labour parties throughout the 'non-socialist' world. These organizations had attempted to reconcile national planning and a limited dose of public ownership with private enterprise in what became known as 'mixed economies'. Here, governments, particularly those founded on the support of organized labour, committed themselves to industrial modernization, the maintenance of full employment and the construction of welfare states. From the late 1960s onwards, however, the achievement of such objectives was increasingly brought into question as centre-left administrations grappled with outbursts of overt class conflict, inflation, erratic economic growth and, from the mid-1970s, rising unemployment. The response, pursued most vigorously in Britain and least enthusiastically in France, was to scale down planning and expand the role of private enterprise through support for deregulation, privatization of state concerns and the removal of barriers to international trade. It all amounted to another vote of confidence in the free market.

The collapse of the Soviet Union and the waning of social democracy in favour of free markets led a senior member of the United States' Department of State to suggest in 1989 that humanity had reached 'the end of history'. There were no serious ideological conflicts left; capitalism had proved its superiority to the alternatives. Liberalism in economics and politics would sweep the world as nations sought to emulate the American model, a surefire recipe for peace and prosperity. During the Bush and Clinton presidencies (1989–2001), Washington encouraged western bankers, working both for private institutions and for public organizations such as the IMF, to provide capital to the new non-socialist regimes in return for deregulation, privatization and drastic cuts in government spending. These initiatives were paralleled by a campaign for inter-national economic liberalization, which saw the General Agreement on Trade and Tariffs (GATT) and its successor the World Trade Organization (WTO) push for the removal of barriers to trade in manufacturing, services and agricul-ture, while the IMF sought increased mobility for international capital. Indeed, in May 1997, the IMF announced its intention to alter its Articles of Agreement – its constitution – in order to allow for promotion of capital account liberalization to become one of its key functions and to give it jurisdiction over capital movements.[3]

The aim of these reforms was to create a world economy built on the prin-ciples of the 'open door'[4] – equal access for all to the world's markets and raw material resources. It was a vision that had informed American foreign eco-nomic policy throughout the twentieth century. Thus after the First World War, the era of 'isolationism' notwithstanding, successive US presidents of the 1920s attempted to resurrect the gold standard system of the nineteenth century. Flows of capital would cross national borders without restriction, states would dismantle barriers to the inflow of goods, particularly barriers that singled out produce from one particular source (this was 'discrimination' and was not compatible with the open door), and currencies would be convertible into each other at fixed rates of exchange. Countries in deficit should not devalue or impose trade restrictions; instead they should inject deflation into the economy with the object of lowering demand for imports – even if the cost was high unemployment. The gold standard system fell into disrepute after 1929, but the free market international economy it sought to guarantee remained the objective of American foreign economic policy. By the end of the 1990s the case had been reinforced by the apparent success of American capitalism, along with the failure of the alternatives. Now a number of well-informed commentators argued that it had left behind the era of the business cycle and had entered a 'new age' characterized by continuous expansion.[5]

Such confidence in the future of free market capitalism may not be justified. The economic crises that overwhelmed Asia, Russia and much of Latin America in 1997–8 sparked a return to interventionism and economic nationalism. By 2000 there were increasing anxieties about the prospects for sustained growth in a US economy characterized by low levels of private savings, overvalued stock market valuations and a growing balance of trade deficit. The fragility at the heart of the international economy and the ongoing crisis throughout a significant proportion of its periphery therefore suggest caution about an approach to the future based merely upon extrapolation from the present, a wariness supported by the experience of history itself. Thus in 1927 John Moody, founder of the credit agency, argued that the continuous prosperity of the period since 1921 should lead to confidence that Americans were now 'living in a new era'. In 1929, just a few weeks before the Wall Street Crash, the economist Irving Fisher declared that stock prices had attained a 'permanently high plateau'.[6] So 1989 was not the first year in which humanity reached the 'end of history'.

Fisher's declaration was followed by the Great Slump and a widespread collapse of confidence in the capitalist system. Stock market prices dived from their 'high plateau' and the 'new era' gave way to a long period characterized by falls in industrial output and levels of unemployment unprecedented in the experience of the advanced economies. In the United States, industrial production dropped by 50 per cent between 1929 and 1932, with steel output operating at 12 per cent of capacity by the end of the period; by 1933 unemployment had reached 25 per cent of the workforce. Joblessness in Germany by this time had risen to 29.9 per cent of the workforce and in Britain it stood at a figure of 23 per cent.[7] The international economy of the 1930s was characterized not by the open door but by protectionism and fragmentation into regional blocs, each with its own hegemonic power – Germany in central and eastern Europe, Japan in East Asia, the United States in the American continent, and the United Kingdom throughout the British Commonwealth and Empire. The 'end of history' gave way to a decade of ideological struggle between fascism and Marxism, philosophies that, in their different ways, not only produced explanations for what was wrong with capitalism but offered alternatives to it. Italy, Germany and Japan all adopted varieties of the former, while the Soviet Union pursued an experiment in the latter. It contracted out of the international economy and embraced 'socialism in one country', an isolationist strategy whose purpose was the country's transformation into a great industrial power. Even the United States abandoned faith in unfettered free enterprise as the federal government sought, through the 'New Deal', to generate jobs and protect living standards through public works projects and social security legislation.

The new politico-economic approaches had mixed results. In Germany unemployment disappeared as the Nazi administration increased public expenditure on rearmament and social overhead capital. It was a policy that generated high levels of internal demand, and pressures on Germany's external finances resulted. These were contained with the assistance of exchange controls and bilateral agreements negotiated by Hjalmar Schacht, President of the Reichsbank from 1930–9, with trading partners. Japan, having devalued the yen by 40 per cent in 1931, embarked on a successful export drive. This, in combination with a military build-up, stimulated economic growth so that the net national product increased by 50 per cent between 1929 and 1936.[8] However, economic expansion was accompanied by imperialism as Japan sought to monopolize markets as well as raw material and mineral resources in China. This was a strategy that led first to the invasion and occupation of Manchuria in 1931 and then provoked the Sino-Japanese war from 1937 onwards. In the United States joblessness fell from 15 million in 1933 to 9 million in 1939, a record that did little to restore the faith of economists in capitalism's future. It appeared that only the Soviet Union, of the large industrial economies, had discovered how to promote national prosperity without embarking on an adventurist and aggressive foreign policy that reduced other nations to economic colonies. Here, under a succession of Five Year Plans, production rose throughout the decade while full employment was maintained. It was a record that seemed to encourage endorsement of Marxism's claim to offer humanity a future characterized by efficiency, increasing affluence and peace.

Although the years 1933–9 saw recovery from the depths of the slump almost everywhere, there were still large pockets of poverty and deprivation throughout the developing as well as the industrialized world at the end of the decade. For example, falling raw material and food prices had brought poverty to British colonies whose welfare was dependent on their exports. Two examples were West Africa, which specialized in palm oil production, and the West Indies, traditionally a producer of sugar and bananas. Diminishing returns from these commodities were reflected in falling living standards and, ultimately, in waves of rioting throughout both regions. Of the developed countries, only Sweden appeared to have successfully reconciled a return to full employment with the maintenance of liberal democracy. In the end it was not the New Deal, nor fascism, nor Marxism that propelled the world out of depression: it was war. And, during the Second World War, the leading belligerent powers determined that there should be no postwar return to the failed liberal order of the era after 1918. All had their own visions of how a reborn international economic system should work, but ultimately it was the American version that prevailed.

◆ The Aims of this Book

The theme of this book is the unfolding of the project to build a world safe for the open door. Chapter 1 covers the wartime quest for a new international economic order and follows the stages by which American plans for an open-door world shaped the agenda for reconstruction. Chapter 2 discusses the failure of this project and its replacement by the Marshall Plan, a US government initiative that aimed to make western Europe the centre of a world committed to multilateralism. Chapter 3 argues that the emergence by 1958 of a single trade and payments system for the non-Soviet world was governed by the determination of the postwar nation state to build an international environment more conducive to national full employment policies than to non-discrimination. Chapter 4 discusses how and why the postwar international economic order – based on the dollar's pre-eminence, international monetary co-operation between the advanced industrial nations, and trade liberalization – ran into trouble in the 1960s before collapsing in 1971. Chapter 5 tells the story of efforts to build a 'new international economic order', on socialist or social-democratic principles, in the 1970s and how these were frustrated by the emergence of neo-liberal economics in the USA and the UK. Chapter 6 follows the continuation of the free-market revolution, enthusiastically promoted in Washington by the US government, the Bretton Woods institutions and multinational capital, and its extension into the so-called 'Third World' in the 1980s. Chapter 7 analyses the arrival of globalization in the 1990s, the apparent fulfilment of plans for an open-door world, and how this transformation generated an economic instability and political opposition that, by 2000, was threatening to undermine it. The Conclusion surveys the development of the world economy from the 1940s to 2000, and discusses future prospects.

◆ Notes

1. See Alastair Couper, 'Globalization: the third shipping revolution is underway', *Maritime Review* 1999, 5–7.
2. Anthony Giddens, *Runaway World: How Globalization is Shaping our Lives* (London: Profile, 1999).
3. Jonathan Kirshner, 'Keynes, capital mobility and the crisis of embedded liberalism', *Review of International Political Economy* 6(3) (1999), 316.
4. See for example William Appleman Williams, *The Tragedy of American Diplomacy* (New York: W.W. Norton, 1988). Williams' study was first published in 1959.
5. See Larry Elliott, 'History points the way to another crash landing', *Guardian* (28 February 2000).
6. Ibid.
7. See William E. Leuchtenburg, *Franklin D. Roosevelt and the New Deal* (New York: Harper & Rowe, 1965), 1; V. R. Berghahn, *Modern Germany: Society, Economy and Politics in the Twentieth Century* (Cambridge: Cambridge University Press, 1988), 284, Table 18; Sidney Pollard, *The Development of the British Economy 1914–1990* (London: Edward Arnold, 1992), 122–3.
8. J.K. Fairbank, Edwin O. Reischauer and Albert M. Craig, *East Asia: The Modern Transformation* (London: George Allen & Unwin, 1965), 499.

1
NEW ORDERS, 1940–1946

◆ Continental Blocs?

During the Second World War all the leading belligerent powers apart from the Soviet Union floated alternatives to the liberal capitalist model of international economic co-operation that had collapsed after 1929. Indeed the Japanese and the Germans claimed that they were not simply calling for the existence of what they both called a 'new order' once hostilities had finished: they were implementing one even as the fighting progressed.

During the 1920s Japan had been a liberal-constitutional state. For much of the decade it had collaborated with Anglo-American efforts to spread disarmament and the open door throughout Asia. However, the country's agricultural sector had been hard hit by the Depression, with sharp falls in rice and silk cocoon prices, and rural cash incomes fell from an index of 100 in 1926 to 33 by 1931. These troubles were compounded by the government's determination to enhance the international competitiveness of the economy through joining the gold standard – a decision that resulted in the collapse of exports, whose value fell by 50 per cent between 1929 and 1931. The economic crisis stimulated a reaction against parliamentary politics, especially in the armed forces and in the countryside. In the 1930s the army took an increasingly prominent role in government, frequently precipitating violent changes of regime, its support for any administration conditional on commitment to a nationalist political and economic agenda. This was expressed in aggression against China (the occupation of Manchuria in 1931, followed by the outbreak of a general war in 1937), withdrawal from the League of Nations, the formulation of an economic policy that aimed to turn East Asia into a Japanese protectorate, and the deterioration of relations with the British and the Americans.

The Japanese Cabinet in fact proclaimed a 'New Order in East Asia' in 1938. This rejected liberal commerce and called for the establishment of a large trading area embracing Japan, China and the Japanese puppet state of Manchukuo (until 1931 known as Manchuria and part of China). Protectionist measures to exclude textiles, which accounted for 60 per cent of all Japanese exports in 1937,[1] from markets in the British Empire and the United States generated a reaction in Japan that played into the hands of the nationalist and imperialist lobby centred on the armed forces. This group called for a reorientation of the economy away from the wider world and towards the construction of a self-sufficient East Asian bloc; the region contained crucial raw materials, such as iron ore and coal in China and tin, oil and rubber in South-East Asia,[2] which Japan could pay for by treating it as a captive market for exports.

Clearly the economic logic of Japanese policy pointed to a larger bloc than had been contemplated when the 'New Order' had been announced, but there was, in addition, a strategic case. Throughout 1938 and 1939, as the war with China intensified, and relations with Britain and America consequently failed to improve, the case for southward extension was made with increasing strength by the military and by various research groups affiliated to the army or the navy. These argued that Japan needed access to the raw materials and markets of all of East Asia, not just to insulate it from unstable global economic influences, but also to guarantee its capacity to survive and fight in an international environment characterized by steadily increasing tension. They established increasing influence over Tokyo's foreign economic policy, and in August 1940 the 'Greater East Asia Co-Prosperity Sphere' was proclaimed.

The Greater East Asia Co-Prosperity Sphere was intended to include Korea, China and Manchukuo, all of South-East Asia, 'southern areas such as the Netherlands Indies', Australia, New Zealand and, if possible, India.[3] The aims of its apologists were not unlimited: they assumed that the future course of world history would be determined by co-operation between regional blocs each dominated by one hegemonic power. If the USA were to control the whole of the American continent as well as the western Pacific, and Germany to dominate Europe (including the Soviet Union as far as the Ural mountains), then Japan would be the dominant power in Asia. Premier Konoye Fumimaro and Foreign Minister Matsuoka Yosuke attempted to legitimize what was, in reality, naked self-interest by calling on the peoples of Asia to break free from western imperialist control under Tokyo's leadership. It was a call that had some resonance in the region; nationalist groups opposed to French rule in South-East Asia, Dutch administration in Indonesia, or the British presence in India, Burma and Malaya were not unsympathetic to the idea of 'Asia for the Asiatics'. When the Japanese Army swept down through Burma and Malaya, and across the Pacific to take the Philippines and invade New Guinea during 1941–2 it appeared as if the vision of the Co-Prosperity Sphere was to be translated into reality.

But the project was a failure. For a start, the Japanese fared poorly in the propaganda war – they revealed themselves to be at least as and sometimes much more brutal and exploitative than the imperialist rulers they had replaced. In China, for example, numerous atrocities, including scientific experiments on live

TABLE 1.1: IMPORTS OF STRATEGIC RAW MATERIALS INTO JAPAN, 1941–1945 (IN THOUSANDS OF METRIC TONS)

Commodity	1941	1942	1943	1944	1945
Coal	6459	6388	5181	2635	548
Iron ore	6309	4700	4298	2153	341
Bauxite	150	305	909	376	15
Iron and steel	921	993	997	1097	170
Raw rubber	68	31	42	31	18

Source: Milward, *War, Economy and Society 1939–45* (London: Penguin, 1987), 167, Table 23

human subjects, were carried out against the population. The result was the alienation of the local peoples and growing support for resistance movements backed by British and American intelligence and sabotage organizations. Second, even as backing for the Co-Prosperity Sphere crumbled it was failing in economic terms. The needs of war worked against the development of East Asia by Japanese capital, and most of the area was simply plundered for its raw materials. The level of imports fell dramatically as the war progressed because Japan, in suffering massive naval defeats during the course of 1942 and 1943, lost control of the Pacific supply routes (Table 1.1). The result was especially serious for stocks of iron ore, coking coal and bauxite, for example, since there was virtually no indigenous production of these commodities. By the end of 1943 at the latest, Japan was cut off from its overseas conquests and unable to export significantly because of the requirement to specialize in military production. Meanwhile, plans to introduce a new division of labour in the region were left largely unrealized. It was only in Korea where Japanese efforts had any notable success, and this was largely because the industries were both of strategic significance (for example, synthetic oil), had long been controlled by Japanese capital and were accessible by sea until very late in the war. In general the record was one of resources neglected or destroyed, and disrupted transportation networks. As a result, trade throughout the Co-Prosperity Sphere sank well below its prewar level and much of the region suffered from shortages, regressing to standards of living that barely met subsistence levels. Japan's attempt to build its own 'New Order in East Asia' had almost completely disintegrated long before its formal unconditional surrender on 2 September 1945.

The German 'new order' was also characterized by savage exploitation of the local populations, despite attempts to galvanize enthusiasm for a European economy that would guarantee markets and jobs. In 1940 the German Finance Minister Walther Funk attacked the gold standard system and called for a 'new order' based on the creation of a tariff-free area in Europe with a planned integration of the old national economies into one unit dominated by a heavy manufacturing core in Germany. Funk's plan was backed by a group of businessmen, civil servants and publicists in the Nazi establishment, as well as by large firms such as the Zeiss concern and I.G. Farben.

The call for a continent-wide reorganization followed the fall of France: it was not merely a propaganda stunt (although it was partly this) but was, in its turn, related to interwar moves to Franco-German economic union such as French President Aristide Briand's 1930 call for European unity based on a Franco-German partnership. The plan did not proceed, largely thanks to political instability and the rise of Nazism in Germany. Yet in its relatively short life it generated considerable interest. Briand had suggested an alternative to the open-door model for international economic relations favoured by the Anglo-Americans; it was a response to the overcapacity and falling prices generated by the downturn in the international economy. At the same time Briand's proposal looked to the longer term, since it was a strategy not just for European co-operation but for the transformation of the continent into a powerful economic bloc dominated by producers' cartels capable of competing with the United States. Unsurprisingly, therefore, Briand had been supported by business lobbies, such as the Douanière Européenne and the Comité Franco-Allemand d'information et de Documentation, composed of leading figures from German and French banking and industry.[4] These were the circles Funk and his associates wanted to cultivate in their campaign for a new division of labour on the continent.

During the period 1941–5, some efforts were made in the direction of creating an integrated European economy. These were, however, very modest and were disrupted, first by Blitzkrieg and then by Nazi ideology. The point of the Blitzkrieg strategy was to achieve rapid victories and avoid the drawn-out war that would put German living standards under strain (Hitler believed this had been a central factor in the debacle of 1918). As a result there was no room for long-term plans, and conquered territories were seen as ripe merely for immediate economic exploitation for Germany's benefit. Despite Funk's rhetoric, and occasional musings by Hitler himself, there was no fundamental shift in approach until it became obvious at the end of 1941 that the Blitzkrieg strategy had failed to effect the rapid defeat of the USSR and that the conflict would last for several years after all. Now there was a growing interest in the reorganization of Europe so that its resources could be mobilized to fight a total war. The Nazi regime could not, however, settle on one way forward and the question became one of what sort of Europe was consistent with the survival of the Nazi regime and its long-term ideological objectives.

This question was never completely resolved. To party ideologues such as Fritz Sauckel (Commissar-General for Labour from March 1942), the defeated nations of Europe provided a massive resource of slave labour that could be drafted in to German factories to boost arms production. Meanwhile, in conformity with Nazi racial theory, the rural populations of Poland and the occupied USSR were allowed to starve so that the land could feed the German armies, while the Jews were massacred. It was an approach that, as some administrators lamented, left no farmers and indeed no one to work with at all.[5] The result was to generate widespread discontent and disruption in the occupied territories as well as to boost recruitment to resistance organizations. Agricultural output dropped in eastern Europe and, in 1941–2, there was famine in the Ukraine and Galicia.

The chaos involved in this genocidal attack on local communities and in Sauckel's labour drives was a stimulus to the Europe-wide planners, who had a powerful advocate for their ideas in Albert Speer, Minister for Armaments after 1942. Speer argued that Germany was wasting resources: it needed to build a 'European war economy' in order to survive the two-front war against the USSR and the Anglo-Americans, and the only way to do this was by working with foreign governments and business organizations rather than alienating them, and by creating a well-motivated, well-fed and skilled workforce. It therefore made sense for Speer to call for transnational planning, which meant that the continent's raw materials and labour would no longer be plundered for the benefit of Germany but diverted to cultivate industrial production elsewhere. Funk's 'new order' was revived as Speer called for the transformation of north-western Europe into a large economic area surrounded by a low tariff, with France and the low countries specializing in light industry, consumer goods and agriculture, Germany in heavy industry and war production, and Norway in raw materials (mainly aluminium) and foodstuffs.[6] The vision extended to the construction of combines embracing power generation and producers of coal, iron ore, aluminium and motor vehicles throughout 'Germany, France, Belgium, Holland and Bohemia, etc'. Production and prices in this network of cartels would be regulated by a high authority, 'a production planning council on a pan-European basis',[7] according to Speer, and peripheral countries such as Portugal and Sweden would be encouraged to participate.

There were some modest steps towards the creation of a European economic community (there can be no dodging the truth that some of Speer's, and Funk's, ideas, anticipated the European Coal and Steel Community, established in 1950). German economic interests took control in the Protectorate of Bohemia and Moravia (Czechoslovak territory between the wars), taking over the coal mining, cement and paper industries almost completely, and acquiring about half of the territory's industrial share capital. In Norway there was heavy German capital investment designed to increase production of aluminium, while long-term plans were established to transform the country into a major agricultural supplier specializing in sheep and frozen fish. In France, German and French producers of dyestuffs agreed on the establishment of a new combine, Francolor; 51 per cent of the capital in Francolor was German but, all the same, the negotiators agreed that the company would monopolize the French markets, domestic and colonial. By the end of the year, between 40 and 50 per cent of French industrial output, both consumer goods and war production, was destined for Germany.[8]

Hitler's racism prevented him from ever giving unequivocal support to Speer. Sauckel's contempt for non-Germans and distaste for corporate capitalism had considerable support in Nazi ranks. Many of the most committed party members, from the land and the 'Mittelstand' – composed of peasants, farmworkers, shopkeepers, clerks, small businesspeople and handicraft workers – had come into the Nazi fold because they had been threatened by capitalism. In the wake of the 1923 hyperinflation and then the Depression it became identified with inflation, unemployment, unpredictable prices for farm and factory output, and with the crushing of the self-employed and the 'little people' between the wheels of finance, big business and organized labour. All these malign forces were being manipulated by alien, non-German influences – meaning the Jews, who were seen, simultaneously, to be defenders of the capitalist system and advocates of communist revolution. In its place the rank-and-file Nazi supporter, of which Sauckel was a typical example, wanted not socialism but a non-materialist, racially pure utopia. This ideal society was to be presided over by a prosperous, fully employed middle class and a sturdy, hard-working peasantry that would be justly rewarded by the state for its efforts.[9]

Hitler not only realized how strong this outlook was: he shared it. He had never been comfortable with Funk and then Speer's version of the new order, but had supported Speer because he had produced what seemed to be a viable strategy for sustaining the war effort. But when the Führer saw that the efforts to encourage production in France were failing because the authorities there were increasingly preoccupied with the activities of the resistance, he finally threw his weight behind Sauckel. As a result the labour drives, which had slackened off during the second half of 1943, intensified dramatically from March 1944.[10] Prospects for a rational exploitation of what was in any case a shrinking Nazi empire disappeared completely when Hitler called for a scorched-earth policy in the face of advancing Allied armies during the autumn of 1944. By the end of that year it was clear that the only new order of interest to Hitler was not one that sought to reorganize international economic relationships but one that gave priority to Nazi racial objectives; the 'final solution' went ahead even as the efforts of the planners were frustrated.

◆ The Road to Bretton Woods

The collapse of Germany and Japan in 1945 meant that the postwar international economic system would be constructed by the victorious Allied powers. The Soviet Union eschewed grand designs and focused on the creation of a European system that would guarantee its own security. To this end the USSR worked for a restoration of the frontiers in existence prior to the German invasion of 22 June

1941, and for the transformation of countries around its border into buffer states. There was much *Realpolitik* and very little idealism in Soviet planning for reconstruction, but Moscow did lend largely passive support to the more ambitious Anglo-American vision of the future. Both in Britain and the United States there was a reaction against Japanese and German attempts to establish continental blocs. Anglo-American international economic policy concentrated not on building a postwar world divided into spheres of influence but on the creation of one in which global organizations would facilitate international co-operation to promote peaceful commerce and rising prosperity all round. However, the attempt to meet so general an aspiration exposed profound differences between London and Washington. When the shape of this anti-fascist new order was revealed in 1945–6 it turned out to be very different from what had been envisaged in the early part of the war: British plans had made the running, but in the end the architecture was almost exclusively American.

When Funk issued his call for a 'new order' in 1940, Britain stood alone in Europe against a seemingly invincible Germany, whose dominion over the continent extended from the Pyrenees to the Arctic Circle. In London it was accepted that the struggle for the hearts and minds of populations in occupied Europe would be central to the final outcome of the war, and as a result the Ministry of Information asked the distinguished British economist John Maynard Keynes for a response to Funk that would prove attractive to the millions now living under Nazi domination.

Three fundamental influences operated on Keynes as he formulated his vision of the future: his own work, the shifting balance of forces within wartime British society, and the development of Britain's wartime international financial position. The first of these has been the subject of considerable misunderstanding, most of which has turned on the relationship of a famous article, 'National self-sufficiency', published in 1933, to Keynes' previous and subsequent labours in the cause of international economic co-operation. 'National self-sufficiency', which appeared when the Great Depression was at its most intense, mounted a powerful critique of the post-1918 international financial order. Keynes argued that it was characterized by footloose capital charging around the world in search of the highest rate of return. The result was anarchy. Under the restored gold standard, governments and central banks struggling to prevent a loss of reserves could only put up interest rates and cut back spending on consumption and investment, thus provoking high unemployment, or scramble competitively for foreign markets and pursue economic imperialism in order to achieve trade surpluses. The system had generated deflation, wrecked efforts to sustain international economic co-operation and prevented the full exploitation of the wealth-creating potential afforded by technological progress. This was why, in a famous passage, Keynes appeared to turn his back on the eternal verities of liberal economics, arguing that it was 'ideas, hospitality, travel' that were in themselves international, but that goods should be 'homespun whenever it is reasonably and conveniently possible' and that 'finance [should be] primarily national'. Keynes accepted the 'inevitability of a considerable degree of international specialisation' but nevertheless claimed that modern mass production could be conducted 'with almost equal efficiency' in 'most climates or countries'. It was time for a turn to national economic planning, which would generate employment through the cultivation of home industries, urban renewal and agricultural protection.

Most commentators have seen 'National self-sufficiency' as a temporary aberration on Keynes' part, a product of despair at the failure of the 1933 World Economic Conference to produce a co-ordinated global response to the Depression. The article subsequently led to Keynes being accused of embracing economic isolationism, and even of flirting with 'fascist or communist economics'.[11] But 'National self-sufficiency' did not flirt with fascism or communism. It did not advocate economic isolationism. Nor was it a reaction to the failure of the World Economic Conference, since both before *and after* the article's publication Keynes was promoting a scheme for international expansion based on the creation of a gold-backed international currency issued by the Bank for International Settlements. This seeming inconsistency can be explained once we appreciate that Keynes was currently embarked on the search for a new political economy, which argued that the test of capitalism's success or failure was its ability to guarantee full employment of resources and an equitable distribution of wealth, and that these objectives could only be achieved by conscious state action. Since the national autonomy required for the pursuit of this new, socialized capitalism (or 'liberal socialism', as Keynes sometimes described it) was incompatible with membership of the current international economic order, either the rules of the game had to be changed or nation states had to contract out of it. The point was not that national self-sufficiency was preferable to membership of a global system but that both it and the international currency plan were alternative means to the same end: a society where rising levels of abundance and prosperity were continuously being generated by the use of all productive forces.

When Keynes' search for a new political economy was completed with the publication of *The General Theory of Employment, Interest and Money* (1936) it became clear that 'National self-sufficiency' did not represent an aberration after all. Once again, Keynes rehearsed his criticisms of the prevailing international economic order. He complained that economists had played 'a part disastrous to the latest act' by urging deflation rather than the restoration of control over the bank rate via managed currency depreciation and the imposition of exchange controls. Their advice had been the opposite of what was required:

> It is the policy of an autonomous rate of interest, unimpeded by international preoccupations, and of a national investment programme directed to an optimum level of domestic employment which is twice blessed in the sense that it helps ourselves and our neighbours at the same time.[12]

The struggle against the slump and the international economic rivalry associated with it had to begin with economic nationalism. Once countries had individually embarked on full employment policies trade would become not a struggle to corner markets and restrict imports but a genuine exchange necessitated by the imperative of paying for what each nation state wanted to buy. The end result would be a world where full employment and the peaceful, co-operative commerce that would flow from it would be the norm; in the *General Theory* Keynes called this a 'visionary hope'.

The Ministry of Information's request for a response to Funk's 'new order' gave Keynes the chance to set about translating his vision into reality. Given the theoretical background to Keynes' own work it is hardly surprising that he sympathized with a good deal of the economics behind Funk's proposals: he wrote that 'In my opinion about three-quarters of the passages quoted from German broadcasts would be quite excellent if the name of Great Britain were substituted for Germany or the Axis'. The way to respond to them was by casting 'doubt on their *bona fides*' and by offering an alternative, democratic version of the 'new order' that would guarantee full employment and social security for all.[13]

The second influence operating on Keynes was the changing climate in Britain, which produced a political culture receptive to his new, interventionist economics. Britain started the war under a right-of-centre national government presided over by Neville Chamberlain. The military disasters of spring 1940 – defeat in Norway above all – discredited this administration, which was replaced in May of that year by a coalition led by Winston Churchill. Churchill was committed to fighting total war and set about mobilizing all of British society's resources of capital and labour to this end. Prewar governments had generally tried to cover expenditure out of revenue (the 'balanced budget'), committed as they were to the view that deficits were inflationary. However, the balanced budget was abandoned as the Churchill coalition embraced the Keynesian policy of national income accounting. The new financial strategy focused on the total volume of goods and services flowing through the economy: it allowed for substantial increases in public expenditure, inflation now being understood to result from the difference between the value of goods and services produced and total money demand in the economy, rather than the discrepancy between government outlay and income.

The war-generated expansion of public investment had a dramatic economic and social impact. First, it stimulated an expansion of output in arms and arms-related industries such as aircraft, vehicles, electronics, engineering and metal manufacturing.[14] The requirements of military service notwithstanding, there was a demand for labour, and in 1941 full employment returned for the first time since 1919–20. Second, there was, as a result of the renewed activity, an increase in trades union density, with membership of trades unions growing from 6.25 million in 1939 to over 8 million in 1944. Third, good wages, combined with progressive taxation and price controls to contain inflationary pressures, ensured a redistribution of income away from the wealthy. After tax, middle-class income fell by over 7 per cent, while working-class income rose by 9 per cent. By 1948, purchasing power in the hands of the best-paid one-sixth had fallen by 30 per cent but had increased by 25 per cent for the rest of the community.[15]

The war economy gave organized labour in Britain a self-confidence it had not possessed since the collapse of the 1926 General Strike. Its leading officials became involved in the formulation of industrial policy, while Ernest Bevin, the General Secretary of the Transport and General Workers Union (the largest one at that time), was appointed Minister of Labour in 1940. Recovering from the political setbacks and unemployment of the 1930s, both the trades unions and their political arm, the Labour Party, campaigned for a better deal for working people after the war. They called for child allowances, higher old-age pensions, job security, more housing, and for free medical treatment and secondary educa-tion. These demands received a sympathetic response from employers and civil servants as well as from politicians, partly because it seemed reasonable that a population that had suffered the terror of the Blitz and the hardships of war should be able to face a future characterized by social justice, and also because the successful experience of wartime economic management seemed to show that interventionist economics could not only deliver this but was efficient into the bargain. It was not surprising that Sir William Beveridge's report on *Social Insurance and Allied Services*, which set out a scheme to provide comprehensive social security 'from the cradle to the grave' was greeted with widespread enthu-siasm and quickly became a best-seller after its publication at the end of 1942. Beveridge's proposals became the agenda for postwar reconstruction; Keynes' new economics provided the means to their implementation.

Keynes himself was, however, more aware than most that there was a mas-sive obstacle in the way of postwar prosperity: Britain's war-created external indebtedness. This was the third major influence on his planning for a demo-cratic version of the new order. Domestic expansion and production for mili-tary use rather than for exports (which had collapsed to 30 per cent of their 1938 levels by the start of 1945) generated a rapid depletion of reserves, which were spent on supplies of food, raw materials and capital goods, imported in large part from the United States. At the same time, though, the costs of finan-cing overseas bases and military operations as well as non-dollar imports led to a deficit of £2723 million with the sterling area by the end of the war (this was equivalent to 33 per cent of the Gross Domestic Product).[16] The sterling area was made up of British Commonwealth (except for Canada, in the dollar zone) and Empire countries, plus a handful of others (such as Egypt, Iceland and Iraq) which had close trade or political links with the United Kingdom. Its mem-bers held their reserves and traded in sterling and banked in London. The long and intimate connection with Britain allowed London to escape from having to provide immediate payment for goods and services provided by sterling area members; they settled for sterling IOUs, which accumulated in London and were known as 'sterling balances'.

Despite the mounting external deficit, Britain was able to sustain its war effort, but it had taken emergency measures to do this, and there was no certainty that these could be prolonged for many years into the reconstruction period. For a start there was the problem of the sterling balances. It was very unlikely that the creditors would allow them to accumulate further after the war – so would they be written off, would Britain run them down through exports of goods, or honour them in whole or in part with convertible currency? Then there was the question of foreign economic policy, which had been dramatically changed at the outbreak of war on 3 September 1939. From this point sterling became an inconvertible currency. It could still be used freely within the area itself, but purchases from outside could not occur without official approval. Permission to import from the dollar area was only granted if the goods were vital to the war effort; resources of gold and convertible foreign exchange were stored in the 'sterling area hard currency pool', which could be drawn on only for approved purchases, mainly of US-made commodities. Meanwhile the Churchill coalition encouraged the development of non-dollar supplies where possible – mostly in Africa, where it established programmes of investment in cotton and tobacco production, and in mineral exploitation.

The turn to discriminatory practices was reinforced by use of bilateralism, whereby Britain made trade and payments agreements with non-sterling suppliers intended to provide for an exchange of goods up to roughly equivalent values (since British exports fell steadily throughout the war it is not surprising that, quite apart from the sterling balances, the country was left owing £632 million to its non-sterling creditors at the close of hostilities).[17] The point was, the discriminatory trade strategy had protected Britain's external finances during the war and in 1945 all the arrangements were in place for its continuation into peace, when, ideally, it would once again be possible to operate the economy at full capacity without running out of foreign exchange. However, it was not clear whether the special circumstances that had applied during the war would be sustainable once it was over. For a start, unless Britain could quickly boost its exports it would be unable to provide much of an incentive to its trading partners for the renewal or continuation of the agreements.

There was a further problem that threatened Britain's ability to sustain its discriminatory external economic policy into the reconstruction period: the attitude of the United States. Britain could not afford to ignore this because of its dependence on American supplies during the conflict. Despite exchange controls and sterling balances, the reserves sank to danger level in 1941 and in order to maintain the flow of supplies across the Atlantic, the United States and Britain established the Lend-Lease system. Under the Mutual Aid Agreement (February 1942), which governed the workings of Lend-Lease, Britain would not need to pay cash for American goods. It was agreed, however, under Article VII of the Mutual Aid Agreement, that after the war there would be Anglo-American co-operation in the creation of a world economy characterized by non-discrimination in trade and currency policy.

Article VII was the result of pressure from the United States. It reflected Washington's long-term commitment to a world based on the principles of the open door. Secretary of State Cordell Hull was convinced that 'unhampered trade dovetailed with peace; high tariffs, trade barriers and unfair economic competition, with war'.[18] A system of non-discrimination, in which nations enjoyed equal access to the world's raw materials and markets, would guarantee economic co-operation between the leading industrial powers. The rise of economic nationalism in the 1930s was viewed as unhealthy by Hull: to him it brought with it the attendant evils of tariffs, protectionism and discriminatory trade practices, which had conspired to deepen the slump. At the same time the trade and currency blocs established by Germany and Japan, and even by Britain with its imperial preference system, had provoked international rivalry and, in doing so, had played a part in the drift to war between 1931 and 1939.

This liberal anti-imperialism was, however, motivated by self-interest as well as by idealism. Within the US administration there were influential figures such as Dean Acheson (Assistant Secretary of State) who pointed to a risk that the Depression might return once the war, and all the government-inspired demand that went with it, had finished. One way to deal with this was by a redistribution of wealth and power in the United States so that production and consumption would balance at full employment – but this would involve the federal government in taking powers over the economy that would not be compatible with the free enterprise system. Therefore, a better solution to any crisis of overproduction could be found in establishing an open international economy. American farmers and manufacturers would gain access to overseas markets while the general reduction of barriers to trade, not least in the United States itself, would allow trading partners to pay for their imports through an expansion of exports. It was a pragmatic economic liberalism, which was supported by financial and business lobbies (such as the National Association of Manufacturers); a widespread hostility to discrimination developed and was reinforced by Britain's adoption of sterling inconvertibility and turn to bilateral trade after 1940.[19] There was in fact a consensus in Washington that the key to prosperity in the United States and the world at large, and therefore to lasting peace, was the liberalization of international economic relations – and once Germany and Japan had been defeated, Britain, at the centre of the sterling area and the imperial preference system, would be 'the biggest obstacle ... to a freer trade world'.[20]

Keynes and the British government were uncomfortable with Article VII. They regarded it as doctrinaire and, if taken literally, likely to deprive them of the ability to protect the external financial position after the end of hostilities: massive deflation would result. But the British would need dollars for peace just as they did for war. Without hard currency to pay for continuing imports of raw materials and capital goods the factories would not work and living standards would sink beneath wartime levels. Exports needed time to reach levels that would generate enough dollars to support the reconstruction programme. It followed that access to significant foreign assistance from the USA would be necessary. In consequence, despite their misgivings, the British had little alternative but to sign Article VII. The final draft did provide some reassuring words about 'the expansion, by appropriate domestic and international measures, of production, employment and the exchange and consumption of goods', but this was not enough for Keynes, who spent the rest of his life fighting against American attempts to implement the most liberal interpretation of Article VII.[21]

Keynes, supported both by the Churchill coalition and by the Labour administration of Clement Attlee that succeeded it in the summer of 1945, attempted to follow a twin-track approach. On the one hand he produced two major initiatives designed to reconcile the non-discriminatory bias and economic internationalism of the United States with the autonomy he had identified both in 'National self-sufficiency' and in the *General Theory* as essential to the maintenance of full employment. On the other hand he was aware that if the United States either retreated into isolationism or demanded unacceptable concessions concerning British economic policy, then a bilateralist strategy must be available. This would involve an intensification of exchange controls and of dollar rationing, the blocking of sterling balances, a determined effort to prioritize production for exports – especially those likely to earn dollars – and the exploitation, in concert not just with Commonwealth and Empire countries but with liberated Europe, of non-dollar sources of supply for all classes of imports. Life would be painful and the social aspects of reconstruction would suffer from lack of investment during the crisis period – but there would be no going back to prewar *laissez-faire*. Keynes worked sporadically and secretly on this radical approach right up to the last weeks of his life.

Clearly, however, the bilateral strategy involved prolonged austerity, and after the privations of total war there were few who were prepared to opt for it out of choice if a reasonable bargain could be struck with the United States. It followed that, in practice, from 1943 to 1945, Keynes and the British governments of the time devoted most of their energies to the pursuit of an acceptable settlement. Because of British reluctance to phase out the imperial preference system in the absence of American commitments to reduce tariffs after the war, commercial talks moved slowly, while between 1943 and 1944 international financial discussions focused on Keynes' first major initiative, the 'Clearing Union', and the American response, a proposal for a Stabilization Fund and an International Bank for Reconstruction and Development (later, World Bank). The issues were not finally resolved (or so it appeared at the time) until the Bretton Woods conference, held in the summer of 1944, saw delegates from all the nations represented there agree to recommend to their governments membership of an International Monetary Fund and an International Bank for Reconstruction and Development.

Britain's *Proposals for an International Clearing Union* were published by HM Treasury in 1943. It was a scheme descended from the abortive plan for international expansion Keynes had launched in 1933, and its objective was to provide the financial architecture of an expansionary postwar global economic order that sustained, and was sustained by, national full employment policies. To this end the Clearing Union would be designed to function as a world central bank, creating for each nation an internationally acceptable currency, known as 'bancor'. Each member of the Union was to be assigned a quota, proportionate to its share of prewar world trade. Keynes' hope was that the total amount of resources in the Union would initially be $26 billion (£4.5 billion, equivalent to 54 per cent of British GNP in 1945), since only so large a sum would permit countries to maintain domestic expansion even when their balance of payments was running in the red.[22] A British Cabinet memorandum explained how the Union was supposed to operate:

> A member State which on balance owed to countries payments which it was not in a position to discharge would be given facilities in the nature of an overdraft. A member State, on the other hand, which on balance was owed money by the other member States, could not recover it except by accepting goods or services from the rest of the world.[23]

With access to large overdraft facilities, debtor countries that were members of the Union would not be pressured into taking deflationary measures in order to return to equilibrium. Creditors, on the other hand, would be encouraged to reflate, reduce tariffs, invest overseas and possibly even revalue their currencies – all measures designed to increase demand for the exports of deficit countries and so ensure that the overdrafts provided by the Union would be cleared automatically.

While the Clearing Union was, of course, a plan for a British new world order in which every nation would be free to pursue its own New Deal, it also offered a lifeline to countries whose commitment to reconstruction would be threatened by a postwar shortage of foreign exchange. Britain was itself one of these but it was clear that most of its allies would be in a similar position after liberation. Even by 1943–4, the combined effects of Nazi and Japanese genocide, occupation and plunder, Allied strategic and saturation bombing, and of sabotage on the part of resistance groups were obvious: export markets had been lost, transport infrastructures had been disrupted, factory plant and equipment had been wrecked, housing had been destroyed. It followed that reconstruction, not just in Britain but throughout most of Europe and indeed Asia, would be dependent on the United States since, in the early postwar period, only the economy of what was now indisputably the world's leading industrial and military power would be capable of producing essential foodstuffs, raw materials and capital goods on the scale required. This reality was appreciated in Washington, both in the Treasury and the White House, where it was calculated that the United States, as the world's largest creditor, might be liable for $23 billion of the initial overdraft facility of $26 billion.[24] US Treasury officials told their British counterparts that Congress would never support American membership of any international financial organization on such terms.

Within the administration of President Franklin D. Roosevelt most of the constructive work on planning for postwar international reconstruction had been done by Harry Dexter White, Assistant Secretary to the Treasury. White personally sympathized with much of the idealism in Keynes' plan and was responsible for the counter-proposals of the Stabilization Fund and the Bank. These two institutions were, respectively, to be responsible for providing foreign exchange to nations in balance of payments difficulties and for long-term financial assistance to war-damaged and developing countries. But with $5 billion in the Fund and $10 billion in the Bank, they would be equipped with much more modest resources than the Clearing Union. In addition, the Fund, unlike Keynes' Clearing Union, worked on the basis of subscription: a member running a deficit with another member would be able to purchase as much of its creditor's foreign exchange as it required with the gold and convertible currency it had placed in the Fund. Although the Bank would be able to lend, there was no room for the overdraft principle in the Fund. Here, borrowing in excess of a member's subscription would need ratification by four-fifths of all the members' votes. The British argued their case throughout 1943, but it became clear that there would be no consensus unless they abandoned the overdraft principle that had been central to the concept of the Clearing Union.

At Bretton Woods it was clear that the IMF would operate on the same principles as the Stabilization Fund. Although it was finally agreed that the Fund should hold $8.8 billion rather than the $5 billion suggested in White's original plan, neither it nor the Bank would provide the generous credit advocated by Keynes. Voting rights in the Fund were to be determined not by shares of world trade but by the size of each subscription. Since the largest subscriber to each organization was the United States ($2.75 billion to the Fund and $3.175 billion to the Bank), there was a clear possibility that members applying for assistance would not receive it automatically, as Keynes had proposed, but would instead be required to conform to rules made in Washington. Given that, from the perspective of the United States, the fundamental task of the Fund was to guarantee a global financial environment characterized by non-discrimination, this would mean commitment to fixed exchange rates and currency convertibility. Indeed, following a postwar 'transition period', expected to last five years, all members would be obliged to remove exchange restrictions on current transactions. Par values were to be expressed in terms of dollars or gold, itself to be convertible into the dollar at $35 to the ounce; members would be required to accept gold in settlement of account. Debtors in receipt of help would be expected to scale down their import requirements more by orthodox liberal measures such as reductions in public expenditure and the introduction of tighter credit conditions than by devaluation and the intensification of existing physical barriers.

Despite these disappointments, the Bretton Woods conference showed that White and the Treasury had gone some way towards meeting British objections.

First, there was the five-year transition period during which members were relieved from the obligations of currency non-discrimination. Second, the commitment to fixed rates of exchange was not immovable. In fact an automatic right existed to devalue by up to 10 per cent; anything larger required agreement on the part of the Fund's executive directors to a claim from the member in question that its currency was in a state of 'fundamental disequilibrium'. Third, exchange controls on capital movements were to remain. Fourth, debtors would be permitted to impose quantitative import restrictions. But the most important American gesture appeared at the time to be the 'scarce currency clause'. This ensured that the Fund retained one of the key components of Keynes' Clearing Union scheme: the ability to exercise pressure on countries whose policies led them to have a persistently favourable balance of payments surplus. The clause declared that if a member's currency became so scarce that the Fund's ability to supply it to others was threatened, it could formally be declared 'scarce' and rationed out to them. This would automatically give the recipients the right to apply exchange restrictions against the surplus country. It was a provision which satisfied Keynes that under the Bretton Woods rules the burden of adjustment to any disequilibrium would be carried by the creditor after all, since, out of self-interest, the creditor would adopt measures of internal expansion, tariff reduction and lending to avoid being faced with the scarce currency sanction.

There is no doubt that the delegates at Bretton Woods believed they were indeed creating the architecture for a new international economic order that would reconcile full employment with multilateralism. The final shape of the proposals was certainly very different from what Keynes had envisaged with his Clearing Union scheme – yet it did represent an ingenious compromise between the original British and American plans. The events of the next two years were, however, to undercut much of the achievement; by the spring of 1946 many elements of the compromise had been nullified, leaving in place a system that owed more to Cordell Hull and the American liberals than it did to Keynes' vision.

◆ Pax Americana

Two obstacles stood in the way of an internationally concerted early move to a world economic system based on Bretton Woods rules. First of all national governments had to ratify the proposals. The behaviour of the British and American administrations would be central to this process. Without American membership the organizations would not have the resources to function. Given Britain's position at the centre of the Commonwealth and Empire, not to mention the sterling area, its absence from the Fund and the Bank would influence many other nations to keep away. In addition, the leading roles taken by Britain and America in creating the Bretton Woods proposals notwithstanding, both administrations had trouble securing acceptance of them at home.

There was opposition to Bretton Woods in Britain, stemming partly from those who advocated the creation of a self-sufficient imperial economic bloc and partly from the Bank of England, which prioritized the payment of Britain's creditors in the sterling area over ambitious schemes for international currency convertibility. Neither position was in tune with the political enthusiasm for reconstruction and both failed to receive backing either from the wartime coalition government or from its Labour successor. All the same, there was no rush to bring the agreement before Parliament, a delay provoked by its uneasy reception in combination with technical problems arising from drafting errors.[25]

Opposition in the USA was more profound, and was centred in the American banking community, which from the moment Harry Dexter White's plan had first seen the light of day had shown little enthusiasm for either the Fund or the Bank. Indeed the American Banker's Association (ABA), a venerable and prestigious pressure group whose membership embraced small and large organizations, such as the Chase Manhattan Bank, opposed the whole concept of Bretton Woods. It resented the intrusion of two publicly funded interventionist agencies into the areas of reconstruction finance and international exchange-rate stability traditionally reserved for private bankers, especially in view of the lucrative business likely to develop from the near certain worldwide need for American capital after the war. The American bankers were interested in establishing free flow of capital and in the privatization of international finance; if the Fund had to stay they would live with it comfortably only on strict conditions that, if respected, would leave it with a very limited role.

The private bankers were not only worried about being sidelined; they also believed that the reconstruction plans were inherently inflationary, since even after Keynes' Clearing Union had been scaled down into the Fund and the Bank they allowed too much room for domestic economic expansion. Focusing on the scarce currency clause, the five-year transition period and the right to retain exchange controls over capital transactions, the ABA argued that the Bretton Woods arrangements contained no serious anti-inflationary discipline. In the old days of the gold standard, trade deficits were conventionally attributed to high costs and uncompetitive practices on the factory floor. The answer was deflation via public spending cuts and tight money policies, so that imports would fall as a result of reduced demand. Higher unemployment would bring down the price of labour; falling prices and costs would ensure that producers regained their competitive edge and exports would grow, bringing in gold and convertible currency. The bankers thought it was wrong that under the new proposals debtors would not have to make such drastic adjustments. The inbuilt expansionary bias of the Bretton Woods institutions, they argued, would lead to the accumulation of unsustainable deficits by debtor countries. Inflation and exchange rate depreciation would follow, bringing international economic instability. The President of the ABA, Randall Burgess, expressed the

view of his members, namely that there should be a return to currency convertibility at fixed rates of exchange and that drawings on the Fund should
occur only when creditor countries were satisfied about the debtor's economic
policies (in other words, they should be of the kind that had prevailed in the
gold standard era). Moreover he argued that the Bretton Woods institutions
were too independent – there should be a guarantee that their decisions would
be taken in accordance with the long-term US objectives of non-discrimination
and liberalization.[26]

The direct assault was headed off. White ensured that Congress accepted
a compromise position, leaving the Bretton Woods organizations in place
but establishing a National Advisory Council on International Monetary and
Financial Policy. This was to be chaired by the Treasury Secretary and had the
mission of guiding the policy of US representatives on the Bank and the Fund.
In addition, there was a nod in the direction of old-fashioned orthodoxy, with
an acceptance that convertibility be prioritized over expansion by limiting the
Fund's power to lend to those occasions when external deficit was attributable
to 'seasonal, cyclical and emergency fluctuations'.[27]

The second obstacle to rapid erection of the Bretton Woods architecture was
the absence within it of provision for the postwar transition. During the discussion leading up to the conference it had been accepted, largely as a result of
American pressure, that the requirements of this period would be too extensive
for the resources at the disposal of the Fund and the Bank. Yet in the absence
of financial assistance from the United States, Britain – along with the sterling
area, as well as liberated Europe – would be likely to maintain exchange controls and anti-dollar discrimination not just for the five years allowed by the
Bretton Woods agreement but for the foreseeable future. If countries were to
commit themselves to fixed exchange rates and convertible currencies they had
to have hard currency. On both sides of the Atlantic it was appreciated that
there had to be some kind of bridge to the Bretton Woods era, and on both
sides the need for this was seen as an opportunity to renegotiate what had
apparently been agreed in July 1944.

As far as Keynes was concerned, the moment provided him with the chance
to propose a new scheme infused with the same ambitious spirit and objectives
as the Clearing Union. The United States, the world's main creditor country,
could not leave adjustment to the problems of the postwar era to the world's
debtors, especially not to Britain, the largest of them. Instead Keynes proposed
that the USA provide a grant of $3 billion and a loan of $5 billion to Britain.
The grant would assist settlement with the sterling area creditors on the basis
of a three-part deal – in each case a portion of the balances was to be funded,
a portion written off and a portion released to provide convertible exchange
for current transactions. The loan was to bolster British reserves during the
reconstruction period. Aware that Washington would need an incentive if it
were to make so expansive a gesture, Keynes argued that with aid on this scale
Britain would be able to move in the direction of Article VII without waiting

the full five years of the transition to Bretton Woods rules. In particular, it would be possible to implement a limited form of convertibility, namely sterling area resident convertibility for current transactions. Non-resident convertibility, which would have allowed Britain's non-sterling area creditors access to hard currency for current transactions, was not contemplated during the transition period and exchange controls on capital transactions were to be retained indefinitely. The extra dollars, together with the restrictions Keynes insisted should remain over convertibility, would ensure that Britain would be able to help in the creation of a postwar world based on multilateral principles without taking risks with its full employment policy.[28] The package would be completed by a modest Canadian contribution, already discussed in positive and encouraging terms with Graham Towers, Governor of the Bank of Canada.[29]

Both the outgoing coalition and the new Labour government supported Keynes' initiative. After some modifications to the plan (the size of the request was scaled down from $8 billion to $6 billion) he was authorized to lead a team of negotiators to Washington in September 1945. Parliamentary approval of Bretton Woods would be tied to a successful outcome. The mission was attended by a real sense of urgency since, immediately after the conclusion of the war against Japan in August, the new Truman administration (Roosevelt had died in April and had been replaced by his vice-president) had terminated the Lend-Lease programme. Within the British Treasury it had been anticipated that goods and supplies would continue to flow across the Atlantic for another 18 months, the expected duration of the struggle against Japan. But as far as Washington was concerned the atom bomb had, in bringing a sudden end to the war, also removed the rationale for Lend–Lease. This all meant that Britain's external financial position was even worse than had been expected: HM Treasury projections forecast a cumulative deficit of £1700 million ($6.8 billion at the current exchange rate of £1 = $4.03) up to 1949. This figure represented 20 per cent of the 1945 GNP and did not, of course, include the sterling balances; it was a 'financial Dunkirk', as Keynes told the Cabinet before he left.[30]

Keynes' plan failed. Despite the defeat of the Clearing Union and the furious lobbying of the bankers over the Bretton Woods scheme, he had come to believe that under the patronage of President Roosevelt New Dealers had gained the upper hand in Washington over the economic liberals around Cordell Hull. This was not entirely wishful thinking. Some of Roosevelt's leading advisers, such as Lauchlin Currie and Harry Hopkins, as well as Chairman of the Federal Reserve Board, Marriner Eccles, were advocates of Keynesian economics. Their outlook was shared by a generation of mainly Harvard-educated graduates, many of whom had entered federal government service after the Japanese attack on Pearl Harbor had brought the United States into the war at the end of 1941. But Truman's arrival was accompanied by a change of personnel and philosophy. The new president was inexperienced and insecure. To bolster his position he bypassed the New Dealers and turned to figures from the Democratic Party core. Foreign economic policy negotiations were taken over by Assistant Secretary of State Will Clayton, a liberal in the Hullian tradition. Fred Vinson, a Midwestern machine politician with conservative financial views, moved into the Treasury. White's influence began to diminish (after the war he came under suspicion of having been a Soviet agent).

The new team in Washington had their own opinions of how to link the problem of transitional finance to construction of a world based on Article VII. These were certainly not Keynesian, but reflected the influence of Professor John H. Williams of Harvard University. Williams, who was also a vice-president of the Federal Reserve Bank, had supported the criticisms of the Bretton Woods proposals made by the ABA and now advanced what were called the 'key currency' proposals. The 'key currency' concept was founded on the fact that the pound and the dollar were the world's two principle trading and reserve currencies – it was their behaviour that influenced that of all the others. Williams therefore proposed to the Senate Committee on Banking and Finance in June 1945 that the United States make a substantial loan to Britain, the second 'key currency' country, on two conditions. The first was that London liberalize the sterling area. Such a requirement could only be fulfilled by the introduction of sterling convertibility, a measure that, according to the theory behind Williams' plan, would encourage less powerful economies to dismantle their own control regimes. With sterling convertible the old sterling area dollar-pooling arrangements would become obsolete. Countries inside and outside the area would be able to use the foreign currency they earned in trade with Britain to purchase goods from the dollar area: sterling–dollar convertibility would automatically lead much of the world into a system based on the principles of the open door. At the same time progress towards this new era would be accelerated if Britain accepted the second condition, namely the pursuit of a postwar trade policy based on the principles of non-discrimination – a commitment that was incompatible with the long-term survival of Imperial Preference.[31]

The questions of how many dollars the British should have and on what conditions they were to have them were discussed at the Washington talks of September–December 1945, concluding in the Anglo-American Financial Agreement, signed by President Truman on 15 July 1946. It was the Williams rather than the Keynes agenda that dominated the proceedings. The British delegation ran into a tide of economic liberalism and conservative isolationism, strengthened by a popular enthusiasm for bringing home the troops and scaling down international commitments now the war was over. Keynes became increasingly depressed; at one point he even considered abandoning the exercise and returning home.[32] The amount of money on the table never approached even the $6 billion Keynes had suggested at the start of the negotiations, let alone the $8 billion for which he had originally hoped. The best Vinson and Clayton could do was offer an interest-bearing loan of $3.75 billion, plus $650 million as a final settlement of Lend–Lease. There was a welcome Canadian contribution of $1.25 billion, but this had been anticipated right from the start of the loan conversations and could not compensate for the shortfall of dollars from the United States.

In return for the American assistance Britain was obliged to embrace not just resident but non-resident convertibility for current transactions, to be operational one year after the President's signature of the Financial Agreement. This represented an unwelcome widening of convertibility and was, at the same time, a drastic curtailment of the transition period.[33] There was to be no separate cover for the sterling balances, merely a British agreement to negotiate reductions in them with the owners. This meant that the sterling balances negotiations over the subsequent two years achieved very little since Britain could not offer its creditors an incentive to scale down their claims. Indeed the looming deadline for convertibility gave sterling balance holders a positive reason for holding onto their balances, since it was obvious that before long there was a good chance it might be possible to exchange some of them for dollars.

The Agreement was a triumph for the economic liberals in Washington. It was also reassuring both for the bankers, whose relationship with the Bretton Woods institutions had been so equivocal, and for the exporters who had long been frustrated by the dollar pool and Imperial Preference. It represented a setback to those who supported the establishment of an international order built on Keynesian principles. Under convertibility, a Britain running a large payments deficit with the United States – and this remained a likely scenario given the limitations of the Financial Agreement – would not be able to introduce exchange controls on transactions with the dollar area. The rules permitted only old-fashioned orthodoxy, of the kind familiar to advocates of the gold standard system. During the Washington talks the American negotiators had tried to write into the loan agreement a clause depriving Britain of the advantages of the scarce currency provisions agreed at Bretton Woods. They had failed in this after vigorous protests from the British delegation and the Labour Cabinet in London. In fact, signature of the Financial Agreement would make this concession meaningless, in the short term at least, since it could only be invoked when there was a shortage of dollars in the International Monetary Fund; and it had been agreed at Bretton Woods not only that the Fund would be largely inactive during the transition period, but also that it would not thereafter become involved in the provision of reconstruction funds.

The British government recommended parliamentary approval of the loan and therefore membership of the Bretton Woods institutions; but it did so without any enthusiasm. There was a good deal of criticism in the press. The parliamentary debate was at times bitter. Keynes made a rather apologetic defence of the loan in the House of Lords; it may be asked why both he and the Cabinet were prepared to support it at all, if it fell so far short of the hopes they had held just a few months earlier. There were a number of reasons. First of all, it was appreciated that the dollars would make life easier for the population at a time when many were hoping for some relief from wartime austerity. Second, the loan was seen by both Keynes and leading Cabinet members as essential if the government's reconstruction programme was to be carried out. Third, Keynes and Hugh Dalton (the Chancellor of the Exchequer) both felt that there was a good chance of further, more generous, American aid if the Agreement failed after the British had at least tried to make it work. On the other hand, if Britain rejected the loan, refused to honour its commitments to Article VII and pressed on with bilateralism and the wartime sterling arrangements, there was no chance of future help from Washington and a risk of trade war instead.[34] In private, Keynes realized that bilateralism remained an option – but he preferred to hold it in reserve against an American Congressional failure to ratify the loan. Fourth, Keynes reckoned that if the government and the Bank of England listened to him and took some tough decisions – the former about overseas military commitments and the latter about the sterling balances (he advocated blocking for five years all balances accumulated up to 31 December 1946) – there was a chance the agreement might be adequate.

Finally, although Keynes made no secret of his disappointment, he did argue that there were encouraging signs it would still be possible, through Anglo-American co-operation, to reach 'the goal of international economic order amidst national diversities of policies'. And there was some evidence for his belief that there were still forces sympathetic to his viewpoint prominently placed in the United States. This had come out of the Anglo-American commercial talks held in Washington during the autumn of 1945, running in parallel with the financial negotiations. Here the British had successfully fought off an American attempt, led by the State Department, to press them into an International Trade Organization (ITO) that would outlaw not just imperial preference but also the use of import restrictions. What emerged was American agreement that measures to liberalize trade should not be unilateral but linked to all-round tariff reductions and to international economic expansion. The American negotiators accepted that the United States had a duty to maintain a high level of employment at home and that the charter of the new organization should contain escape clauses under which deficit countries would be permitted to maintain discriminatory trade controls. These commercial talks, therefore, did seem to show, in part at least, that Washington shared the Keynesian thesis that flourishing multilateral trade was dependent on the maintenance of buoyant internal economic conditions. On that basis, the British agreed to join the United States in a conference to establish the ground rules for a working ITO. The result was truer to the spirit of wartime optimism than the financial discussions; there was little doubt that this genuinely hopeful sign for the future would not survive rejection of the loan.[35]

Remaining hopes that the United States and Britain could together build a new international economic order were soon, however, to be dashed. In February 1946, Keynes was appointed British governor both of the Fund and of the Bank. The following month he went to the inaugural meeting of the governors of the two organizations, at Savannah, Georgia, USA. It was a depressing experience for Keynes and left him pessimistic about the prospects for future international economic co-operation.[36] Right from the start of the meeting, the Americans exerted pressure to have the headquarters of the Fund located in Washington. Keynes argued for New York. He pointed out that in Washington the Fund's independence would be compromised and it would become vulnerable to political pressure. Additionally he believed that the executive directors of the Fund should be part-time, selected from the top ranks of members' treasuries and finance ministries. But the Americans insisted on full-time executive directors, who would be paid generous tax-free salaries. Vinson succeeded in railroading this through the meeting with the help of extremely compliant delegations from China and Latin America.

The Anglo-American dispute about the staffing and location of the Fund was not trivial. It reflected a fundamental difference in philosophy. This had been present at Bretton Woods, had been glimpsed in the creation of the National Advisory Council, and had become increasingly prominent as the New Deal faded. It had soured the loan discussions and now threw a shadow over the Fund and the Bank right at the start of their careers. The Americans wanted an IMF whose operations would reflect the imperatives of their own foreign economic policy; in other words, its mission was to exercise constant pressure on members in the direction of currency convertibility, fixed exchange rates and non-discrimination in trade.[37] The British, on the other hand, inspired by Keynes, had believed that the Fund's deliberations would always be led by national policy programmes, rather than the reverse. Accordingly, Keynes envisaged a neutral organization that would allow the automatic use of drawing rights and meet to consider exchange rate alterations – something he thought unlikely to occur very often. It was an argument settled in the end by simple power politics: the British lacked both the international influence and the financial clout to make their views prevail either in Washington or Savannah.

The Savannah conference left Keynes disillusioned because it seemed clear to him now that Washington did not share his vision at all. There would not be a 'new order' in which every nation could pursue its own New Deal. Such an environment was politically unattractive in the United States, where there was a growing suspicion not just of expensive international commitments but of political experiments that smacked of 'socialism'. The organization of the Fund and of the Bank was designed to keep members from straying too far in this direction, and reflected the priorities both of American bankers and of State Department liberals. Returning to Britain, Keynes appears to have considered recommending to the Cabinet that the country withdraw from the Fund, an action that would, at the very least, have left a question mark over the future of the loan agreement and that pointed to adoption of the austere alternative economic strategy he had hoped to avoid. He was talked out of this by colleagues, contented himself with a rather cool report on the proceedings and died from a heart attack within a matter of weeks.[38]

In the end the 'new order' that emerged from the war was Washington's version. It owed more to pre-1939 orthodoxy than had seemed likely during the 1941–4 period. Yet this too was doomed to fail because it was out of step with the aspirations of the millions of people who looked to a better future now that the dictators had been vanquished. Whatever arrangements were to be made for the new era had to include provision for a system that generated jobs, houses and social security out of the wreckage left by the Second World War: 'freedom from want and freedom from fear', as President Roosevelt called it. It did not take long to become clear that the British loan and the Bretton Woods institutions were incapable of such a task: they were not designed for it, in terms either of their resources or of the politico-economic project they were supposed to fulfil. As a result Washington had to find a new way of retrieving the goal of a non-discriminatory world, or face its disappearance over the political horizon. By 1950 it was providing billions of dollars in reconstruction aid, mostly to western European states committed to economic policies that could not work in the absence of anti-dollar discrimination – and all of it in the name of Article VII!

◆ Notes

1. See J.K. Fairbank, Edwin O. Reischauer and Albert M. Craig, *East Asia: The Modern Transformation* (London: George Allen & Unwin, 1965), 501.
2. Ibid., 500.
3. Joyce C. Lebra (ed.), *Japan's Greater East Asia Co-Prosperity Sphere in World War II* (Kuala Lumpur: Oxford University Press, 1975), xiii.
4. See Robert W.D. Boyce, 'Britain's First "No" to Europe: Britain and the Briand Plan, 1929–30', *European Studies Review* 10 (1980), 17–45.
5. See Mark Mazower, *Dark Continent: Europe's Twentieth Century* (London: Penguin, 1999), 157.
6. Alan S. Milward, *The New Order and the French Economy* (Oxford: Oxford University Press, 1970), 146.
7. Albert Speer, *Inside the Third Reich* (London: Weidenfeld & Nicholson, 1970), 310.
8. Mazower, *Dark Continent*, 160.
9. See Alan S. Milward, 'Fascism and the economy', in W. Laqueur (ed.) *Fascism: A Reader's Guide* (London: Penguin, 1979), 420–4.
10. Alan S. Milward, *The New Order and the French Economy* (Oxford: Oxford University Press, 1970), 170, Table 23.
11. Robert Skidelsky, in *John Maynard Keynes, Vol. II The Economist as Saviour* (London: Macmillan, 1992), 476–9, accuses Keynes of flirting with fascism or communism. The full text of 'National self-sufficiency' can be found in *Collected Works of J.M. Keynes*, ed. D.E. Moggridge,

XXI, 233–46. The *Collected Works* (hereafter *CW*) were published by Macmillan (London) between 1971 and 1989.

12. John Maynard Keynes, *The General Theory of Employment, Interest and Money* (London: Macmillan, 1973 edn.; first published 1936), 349.
13. See Mazower, *Dark Continent*, 189.
14. Milward, *War, Economy and Society, 1939–1945*, 91. The impact of the Second World War on British politics is discussed at length in Paul Addison, *The Road to 1945* (London: Quartet Books, 1975) and, more briefly, in Scott Newton and Dilwyn Porter, *Modernization Frustrated: The Politics of Industrial Decline in Britain since 1900* (London: Unwin Hyman, 1988), Ch. 4.
15. Newton and Porter, *Modernization Frustrated*, 103.
16. Scott Newton, 'A "visionary hope" frustrated: J.M. Keynes and the origins of the postwar international monetary order', *Diplomacy and Statecraft*, Vol. 11 (2000), 193.
17. Newton, ibid., 194.
18. Quoted in Richard N. Gardner, *Sterling–Dollar Diplomacy: Anglo-American Collaboration in the Reconstruction of Multilateral Trade* (New York: Columbia University Press, 1980), 9.
19. This is covered by Richard N. Gardner in *Sterling–Dollar Diplomacy* and by the 'revisionist' historians whose work started to appear in the 1960s. Characteristic examples are Gabriel Kolko, *The Politics of War* (New York: Harper & Rowe, 1968) and Joyce and Gabriel Kolko, *The Limits of Power: The World and United States Foreign Policy 1945–1954* (New York: Harper & Rowe, 1972).
20. See the interview with Paul Sweezy by Christopher Phelps and Andros Skotnos in *Monthly Review*, Vol. 51 (1999), 39–40. Sweezy, a distinguished scholar on the American Left, worked in the London office of the OSS (Office of Strategic Services, forerunner of the postwar CIA) from 1942–5.
21. See Scott Newton, 'John Maynard Keynes and the Anglo-American special relationship: a reinterpretation', *Lobster* 36 (1998/99), 27–38; also Scott Newton, 'A "visionary hope" frustrated: J.M. Keynes and the origins of the postwar international monetary order', *Diplomacy and Statecraft*, Vol. 11 (2000), 189–210.
22. Gardner, *Sterling–Dollar Diplomacy*, 92–3.
23. Public Record Office, Kew, London (hereafter PRO), Cab66/23, WP (42), 10 April 1942, 159.
24. See Gardner, *Sterling–Dollar Diplomacy*, 93.
25. See, for example, PRO T247/40, Keynes to Beaverbrook, 24 April 1945; D.E. Moggridge, *Maynard Keynes: An Economist's Biography* (London: Routledge, 1992), 734–5, 750–3.
26. Fred Block, *The Origins of International Monetary Disorder* (Berkeley: University of California Press, 1977), 50–5. See also Stanley W. Black,

A Levite Among the Priests: Edward M. Bernstein and the Origins of the Bretton Woods Monetary System (Boulder, Colorado: Westview Press, 1991), 50–1 and PRO T247/40, memorandum by Keynes on 'Mr Burgess's address on international financial cooperation', 25 May 1945.

27. See T247/40, memorandum by Keynes on 'Bretton Woods', 14 June 1945.
28. Keynes, 'Overseas financial policy in Stage III', 15 May 1945, in Donald Moggridge (ed.), *CW*, XXIV, 272–3.
29. Moggridge, *Maynard Keynes*, 783.
30. PRO Cab129/1, C.P. (45), 14 August 1945, 112.
31. Block, *Origins of International Monetary Disorder*, 50.
32. See Newton, 'A "visionary hope" frustrated', 200.
33. It is simply false to claim, as the otherwise excellent Block does (*Origins of International Monetary Disorder*, 65) that Keynes 'was not unhappy with this obligation'. The evidence of the Treasury papers and his own files contradicts this statement, which is derived from Roy Harrod's very flawed account of Keynes' views and behaviour in *The Life of John Maynard Keynes* (London: Penguin, 1975). See PRO FO371/45714, UE6249/1094/53, where Keynes is quoted in the minutes of a meeting held in Washington, 26 November 1945. For Harrod's flaws, see Scott Newton, 'Deconstructing Harrod: some critical reflections on the life of John Maynard Keynes', *Contemporary British History* 15 (2001), 15–27.
34. The Chancellor's views can be found in his autobiography: Hugh Dalton, *High Tide and After* (London: Muller, 1962), 89; for Keynes, see 'The sterling area settlement', PRO T247/74, 1 February 1946.
35. See Block, *Origins of International Monetary Disorder*, 67; PRO Cab129/4, C.P. (45), 297, gives the view of the then President of the Board of Trade (Stafford Cripps) on the progress of the commercial talks.
36. Keynes' letter to Kahn is quoted in, for example, Newton, 'A "visionary hope" frustrated', 204; his contemptuous opinion of how the US delegation engineered a majority of votes in favour of their own preferred IMF staffing arrangements and structure was recorded in 'The Savannah conference on the Bretton Woods final act', 29 March 1946, *CW* XXVI, 220–38.
37. Raymond F. Mikesell, *The Bretton Woods Debates: A Memoir* (Princeton: Princeton Essays in International Finance, No. 192, March 1994), 52.
38. Newton, 'A "visionary hope" frustrated', 203–5. The full extent of Keynes' disillusionment was not revealed in Roy Harrod's biography, first published in 1951. The author himself, a staunch pro-American with more sympathy than Keynes for economic liberalism, suppressed some details. On top of this, the text was subject to government censorship. The story is told in Newton, ibid., and 'John Maynard Keynes and the Anglo-American special relationship', *Lobster* 36 (1998/2000), 27–38.

2

THE LIMITS OF LIBERALISM, 1946–1951

◆ The Failure of Universalism

From the late 1940s through to the end of the 1960s the world experienced what economic historians later called the 'golden age'.[1] These were years of consistent growth, full employment and rising affluence. There was an explosion in international trade, particularly between developed countries. In 1951–3 and 1969–71 world trade in manufactured goods rose by 349 per cent, an expansion that exceeded even that of output, growing by 194 per cent over the same period.[2] This process was encouraged by the maintenance of high demand and by successive rounds of negotiated reductions to trade barriers. At the same time the wartime controls on currency convertibility were dismantled, and from 1949 until 1967 fixed exchange rates prevailed throughout the advanced capitalist world. The economic nationalism that had haunted the world economy between the two world wars retreated in the face of progress towards non-discrimination: it seemed that the liberal ambitions of wartime American planners had been fulfilled and their version of a new order had, as their ideology taught them it would, brought unprecedented prosperity to unprecedented numbers. Economists and economic historians gave their approval to this argument, attributing prosperity to the benevolent institutional framework agreed at Bretton Woods. In many textbooks the postwar age of affluence was known as the 'Bretton Woods era'.[3]

In fact, the evolution of the post-1945 international economy owed little to Bretton Woods, and the 'Bretton Woods era' lasted for a very brief time: from 15 July until 20 August 1947. America's campaign for the open door did not take long to fall foul of government policy throughout the developed world. Both the institutions and practices that were conducive to expansion owed as much to resistance against US-inspired economic liberalism as they did to anything that came out of Bretton Woods.

Only a few months after its apparent triumph concerning the world's postwar international financial architecture at Savannah, Washington encountered stiff resistance to its plans for international trade liberalization. The Truman administration proposed that the Economic and Social Council of the United Nations convene an international conference whose aim would be the establishment of an International Trade Organization (ITO). To this end it produced a draft ITO charter that would commit all members to strictly non-discriminatory trade policies. The document was extensively discussed at a series of international conferences between 1946 and 1948, and it quickly became obvious that there was considerable dissent from the American campaign for a speedy all-round dismantling of preferential arrangements, import duties and other forms of trade restriction. The opposition drew together a coalition of states, ranging from the industrial European economies to countries such as Australia and India, which had specialized in food exports and primary production but were now keen to develop sizeable industrial sectors.[4] These two countries were supported by the British, and an American attempt to commit all ITO members to the elimination of import quotas by the end of 1949 – quantitative restrictions on imports of specified commodities – was wrecked.[5]

The tension between the American drive for economic liberalism and the determination of most other parties to the talks to preserve full employment led to the production of a compromise document, signed at Havana by 53 nations in 1948. The Havana Charter declared its allegiance to trade liberalization *and* to the protection of employment; no signatory would have to pursue orthodox deflationary measures on encountering balance of payments problems, but would be permitted to take interventionist steps. The settlement was some way removed from what American negotiators had wanted and, in fact, the US Congress refused to ratify the Charter. In its place there emerged the General Agreement on Tariffs and Trade (GATT), as a result of talks designed to secure reductions in import duties held in Geneva during 1946 and 1947 between the US and 23 other countries. On 30 October 1947 the participants signed a Draft Agreement on Tariffs and Trade, and this was followed by the establishment of the General Agreement in January of the following year.

The GATT was seen as a stop-gap pending the establishment of the ITO, but of course this never happened and the GATT enjoyed a career lasting almost half a century. It had its own administration in Geneva and acted more as 'a forum and a code of rules'[6] than as an organization. It was where governments met to discuss tariff reductions and rules relating to the conduct of international trade policy, and members agreed to observe a common code. This was based on acceptance of two principles. The first was non-discrimination: under the 'most-favoured-nation' clause, concessions made by one country to another covering imports of a specified commodity had to be extended to the imports of the same commodity from other nations. The second was reciprocity so that the benefits of trade liberalization were shared by all parties and could not be unilateral.

There were, however, exception clauses, and the most significant of these fell in three areas. First, membership of the GATT did not preclude the right to take protective measures in the event of balance of payments difficulties or in cases where imports threatened the existence of local producers. Second, no commitment made under GATT rules took precedence over pre-existing national legislation; finally, the 'most favoured nation' rule could be suspended in favour both of regional trading associations committed to reducing trade barriers, such as customs unions and free trade areas, and of preferential arrangements between industrialized and developing countries. From the perspective of the American liberals all this was rather modest – but it did represent a start to postwar international trade co-operation. At the very first meeting, in Geneva in 1947, the USA and Canada made tariff concessions useful to European industrial producers and agreed to the maintenance of quantitative restrictions on their exports so that the reciprocal European tariff reductions made little impact in the short term. The bargaining continued at another five meetings up to 1962, in Annecy (1949), Torquay (1950–1) and Geneva (1955–6 and 1961–2).[7]

The American concessions occurred at a time when US foreign economic policy was increasingly focused not on projects to reorganize capitalism worldwide but on postwar western European economic recovery. This new strategy was being driven by Washington's anxiety about the darkening international picture.

Hopes that the wartime Grand Alliance between the USA, the USSR and the UK would persist into peacetime had proved unfounded. Between 1945 and 1947 there was growing western anxiety about what looked like a Soviet project to turn eastern Europe into a collection of satellite states. A powerful, indigenous communist movement was engaged in a bloody civil war with the centre-right in Greece. Early in 1947 the British, who had supported the anti-communist forces there for three years, announced they could no longer afford to do so. In Washington there was anxiety that a communist triumph would mean the extension of Soviet influence into the Mediterranean.

Meanwhile attempts to work out an agreed future for Germany failed, and in both London and Washington there were suspicions that the USSR, aware of the importance of the German economy to postwar European recovery, was being obstructive in the expectation that economic crisis would overtake western Europe if it was deprived of German capital goods and the German market. It was feared that the powerful Communist Parties in France and Italy, and the German Social-Democrats, would then ride to power on a tide of popular frustration. The European continent would fall under the political, strategic and economic domination of the USSR – Stalin would have succeeded where Hitler had failed, creating a continental bloc, hostile to the USA, of enormous industrial and military potential. In these circumstances the Americans launched, in March 1947, the Truman Doctrine, designed to 'contain' Soviet expansion 'primarily through economic and financial aid'.[8] The new policy meant that Washington could not afford to alienate nation states that might serve as allies in the anti-communist cause, least of all in Europe. It followed that the dogmatic liberalism

of the immediate postwar period had to accommodate itself to the more interventionist politico-economic strategies now being pursued throughout most of
the non-Soviet world.

◆ The Collapse of Bretton Woods

Concentration on western Europe after 1947 was reinforced by the breakdown of
the Bretton Woods initiative to resurrect a global financial system based on the
interconvertibility of currencies at fixed rates of exchange. The key to this new,
open era was supposed to be sterling convertibility, as agreed in the 1945 negotiations that led up to the Anglo-American Financial Agreement. But sterling convertibility, introduced on 15 July 1947, was over within six weeks and with the
failure of this experiment the attempt to build a world safe for Article VII came to
centre on the reconstruction of a new, liberal-capitalist western Europe.

Sterling convertibility foundered on the postwar 'dollar shortage'. This problem was rooted in the upheaval in the world economy that had resulted from the
war, but it was made particularly intractable by the economic policies pursued
throughout much of the world and especially in Europe after 1945. It was not
just in Britain that electorates supported left-wing regimes determined to embark
on social reform, the redistribution of income to the working class, full employment, the modernization of industry, agricultural protection and the construction of a minimum standard of living for all. In liberated Europe most
administrations were socialist led or dominated. In France, the new Fourth
Republic developed its own 'Modernization and Re-equipment Plan' and communists participated in the government. Here, as elsewhere, postwar governments spent heavily on re-equipment, public transport and communications.
They saw investment as the key to national revival and future prosperity; consumption was held down while capital formation was pushed well in excess of
prewar levels in almost every west European state apart from Germany.

The reconstruction of battered and war-torn countries generated a significant
demand for imports of raw materials, capital goods and vehicles. Up to the outbreak of war Germany had supplied a large proportion of Europe's imports of
capital goods, and these had been paid for by reciprocal exports and by trade
surpluses with Britain. But by 1946 the German position in European trade had
been undermined by the effects of the war and by the limits on production
maintained by the Allies. In 1938 what became the American, British and
French zones of occupation after the war had accounted for 16.62 per cent of
all Europe's production – but this prop to the European economy had collapsed
by 1946 (Table 2.1). At the same time the food surpluses that had been produced in eastern and central Europe before 1939 and exported to the western
half of the continent collapsed as a result of wartime disruption. Postwar concentration on national development combined with the rising international tension caused by the emerging Cold War to prevent their reappearance, forcing west

TABLE 2.1: GERMAN POSTWAR PRODUCTION (1938 = 100)

Quarter	1946	Quarter	1947
1	22	1	24
2	26	2	23
3	31	3	37
4	31	–	–

Source: derived from United Nations Economic Commission for Europe, *Survey of the Economic Situation and Prospects of Europe* (Geneva, 1948), 3, Table 1

European states to look elsewhere for a substantial proportion of their foodstuffs. In the circumstances of the time there was only one country where all these commodities could be found in abundance: the United States, whose economy had flourished during the war years. But how were the imports to be financed?

Up to 1914 neither the British nor the continental Europeans had experienced difficulties in affording imports from the United States. The pattern of international settlements had revolved around Britain's ability to finance deficits with both continental Europe and the United States by generating trade surpluses with Australia, West Africa and East Asia (above all India, but also Malaya, which had been an important supplier of rubber to the USA) as well as via invisible income from banking and shipping services centred on the City of London. But this system barely survived between 1918 and 1939. The United States emerged from the First World War as the world's leading creditor nation and in the 1920s Europe's need for dollars was covered by an outflow of short-term funds from the United States. But in 1929 capital flows from the United States to Europe began to peter out and in 1931 they were reversed. The intensifying Depression sharply reduced demand and as a result it became hard to obtain dollars from an American economy that offered neither loans nor market opportunities. The inability of non-dollar countries to sustain large trade imbalances with the United States led to a very sharp contraction of international trade during the 1930s.

The Second World War had administered the *coup de grâce* to this old system. British invisible earnings slumped thanks to the loss of 25 per cent of the country's shipping and almost 50 per cent of its investments.[9] After 1945 it was no longer possible for Britain and continental Europe to pay for dollar goods with offsetting surpluses earned in trade with third countries. The primary producing nations themselves needed to reconstruct their own societies and economies and, like the developed world, they looked to America for the wherewithal to accomplish this task. Much of Asia suffered from shortages of fertilizer and food, which could only be supplied by the USA. India found that many of its needs for

TABLE 2.2: SIZE AND GEOGRAPHICAL DISTRIBUTION
OF US EXPORT (+) AND IMPORT (−) BALANCES,
1938 AND 1946 ($ MILLIONS, HALF-YEARLY
AVERAGES)

	1938	1946
Europe	+380	+1653
Latin America	+39	+201
North America	+104	+273
Asia	−26	+218
Africa	+32	+91
Oceania	+39	−33

Source: Milward, *War, Economy, Society* (London: Penguin, 1987),
358, Table 35

the capital goods essential to industrialization as well as for food could be met
only by purchasing dollar goods. The result was a shift to dependence on dollar
goods throughout the globe (Table 2.2).

The most dramatic surge in US exports was to Europe (including the United
Kingdom). Overall, European imports in 1947 were only 7 per cent higher than
prewar, but the volume of imports from the United States was 130 per cent up on
its 1938 figure.[10]

Nine-tenths of the increase was in goods essential for relief and reconstruction
such as grain, foodstuffs, tobacco, coal, timber, iron, machinery, vehicles, chemicals and ships (Table 2.3). In 1946 the consolidated deficit of all European countries in their current transactions with the rest of the world was $5.8 billion,
rising to $7.5 billion in 1947. The deficits with the United States in each year
were, respectively, $4.2 billion and $5.4 billion, or over 70 per cent of the total.
These were the outward signs of the disruption to the pattern of international
settlements caused by the war and then reconstruction, and in 1946 they were
financed partly through official US government assistance, recycled through the
United Nations Relief and Reconstruction Agency (UNRRA), and partly through
the expenditure of $2 billion in hard currency reserves.

Senior State Department officials, touring western Europe in the spring of
1947, claimed that the economic situation was desperate.[11] The picture painted
was one of economic failure as countries ran out of food and cash, with bombed-
out factories operating intermittently due to shortages of raw materials and
spare parts.[12]

TABLE 2.3: US EXPORTS TO EUROPE PREWAR AND POSTWAR BY
PRINCIPAL PRODUCTS ($ MILLIONS OF PREWAR PURCHASING
POWER)

Product	Prewar	Postwar
1. *Foodstuffs*	*('35 or '37)*	*(1947)*
Grains	10	370
Sugar, refined	5	10
Meat	25	35
Dairy products	–	105
Eggs and products	–	65
Veg. oils, whale oils and other animal fats	15	20
Fish and fish products	10	15
Veg. and preparations	–	20
Tobacco	100	115
Fruit and fruit juices	80	45
Miscellaneous	–	15
Total for foodstuffs	250	815
2. *Raw materials and semi-manufactures*		
Coal and coke	–	200
Non-metallic materials	10	25
Timber and woods (incl. paper)	40	50
Lubricating oils	55	70
Petroleum and products	80	80
Iron and steel	15	80
Copper, raw and manufactured	45	30
Other non-ferrous metals	10	20
Raw cotton	290	150
Other veg. products, inedible	15	20

(Continued)

TABLE 2.3: (*Continued*)

Product	Prewar	Postwar
Wool	–	10
Animal products	30	35
Total raw materials	**590**	**770**
3. *Manufactured goods*		
Textiles and clothing	20	200
Rubber and manufactures	10	40
Iron and steel manufactures	10	25
Chemicals and fertilizer	50	130
Machinery	130	235
Vehicles	130	430
Relief and charity	–	50
Miscellaneous	45	80
Total manufactured	**395**	**1100**
Total 1–3	**1235**	**2695**

Source: derived from United Nations, Economic Commission for Europe, *Survey of the Economic Situation and Prospects of Europe*, 43, Table 27

    This did not represent an accurate analysis. In fact, the early postwar period had seen a vigorous recovery throughout most of western Europe, stimulated by the major capital investment programmes. By the second quarter of 1947 industrial production in all Europe (excluding Germany) had regained its 1938 levels. The 'crisis' was not one of production but reflected Europe's lavish expenditure of dollars and inability to find any significant means of earning them. How long could this continue, given that UNRRA was due to be terminated and that gold and dollar reserves were becoming increasingly scarce?

    In the prewar era the answer to a deficit of such magnitude had been deflation. Yet this course was now anathema and taken only in Italy. Given the general commitment to reconstruction the more usual response was for governments to sustain domestic activity and intervene in the foreign trade sector. Thus gold and dollar reserves were safeguarded for essential purchases, their use limited by foreign exchange controls, as well as by import restrictions that discriminated in favour of capital goods and against consumer goods and luxury items. At the same time the need to conserve hard currency while protecting domestic expansion led most west European governments to negotiate bilateral trade and payments agreements, whose number exceeded 200 by the end of 1947.[13] These bilateral agreements contained provisions for the extension of credit facilities to debtors so that there was no need for the parties to them to pursue a short-term balancing of accounts. Instead a 'swing' beyond strict balance was allowed and as a result the bilateral arrangements helped to sustain some expansion of intra-European trade. But they contained a serious shortcoming. From late 1946 persistent debtor and surplus positions began to emerge – for example, in the cases of France, the Netherlands and Denmark as against Switzerland, Sweden and Belgium. In these cases the creditors were faced with the problem of accumulating inconvertible balances of foreign currency when what they really needed was dollars. The debtors were therefore obliged to pay out of their own gold and hard currency reserves or choke off imports from their creditors, a process that threatened to subject trade to disruptive shocks.

After 1945 sterling convertibility seemed to offer an escape. The formal opening of the Bretton Woods era meant that Britain's trading partners could use current earnings of sterling to finance deficits, especially those with the United States, while in theory Britain's import requirements would be financed by invisibles and its own overseas surpluses. But invisibles had collapsed and Britain not only carried the burden of the sterling balances but ran substantial overseas trade deficits outside Europe (mostly with the USA). On top of this the convertibility obligation extended to *sterling only* so that the British could not use their non-dollar trade surpluses to offset what became an accelerating run on the gold and dollar reserves. The dollar outflow was intensified by the existence of the sterling balances, and although holders had concluded what were called 'gentlemen's agreements' with the Bank of England that these would not be used to finance current import requirements, they paid small attention to these arrangements in practice. The evidence suggests that substantial illicit sterling balance conversions were occurring, given that throughout 1946 Britain only provided $85 million from its reserves to sterling countries but $643 million in just six months of 1947, from the start of April until the end of September.[14] What convertibility had provoked was in fact a worldwide movement out of sterling into dollars, and this was reflected in the British dollar drain, which reached $868.5 million between the start of July and 15 August. By this time it was obvious that with no intervention to stop the run there would be nothing left of the American loan come the end of the year and precious little in the gold and foreign currency reserves. Convertibility had, in short, proved unsustainable and in recognition of this it was suspended by Britain's Labour government on 20 August 1947.

After the suspension of convertibility the sterling area once more became a discriminatory economic bloc. The dollar-pooling arrangements were reintroduced and in September 1947 leading members of the area agreed to tighten both their import restrictions against dollar goods and their exchange controls to prevent leakages of hard currency. Britain negotiated a set of new, bilateral agreements by which both parties agreed to hold specified sums of each other's currency before starting conversions into gold or dollars. Forced to choose between its commitments to Article VII and the continued prosecution of its reconstruction programme, Britain, in keeping with the spirit of the time, chose the latter.

The British measures after 20 August effectively meant, of course, the reintroduction of the wartime sterling area. Trade throughout most of the non-dollar world was now as closely controlled, if not more so, than it had been in the 1930s, and the Bretton Woods 'system' that had been supposed to lead the world to a new, liberal era had foundered. It had indeed proved inadequate in the face of postwar aspirations and economic dislocation. The problem facing the United States in the summer of 1947, therefore, was how to salvage its wartime international economic objectives. Given the coming of the Cold War and the political imperative of reconstruction it was clear that any initiative to rescue the long-term aim of non-discrimination would have to work with postwar governments and electorates, and guarantee the continuation of economic expansion, above all in western Europe.

◆ The Marshall Plan

Europe's economic 'crisis' of 1947, which was in reality a growing foreign exchange problem, generated anxiety in Washington. A State-War-Navy Co-ordinating Committee meeting of early 1947 warned that if US exports were to suffer a decline as a result of other countries' inability to pay for them, then business activity would become depressed and unemployment would rise. These fears led the Truman Administration to the conclusion that nothing less than a major government foreign aid programme was needed to ensure that export levels remained buoyant. Here was the germ of what became known as the Marshall Plan for European recovery, announced to the world by Secretary of State George Marshall on 5 June 1947.

The Plan was, however, more than a mechanism for supporting US exports. It was aimed at the complex of problems that had disrupted Washington's attempt to create a postwar world in the image of liberal capitalism. Thus on one level it was intended as a reinforcement to the Truman Doctrine on the assumption that dollars to help with economic recovery would ease living conditions in western Europe and diminish the appeal of communist parties there. On another level, the Marshall initiative represented an acknowledgement that the west Europeans required a major transfusion of dollars if they were not to embrace planned trade and permanent discrimination against the dollar.

But the dollars were not to be provided unconditionally. The idea was that European governments should pool their recovery efforts, abandoning national recovery plans and instead supplying each other, as far as resources would allow, with US aid filling the gaps until 'viability', or freedom from dependence on extraordinary sources, had been achieved. The target for this was 1952, and thereafter it was hoped that western Europe could take its place in an international economic system based on the principles of Article VII; Marshall Aid was, in effect, money to ease countries through the transition to 'normal' peacetime trade and currency arrangements.

Washington had clear ideas about how this could be done. It envisaged, first, the production by participating countries of combined European recovery plans, which could then be presented annually to the United States up to 1951–2; second, the rehabilitation of the German economy, as a supplier of capital goods and as a market for exports from other European states; third, the liberalization of European trade and payments; and fourth, the formation by participating counties of a 'continuing organization', which would facilitate the maintenance of co-operation between them once the aid programme had come to an end. Unless these four conditions were met there could be no guarantee that the dollars would flow across the Atlantic.

The Marshall Plan, which became the European Recovery Programme (ERP), was a highly ambitious operation whose aim was the transformation of Europe into a liberal-capitalist community. Why did American policy-makers wish to reform the political and economic organization of the continent in so fundamental a way? In essence they believed that without European unity there could be no lasting recovery, or certainly not one compatible with US strategic interests. To begin with, there was the urgency of German economic revival. But achieving this required the reassurance of Germany's recent victims, above all the French. It seemed clear that German reconstruction would only be acceptable if it were to be located inside the framework of a new European structure whose institutions were strong enough to contain the resulting political and economic threat it presented to the rest of the continent.

Even without the need for Germany's peaceful rehabilitation Washington's planners would have championed the cause of integration. This enthusiasm derived from a conviction that Europe's dollar deficit could only be overcome by higher production. But how? Contemporary economic wisdom, in the form of customs union theory, seemed to provide the answer. It was widely held that the most effective way to maximize the efficiency of the factors of production in any given area was to remove any restrictions on their movement. Thus it was believed that the creation of a large single European market would encourage the growth of intra-European trade and in so doing correct the imbalance with the United States. It followed that the bilateral trade and exchange agreements that had grown up on the continent since 1945 should be removed. Not only were they seen as constraints on expansion but US aid to secure the flow of vital imports would render them unnecessary. Economic liberalization could begin and the way would be clear for progress towards an open international economy to be resumed.

Marshall's 5 June speech was addressed to all of Europe, including the USSR. Indeed, the Soviet Union sent a delegation to the Paris Conference of governments interested in exploring the American offer. However, its members complained that Washington was using aid as a tool of its imperialistic determination to extend free market capitalism. After just a week of fruitless conversations the Soviets walked out, an act that guaranteed the economic division of Europe to match the political divide between the western and eastern blocs. Participation in the Marshall Plan was now limited to 16 countries: Austria, Belgium, Denmark, France, Greece, Iceland, Ireland, Italy, Luxembourg, the Netherlands, Norway, Portugal, Sweden, Turkey, the United Kingdom and the western-occupied zones of Germany. Moscow meanwhile embarked on its own plan to integrate the economies of the European states within its own sphere, based on investment in heavy industry and agricultural collectivization, all funded by a vigorous repression of consumption. The upshot was the Council of Mutual Economic Assistance (CMEA), better known as COMECON, formally established in 1949.

The withdrawal of the Soviets, and of the governments within their sphere of influence, from the Paris Conference, was greeted with relief in Washington and London. Indeed the State Department had framed the conditions for assistance in a way designed to encourage Moscow's distrust and in so doing provoke its departure. For a start this made the task of the Truman administration easier when it came to seeking approval for $17 billion for European Recovery Programme funding from an anti-communist Congress. After an initial appropriation of 'interim aid' to those participating in the Marshall Plan, Congress agreed in April 1948 to allocate to ERP a sum of $13.3 billion over four years. Second, the absence of the Soviet Union and its allies squared with the objective of containment since it allowed the build-up of a west European bloc that was allied with the United States both in the quest for multilateralism and in the struggle against communism.

Management of ERP was placed in the hands of the Economic Co-operation Administration (ECA) centred in Washington under Paul Hoffman, President of Studebaker. The ECA also had its own Special Representative (W. Averall Harriman, merchant banker and ambassador to the USSR from 1943 to 1946), who was based in Paris, and it established missions in all participating countries. Assistance was shared between governments according to the size of their respective dollar deficits, which meant that the lion's share was mopped up by Britain and France (23 per cent and 20.6 per cent of the total respectively).[15] The practical emphasis of the scheme was on widening bottlenecks and improving productivity. Thus the aid package, 90 per cent of which was in the form of grants, was intended to guarantee the supplies of the food, animal feed, fertilizer, fuel, raw materials and capital equipment that had taken up such a large share of western Europe's hard currency reserves in the postwar period, in expectation that a continuing flow of vital imports would prevent any setback to recovery. In France and the Netherlands, for example, this meant substantial machinery and vehicle imports; in Britain and Germany there was a heavy reliance on food.[16] At the same time resources were provided to encourage investment expenditure, both in local infrastructure and key industries – an exercise handled through the deployment of 'counterpart funds'. Here aid recipients matched dollar grants with equivalent funds of local currency. These were spent on worthy projects, subject to ECA mission approval, such as the reconstruction of electricity, gas

TABLE 2.4: INVESTMENT OF ECA COUNTERPART
FUNDS BY SECTOR ($ MILLIONS)

Electricity, gas and power	956.0
Transport, communications and shipping	781.3
Agriculture	623.9
Coal mining, mining, quarrying	452.4
Primary metals, chemicals, strategic minerals	332.8
Machinery	164.2
Light industry	64.7
Petroleum and coal products	22.0
Technical assistance	20.3
Other and undistributed	452.1
Total	**3869.7**

Source: derived from Milward, *The Reconstruction of Western Europe,
1945–51* (London: Methuen, 1984), 109, Table 20

and power, the renewal of transport systems, the rebuilding of national coal-mining industries and the modernization of agriculture (Table 2.4).

Unsurprisingly, the disbursement of counterpart funds reflected the priorities of individual governments: there was no common theme but most took advantage of their availability. Their existence relieved the French Modernization Plan from dependence on an unwilling private sector and cautious publicly owned banks, so that the Modernization and Re-equipment Fund used them to finance 33 per cent of its investment expenditure in 1948, 50 per cent in 1949 and 30 per cent in 1950. At the same time, France spent $724.5 million of its overall $1845.3 million on electricity, gas and power; the Netherlands used $138.9 million of its $180.5 million on agriculture; $269.9 million of Italy's $591.9 million was devoted to transport, communications and shipping; Austria devoted just under one-third of its $300 million to the modernization of the transport sector, notably railway electrification. The new Federal Republic of Germany, formed out of the union of the Anglo-American and French occupation zones in 1949, concentrated on heavy industry and spent 43.5 per cent of its allocation on coal mining. The only exceptions were Britain and Norway; both chose to use their allocations exclusively on debt retirement.[17]

There is no doubt that Marshall Aid represented a major transfer of resources across the Atlantic. It was for most recipients a significant fraction of the annual GNP: in its first year it added as much as 14.8 per cent to the Austrian national income, 10.8 per cent to the Dutch, 6.5 per cent to the French and 2.4 per cent to the British. These are substantial figures, exceeding in most cases the annual rate of GNP growth at the time.

The scale of ERP in terms of the imports it financed, together with the investment programmes facilitated by counterpart funds and the obviousness of European recovery after 1948, led many subsequent commentators to claim that it had been a triumphant success. For the best part of a generation it was taken as axiomatic that the plan had built the foundations of postwar European prosperity and in so doing had guaranteed a democratic future for the western half of the continent.[18] This interpretation was challenged by Milward, who surveyed the leading importers of capital goods in Marshall Europe and argued that in the absence of ERP all of them bar France and the Netherlands would have been able to afford 1949 levels of capital goods imports as long as expenditure of dollars on food imports was frozen at the point it had reached in 1947.[19] Yet this is a deceptively modest claim as well as being a rather limited approach. Britain, for example, was not a major importer of capital goods, spending on average over one-third of each annual ERP allocation on food – but even this was not enough to prevent, in 1948 and 1949, rationing of meat, cheese, butter and margarine, cooking fat, sugar, milk and eggs (no one could have more than one egg a week).[20] Absence of Marshall Aid would have meant an intensification of this austerity and a return to bread rationing, which was abolished in July 1948. In France, in 1947, working-class dissatisfaction with frozen living standards led to the resignation of the communists from the government and provoked a wave of civil unrest. How much more serious would this have become in the absence of Marshall Aid? Overall it seems safe to say that the early historians of the post-1945 era overestimated the impact of Marshall Aid but, all the same, ERP generally allowed governments to maintain expansionist economic policies that achieved high levels of investment without putting excessive pressure on consumption. In particular the counterpart funds were a welcome addition to domestic sources of capital. Without the extra dollars reconstruction may still have been achieved – but more slowly and painfully, with lower living standards and in the teeth of popular disillusionment.

◆ Washington Frustrated?

If Marshall Aid cannot be said to have been solely responsible for bringing about the recovery of Europe it is equally difficult to argue that it created the liberal-capitalist Europe desired by the US policy planners who had devised the scheme. One school of neo-Marxist historians has argued that ERP was a broadly successful imperialist exercise that reformed European capitalism and brought it within the orbit of American corporations and finance during the 1950s and 1960s.[21] Yet this argument, along with the claim that Marshall Aid was the foundation of the new, pacific, co-operative Europe of the twentieth century's second half, underestimates the level of resistance to liberalization throughout much of Marshall Europe, and the determination of participants in the programme to shape their own international economic environment.

American policy-makers were encouraged when the participating countries established a 'continuing organization', known as the Organization for European Economic Co-operation (OEEC), in April 1948. The role of the OEEC was to prosecute European integration. There were three principal routes to this objective. The first was through the construction of a long-term economic recovery plan covering all of Marshall Europe, the second involved collaboration on the division of aid between recipients, and the third required significant steps to the liberalization of trade and payments, ending with a single market characterized by fully mobile factors of production. By the end of 1950 the nucleus of an integrated Europe did exist – but ironically its creation owed more to European resistance to Washington's plans than it did to the plans themselves.

The first of the three routes to integration was abandoned fairly rapidly. Work began on the production of a long-term programme during the summer of 1948, but major difficulties soon emerged. These were mostly the product of national economic policy choices on the part of member states, which when put together proved highly incompatible. For example, the French planned a significant increase in food exports by 1952–3, aiming to send a million tons of wheat to Britain alone – an objective that could not be squared with Britain's postwar commitment to the reduction of dependence on imported food and its replacement by domestic agricultural production. High-level Anglo-French talks designed to iron out these discrepancies achieved nothing.[22] At the same time the Belgians ran into criticism within the OEEC for over-reliance on exports to the rest of western Europe, and the Italians were attacked for building up trade surpluses while pursuing excessively deflationary policies that resulted in high unemployment (17 per cent of the workforce by December 1948) and relatively low demand for imported goods.[23] When the final version of the long-term plan appeared it revealed that, overall, members were aiming for a 20 per cent increase in production. This entailed continuing dependence on dollar imports with a deficit of $1 billion foreseen as late as 1952–3, by which time ERP would be finished. The document explained that participating countries would finance the gap by expanding exports to OEEC partners – a futile aspiration, in fact, since the planning exercise had shown that members were reluctant to receive imports from each other! When the 'long-term plan' appeared at the end of 1948 it was obviously going to be unacceptable to the ECA and Congress, so it was quickly redubbed an 'Interim Report' and explicitly denied being a 'joint European recovery programme'.[24] The exercise had collapsed into bathos and was not to be repeated. As far as Washington was concerned the episode confirmed the resilience of *national* planning and the abiding autarkic tendencies of the Europeans; it was a setback to hopes for integration as well as to prospects that 'viability' and multilateralism could be achieved by 1952.

This frustration was to be repeated, and for similar reasons, when it came to trade and payments, and to the division of aid. The ECA, in the persons of

Hoffman and Harriman, was keen to inject increasing doses of liberal capitalism into western Europe, aiming at the replacement of the bilateral arrangements that had proliferated since 1945 with a multilateral clearing system
covering the whole of Marshall Europe. The idea was to start with currency
transferability, whereby OEEC members would be able to trade freely with
each other, balancing surplus and deficit positions not on a country-by-country
basis but with the group as a whole. The ultimate objective, however, would be
complete convertibility, with foreign currency surpluses earned in western
Europe changeable into dollars. At the same time participating countries were
encouraged to agree on the progressive removal of obstacles to trade, notably
tariffs and quantitative restrictions, the result of all this deregulation being the
creation of a West European Customs Union (including the western zones of
Germany).

Washington reckoned its plans could be fulfilled if the British took the initiative in driving forward the process of integration. The United Kingdom was
apparently the most stable and prosperous of all the European democracies, and
was also the most powerful in military terms. Britain's financial problems may
have forced a retreat from Empire but its prestige in Europe was at a high point
following its role in the 1939–45 war, and its position at the centre of the sterling
area ensured that the liberalization of the west European currencies (including
sterling) would embrace most of the non-dollar world outside the Soviet Union
and China. The British could be helped by the 'strong' OEEC with its own
Secretary-General, a figure of Cabinet rank and therefore able to negotiate with
national governments on an equal footing. At the same time the organization's
constitution should allow it to take decisions on the basis of majority votes – in
other words no member would be able to veto a policy if it took a minority view.

In fact the British had no interest in prosecuting this liberal agenda. They
actively opposed ECA attempts to liberalize payments arrangements and succeeded in wrecking efforts to enhance the power of the OEEC. Indeed, British foreign economic policy was driving the country away from western Europe rather
than closer to it. There were a number of reasons for this. First, only 25 per cent
of Britain's trade was with OEEC countries, whereas approaching 50 per cent
both of its exports and its imports went to and came from the sterling area.
Second, the postwar British Labour government encouraged manufacturers to
export more to the United States and Canada in order to earn dollars directly;
trade surpluses in western Europe would only result in accumulation of soft currencies and would not go towards the reduction of Britain's dollar gap. Against
this it could be argued that the UK could have manoeuvred itself into the position of earning convertible surpluses from exports to participating countries if it
had worked in support of the ECA's objectives concerning currency liberalization
and the OEEC. However, this was just what Labour could not do.

The fundamental problem arose from the importance of safeguarding the
gold and dollar reserves from a rerun of the dollar drain that had led to the suspension of convertibility in August 1947. British ministers and civil servants

insisted that the reserves must be held at or above a figure of £500 million ($2 billion)[25] and no economic initiatives that threatened to reduce them below such a level could be contemplated. There were good reasons for this caution. Britain was, after all, banker to the sterling area, so that a run on the reserves would reduce the attractiveness of membership. As it was, with the dollar pool back in business after the convertibility fiasco, members could gain access to more hard currency resources within the area than they would have been able to had they left it. This applied with particular force to independent members such as Australia, New Zealand and India. These countries were able to offset their dollar deficits against the dollar surpluses of dependent sterling area territories such as Malaya, whose rubber exports were by 1948 starting to generate substantial hard currency earnings. If the central reserves were allowed to shrink so far that members could no longer rely on the pool for extra resources but were, by contrast, forced into more stringent controls on dollar purchasing, it was difficult to see why they should stay within the area. And it was feared that once they left the sterling area members would inevitably seek to maximize dollar income by focusing exports on the western hemisphere and cutting down on imports from each other, a recipe for the shrinkage of international trade.

Such a development would obviously have reduced the incentive for independent sterling area members to export to Britain and western Europe since they would have received only inconvertible currency in return. This would have represented a setback for living standards, especially in Britain but also in some continental economies such as the French, Italian, Swedish and Norwegian; Australia, for example, had become a significant supplier of grain, and, with New Zealand, of wool and foodstuffs such as meat, butter and fruit.[26] There was nothing to be gained by risking sterling area reserves, and a good deal to be lost – including both the cultivation of non-dollar sources of supply and the battle for reconstruction in Britain itself. A top-secret report by the British government's Central Economic Planning Staff in the summer of 1947 pointed out that without substantial hard currency reserves Britain would have to cut back on food and raw material imports, intensify rationing and reduce its building programme. The need to expand domestic food production would necessitate the use of child labour in agriculture, while shortages of capital goods would be likely to interrupt factory production, leading to a surge in unemployment (the document suggested this figure might temporarily reach four million).[27] Clearly the flow of Marshall Aid would insulate the British economy from quite so profound a shock, but even so it is hard to see how the Labour government's commitment to full employment and the construction of a welfare state could have survived the collapse of the gold and dollar reserves and the disintegration of the hard currency pool.

Why should trade and payments liberalization have threatened the future of the sterling area in this way? The problems derived partly from the existence of sterling balances held by OEEC countries with whom Britain had negotiated bilateral agreements. The bilateral deals allowed both parties to hold each other's currencies without demanding conversion into dollars – but only up to a certain level, often known as the 'gold point'. Britain's problem was that if these balances were swept into clearing arrangements covering all participating countries, several gold points could be exceeded, leading to an outflow from the central reserves. But the difficulties did not stop there. The ECA's suggestion that OEEC states offer each other transferable credits (known as 'drawing rights'), which would be matched by dollars (called 'conditional aid'), also represented a danger since in this scheme there would be nothing to stop a recipient of sterling credits that did not want to purchase much from Britain or a sterling area member from transferring them to another country that already held sterling up to the gold point. As it happened, both Switzerland and Belgium fell into this category. Unsurprisingly, the ECA was unable to make much headway against British determination to preserve its post-20 August 1947 system of anti-dollar discrimination and bilateralism in the face of pressure for currency liberalization; as a result Britain failed to play the unifying role in Marshall Europe that Washington had assigned it.

The British position was supported by France, itself a debtor in intra-European trade. No more than Britain did France wish to see its creditors given the chance to convert its currency into dollars or gold. The Anglo-French axis on liberalization was backed up by the Dutch, who shared the commitment to full employment policies, and the Scandinavian economies, all of which traded heavily with Britain and were prepared to hold large balances of inconvertible sterling as a result. It followed that the ECA's efforts to strengthen the powers of the OEEC in order to undermine opposition from national governments were repeatedly thwarted. American enthusiasm for a turn towards the free market only found a consistently sympathetic audience in Belgium and Italy, and this was not enough to guarantee significant moves away from bilateralism. Indeed, the strength of national policy commitments throughout Marshall Europe proved so powerful that the division-of-aid exercise, difficult in 1948, was acrimonious and almost impossible in 1949, until the ECA started to make threats about the future of the aid programme, side-lined the OEEC and took over the division-of-aid exercise itself. By the end of 1949 western Europe was not much nearer to a free single market than it had been two years earlier.

The British did suggest a way out of the impasse. Their proposals were rooted in the belief that the Marshall Plan, while welcome, was misdirected and inadequate. London argued that the real problem was not a European failure to recover rapidly enough but the worldwide economic upheaval that had resulted from the war. British policy-makers repeatedly argued that if the United States embarked on a foreign economic policy designed to put dollars in the hands of the food- and raw material-producing states, which had traditionally earned them prior to 1939 (and many of these were sterling area members), not only would anxieties about the reserves disappear but a genuine revival of international trade would be stimulated. British and European exports to Asian and African states and colonies would generate convertible income that could be spent on western hemisphere imports, while at the same time providing Britain with the security to take a more liberal approach to European payments. The Chancellor of the Exchequer, Sir Stafford Cripps, suggested in July 1949 a new Anglo-American economic alliance whereby Britain would move rapidly towards convertibility in return for US commitment to overseas aid, funding of sterling balances, stockpiling of raw materials and an expansionary domestic macroeconomic policy.

Cripps' manifesto was, at root, a call for international Keynesianism: its vision of combining multilateralism with full employment had first been evident in the Clearing Union scheme launched some six years before. Now it was launched against a background of falling sterling area dollar reserves (draining away at an annual rate of £600 million by mid-June),[28] caused by an inventory recession in the USA, which was having a particularly severe impact on the income of sterling area raw material producers. Its initial reception from John Snyder, the US Treasury Secretary, as well as from the State Department and the ECA, was frosty. The consensus in Washington was that the real problems were inflation in Britain and France especially, and European currencies that had deliberately overvalued against the dollar in order to keep import prices down. The idea had been to prevent supplies from being drastically curtailed as a result of the imme-diate postwar shortage of exports, but now, four years on, exports were growing but failing to make headway in hard currency markets because they were over-priced. The answer was devaluation and less ambitious public spending plans. The British reluctantly obliged with a sterling devaluation, from £1 = \$4.03 to £1 = \$2.80, in September 1949; they were followed by most of their partners in the OEEC.

During the summer of 1949 the British had been disappointed at the American refusal to admit any responsibility for the economic crisis. They contemplated adoption of a 'two world' policy, involving an attempt at sterling area autarky, even making a start in this direction when they concluded an agreement in July with Commonwealth finance ministers to cut dollar imports by 25 per cent. But Labour shrank from so radical a departure in the end, reluctant to break with Washington on such a fundamental issue. The results would have meant intensi-fied domestic austerity (Cabinet studies suggested that shortages of raw mater-ials would set back recovery and create unemployment while the national diet would revolve almost entirely around fish and potatoes)[29] and a diplomatic cri-sis at a time when Britain was strategically reliant on the USA for its security as Cold War tension grew. Nonetheless the willingness of the British to consider a complete repudiation of Article VII, not just on a temporary basis as a result of economic emergency but because they believed that the whole project of non-discrimination might be incompatible with domestic social and economic impera-tives, frightened policy-makers in Washington. Given Britain's position at the centre of the sterling area, its defection from wartime pledges to the open door would mean the indefinite postponement of Washington's hopes for a world based on the principles of liberal capitalism. Dean Acheson, Secretary of State from January 1949, took the view that there had to be some kind of Anglo-American economic accommodation, and that this would involve, first, support for the sterling area and, second, a recognition that as long as Britain was seen as the linchpin of west European integration, Washington's ambitions would be frustrated; another agent had to be found, one that had a national interest in European unity.

◆ The Failure of the Marshall Plan I: The European Payments Union

By the end of 1950, Anglo-American co-operation had produced a working multilateral European payments system: the European Payments Union (EPU). At the same time, negotiations were well under way to establish an institution which, it was hoped, would be the first step to the creation of a politically and economically united western Europe: the European Coal and Steel Community (ECSC). At first blush this appears to represent a triumph for US foreign economic policy – but, in fact, both the EPU and the ECSC perpetuated discrimination in trade and currency policy, doing little to advance the cause of the open door.

The EPU arose out of a determined drive by the ECA in the autumn of 1949 to accelerate progress towards a single market. In 1949 and 1950 both the ECA and the State Department promoted the multilateralization of European payments, the proposal being that participating countries would work out their credit and deficit positions against a Clearing Union and settle with it in gold and dollars. The Belgians gave especially strong support and argued that settlements with the Union should be 100 per cent in hard currency. This proposal for, in effect, reinventing the gold standard was too much even for the ECA and the State Department. The USA took the view that while it was certainly time to bring the dollar back into intra-European trade, the process had to be gradual, and for now debtors need only make part payment in gold and dollars while creditors should be prepared to extend a limited amount of credit. Indeed, the Belgians were on their own, with a majority of OEEC nations, led by the British and the French, arguing for generous credit terms and only minimal facilities for payment of debts in gold or dollars.

The consensus across Marshall Europe was that members of a Union without generous credit provisions would be forced into deflation. It was a reasonable position and accorded with the evidence of movements in intra-European trade during the past year. Existing controls on the expenditure of dollars had allowed participating countries to survive the 1949 US inventory recession. When US demand dipped there had been plenty available in western Europe to take up the slack. This was, in turn, a product of full employment (in most of the OEEC), high levels of public expenditure and the capital investment programmes that absorbed so large a proportion of national income. But it was also a function of payments arrangements that had encouraged trade between OEEC members since there had been no great pressure on debtors to part with significant supplies of hard currency and therefore cut back on imports. When the Belgians tried to alter the situation – as they did in all the intra-European payments talks, including those for the EPU – they were thwarted. There were perhaps two reasons. To start with, most OEEC governments were committed to policies that would not work in a deflationary climate. In addition, however, they were increasingly capable of going some way towards meeting each other's needs, a factor that was connected to a rapid spurt of growth in the West German economy after 1948.

The new West German state had returned to European markets as an exporter mainly of raw materials which, at $379.2 million out of $615.4 million, had taken up just over 60 per cent of all its exports to OEEC countries in 1948. By 1951 raw materials had been overtaken by metals and manufactures, and German exports had recovered to prewar levels (Table 2.5). The German economic growth, in turn, had stimulated imports into the country, especially foodstuffs from the Netherlands and Denmark, generating large deficits that

TABLE 2.5: WEST GERMAN EXPORTS TO WESTERN EUROPE, 1938–1951 ($ MILLIONS)

	1938	1948	1951
1. Food, drink and tobacco	29.0	13.3	109.0
2. Raw materials	666.2	379.2	554.8
3. Metals and manufactures	483.4	60.9	614.6
4. Machinery	430.2	42.8	479.3
5. Personal cars	34.4	4.4	77.6
6. Other transport equipment	116.1	7.7	106.0
7. Chemicals	323.0	37.3	345.7
8. Textiles	353.1	47.3	133.6
9. Other manufactures	289.8	21.4	187.4
10. Unspecified	0.6	1.1	–
Total	2680.8	615.4	2608.0

Source: derived from United Nations, *Economic Survey of Europe since the War* (Geneva: United Nations Economic Commission for Europe, 1953), 300–1, Table LV were compensated by American aid, just over half coming in dollars from Government Aid and Relief in Occupied Areas (GARIOA) and the rest from the Marshall programme.[30] But the effects of West German expansion were not limited to its direct trading partners, because the buoyancy created there attracted an increasing volume of goods, setting off a cumulative spiral of intra-European trade involving the Benelux countries, Italy and France.

Resistance to a liberal EPU was strengthened by the British, who supported the campaign against liberalization as a result of their concern to keep sterling balances out of any European clearing. As a result they developed a counter-proposal by which all bilateral agreements would remain in place, with the Union, acting as a 'lender of last resort', being brought into play only when the credit facilities available under the bilateral arrangements had been exhausted and gold payments had become necessary. The scheme was unlikely to prove popular with creditors and indeed there was no chance it would be acceptable to the Belgians. The ECA was depressed by the British position, which could not provide a basis for unity in the OEEC since, by March 1950, even the French, who had usually supported the British line on payments liberalization, had swung round in favour of multilateral clearing. They had been impressed by the ECA's affirmation that creditors would have to adjust to disequilibria either by taking more imports or by extending credits to the Union. Only the Scandinavians now backed the British. Stalemate resulted in the OEEC, with the result that the ECA's hopes for the creation of 'an integrated economy in western Europe' continued to meet frustration.[31]

However, the deadlock was broken in April and May. By this time a series of encouraging balance of payments figures had revealed a sterling area surplus for the first quarter of 1950. Although sterling balances held by OEEC members were still worth $1.1 billion, most of them were with countries that tended to import more from sterling sources than export to them. The change of fortune led London to agree that all balances in the hands of OEEC members on 30 June 1950 could be used to finance net deficits with the Union. It was a major concession and meant acceptance of a Union that would super-sede all the old bilateral deals. The ECA responded with a commitment that the USA would insure Britain against any resulting losses of gold. On top of this it was accepted that Britain would be entitled to introduce quantitative import restrictions if the government had any reason to fear that a deficit with the Union would put the reserves in danger. The initiative reflected the under-standing achieved by the State Department in the wake of the 1949 sterling crisis, that an Anglo-American economic accommodation would be required in order to minimize the risk of plans for multilateralism being derailed by a British lurch towards a 'two world' strategy. On this basis the Union could go ahead as the EPU and, despite some last-minute protests from Belgium, it was formally established on 1 July.

The final shape of the EPU reflected the interests of the European nations that made up its membership more than the long-term priorities of Washington.

The Union revolved around the principle of intra-European currency transfer-ability of course, but only a very limited degree of convertibility into gold and dollars was allowed by its rules. Each participant had a quota, worth 15 per cent of its turnover in Marshall Europe. Only after deficits with the EPU exceeded 20 per cent of this quota would gold payments be expected, the Union extending credits up to that point. Even when a member's deficit with the Union had risen to 100 per cent of the quota it would be receiving 60 per cent in credits, financing the rest in gold or dollars. A creditor, meanwhile, would receive no gold from the Union if its surplus was worth up to 20 per cent of the quota; beyond this, each claim on the Union would be met by equal extensions of credit and receipts of gold. These arrangements not only safe-guarded the position of sterling but provided the architecture of a payments system that permitted the continuation of the growing intra-European trade so noticeable since the last part of 1948. The generous credit facilities encouraged members to trade with each other since they offered no great incentive to use exports as a way of accumulating dollars. Thus the EPU facilitated continued economic expansion in Europe even as it permitted continuing discrimination against the dollar. This was acceptable, though not without misgivings, to the ECA since the creation of the Union could be said to further its mission. It was tolerable for the State Department, always worried about the strategic implica-tions of a break with western Europe. But it all left the US Treasury feeling very uncomfortable; European co-operation was developing, but this soft currency bloc did not seem to have much to do with Article VII.[32]

◆ The Failure of the Marshall Plan II: The Schuman Plan

Once Washington realized that it was not possible for the British to lead west-ern Europe towards political and economic integration, it turned to the French. The new approach stemmed from an understanding in the State Department that if the German recovery, which was essential to the economic future of par-ticipating countries, was to proceed then it had to do so in a manner unthreat-ening to the French. By the second half of 1949 this was an urgent issue. Industrial production in the new Federal Republic (FRG) was close to its 1938 level (in the area covered by the postwar state). Steel production, which had collapsed after 1945, had reached 6 million tons in 1948 and was expected to reach 9 million by the end of 1949. Through their management of the International Ruhr Authority, established in 1948 to control heavy industry in the western zones of Germany, the Anglo-Americans and the French had estab-lished a production limit for steel of 11.1 million tons. However it was clear that this limit would soon be exceeded and that both in London and Washington there was support for raising or even scrapping it. On the other hand such a move was not going to be welcome in France, where there was growing concern that surplus German steel would undermine the ambitions of the Modernization Plan to preside over an increase in French steel production, to 11 million tons by 1950.

The French had responded to German economic recovery by attempting to protect themselves via discriminatory arrangements. In the summer of 1949 they had proposed regional union with the Benelux countries and Italy (known as Finebel) based on currency transferability, floating exchange rates and lower trade restrictions on goods exchanged between each other than on imports from outside the group. The Dutch, keen to retain their lucrative access to the German market, argued that the new FRG should be inside. The negotiations stalled, causing worry in Washington. If the French tried to block West German industrial growth there was a serious risk that the political parties there would exploit resurgent nationalist feeling, possibly seeking reunification with the Soviet-occupied eastern zone. This would be a disaster for containment and would also set back western Europe's economic potential. In the State Department, Acheson responded by encouraging the French to act: they could break European integration but only they could make it, on the basis of an initiative that could harness German resources 'to the security and welfare of western Europe as a whole'.[33]

The initiative came in May when the French Foreign Minister, Robert Schuman, announced his government's support for a European Coal and Steel Community, which would include the FRG as well as France, and invited interested governments to send representatives to a conference that would explore the initiative. Both the State Department, convinced that Schuman's 'plan' was the key to the further integration they had been waiting for, and the ECA, impressed by the liberal rhetoric surrounding the proposal (Schuman had spoken of 'a common market in coal and steel') saw in it the core of a European union.

In fact, like the EPU, the Schuman Plan reflected no acceptance of US designs for the future but rather the national interests of the participants. It offered security and expansion to all who joined, namely France, the FRG, Italy and Benelux. The entire scheme was designed to protect French reconstruction from German competition, while leading both countries away from the path of confrontation. It followed that the 'common market in coal' was to be built on measures that eliminated dual pricing (German domestic coal prices were lower than German exported coal prices) and freight rates that left the price of German coke 46 per cent higher in Lorraine than it was in the Ruhr, discriminating against French steel producers in the process. At the same time the Schuman Plan was designed to increase the French steel industry's supply of coking coal, now being produced at near-1938 levels on the Ruhr, because in the absence of this input bottlenecks were likely to prevent it from meeting the production targets set by the Modernization and Re-equipment Plan.[34]

A failing steel industry had disturbing implications for industrial expansion in postwar France since it was such an important component of finished manufactured goods, particularly, of course, aircraft, cars, trucks, buses, trains and agricultural machinery. The International Ruhr Authority gave the French no access to Ruhr coking coal and no voice in the management of the Ruhr firms. But if French and German coal and steel production were pooled in a single organization that took over the powers of the International Ruhr Authority, then France would gain access to the region's coking coal and influence over the recovery of heavy industry in Germany. It would have succeeded in constructing an international environment that would help French steel producers collectively reach the production targets set for them. Seen in this light the Schuman Plan appears not so much as a foundation stone of Europe united but as a rescue vehicle for the French Modernization and Re-equipment Plan, and indeed Jean Monnet, the head of the planning commissariat that bore responsibility for this, played a major part in the formulation of Schuman's initiative.[35]

All the other participants in the Schuman Plan – which became from March 1951 the European Coal and Steel Community (ECSC) – gained advantages reinforcing postwar national reconstruction. The Italians, whose small, high-cost steel industry depended on the electric arc process and therefore needed scrap, were able to have this included in the common market along with coal, coke, iron ore, and iron and steel. They were protected from the high world price of scrap by agreement on the part of ECSC members to subsidize its cost to Italian producers. The Belgians achieved a fixed price for their coal, while the ECSC offered assistance to Brussels in the form of subsidies to cushion the social and economic costs involved in restructuring what was a declining industry. The Dutch, whose steel industry was small and very competitive, had built a modern steel works at Ijmuiden in a bid to expand capacity and escape from dependence on market gardening and agriculture. Prior to 1939 new-comers to the international steel industry had suffered from price-cutting measures by the more established producers – but the ECSC guaranteed the Dutch protection from what was now deemed unfair competition. For the FRG, the benefits of membership included freedom from the International Ruhr Authority's restrictions on production and exports, a process that assisted the campaign of the government led by Konrad Adenauer for full sovereignty.[36]

Although the State Department had welcomed the Schuman Plan it had been suspicious of what Acheson called its 'possible cartel aspect',[37] and these worries grew as the ECSC negotiations neared completion. However, the talks were conducted against the background of the Korean War, which had stimulated a substantial increase in defence expenditure by the USA. The budgetary requirements of containment in Europe and 'hot war' in Asia were causing political problems in Congress for the Truman administration, which saw greater investment in defence by the west Europeans, a process that should include German rearmament, as a way out of trouble. In these circumstances it became politically impossible for Washington to retract from its early support for the Schuman Plan. American policy-makers could do little except express their concern about the price fixing of coal, the scale of the subsidies and the retention of organizations to distribute coal.[38]

By the end of 1950 it had become clear that, whatever the economic impact of the Marshall Plan, its attempt to found a new global economic order on a reformed, integrated west European capitalism, had failed. As Acheson himself admitted, the end of ERP would see economic recovery in Europe – but it appeared that demand for dollar goods would still exceed the ability of participating countries to pay for them in the absence of American foreign assistance. As late as 1950, one-third of America's exports of $16 billion were being financed through aid. What would happen when this was terminated in 1952?[39] The experience of the years after 1945 did not suggest that the deficit countries would try to reach equilibrium via deflationary measures, although these would have been in keeping with the spirit of Article VII and the open door. First, there had been Britain's reconstruction of the sterling area dollar pool; then, in 1950 and 1951, the two most enduring creations of the Marshall period, the EPU and the ECSC, were deliberately designed as discriminatory organizations that prioritized reconstruction over a return to free markets. From Washington's perspective there seemed no end to the prospect of discrimination. Economic heresy this may have been as far as the US Treasury was concerned, but it had worked and was beginning to allow postwar European governments to meet the aspirations of their tired and hungry electorates. Far from helping Washington bring Bretton Woods back from the dead, Marshall Aid had presided over its burial.

◆ Notes

1. Eric Hobsbawm, *Age of Extremes: The Short Twentieth Century* (London: Michael Joseph, 1994).
2. See Philip Armstrong, Andrew Glyn and John Harrison, *Capitalism since 1945* (Oxford: Basil Blackwell, 1991), 394.
3. See, for example, Ricky W. Griffin and Michael W. Pustay, *International Business: A Managerial Perspective*, 2nd edn (New Jersey: Prentice Hall 1999), Ch. 4.
4. E.A. Brett, *The World Economy since the War: The Politics of Uneven Development* (London: Macmillan, 1985), 74–6.
5. Block, *Origins of International Monetary Disorder*, 76.
6. Brett, *The World Economy since the War*, 76.
7. Herman Van der Wee, *Prosperity and Upheaval: The World Economy 1945–1980* (London: Penguin, 1987), 350.
8. See Joseph M. Siracusa (ed.), *The American Diplomatic Revolution: A Documentary History of the Cold War 1941–1947* (Milton Keynes: Open University Press, 1978), 28.
9. See Sidney Pollard, *The Development of the British Economy 1914–1990* (London: Edward Arnold, 1992), 182.

10. United Nations, Economic Commission for Europe, *Survey of the Economic Situation and Prospects of Europe* (Geneva, 1948), xiii.
11. *United States Department of State, Foreign Relations of the United States* (hereafter *FRUS*), Vol. III, memorandum by Clayton, 'The European Crisis', 27 May 1947, 230.
12. See Milward, *The Reconstruction of Western Europe*, 3.
13. William Diebold, *Trade and Payments in Western Europe: A Study in Economic Co-operation, 1947–1951* (New York: Harper & Rowe, 1952), 19.
14. See Sir Richard Clarke, *Anglo-American Economic Collaboration in War and Peace, 1942–1949* (Oxford: Clarendon Press, 1982), 187–9.
15. Milward, *The Reconstruction of Western Europe*, 95.
16. Ibid., 103–4, Table 19.
17. Ibid., 108–9.
18. See Richard Mayne, *The Recovery of Europe – from Devastation to Unity* (London: Weidenfeld & Nicholson, 1970); H.B. Price, *The Marshall Plan and its Meaning* (Ithaca: Cornell University Press, 1955); and Ernst H. Van Der Beugel, *From Marshall Aid to Atlantic Partnership: European Integration as a Concern of American Foreign Policy* (London: Elsevier Publishing Company, 1966). Charles Kindleberger, *Marshall Plan Days* (London: Allen & Unwin, 1987) is also complimentary but more cautious. Kindleberger was Chief of the State Department's German–Austrian Economic Affairs Group at the time.
19. Milward, *The Reconstruction of Western Europe*, 105–7.
20. See Kenneth O. Morgan, *Labour in Power 1945–1951* (Oxford: Oxford University Press, 1984), 369.
21. See, for example, Gabriel and Joyce Kolko, *The Limits of Power. The World and the United States Foreign Policy, 1945–1954* (New York: Harper & Rowe, 1972).
22. C.C.S. Newton, 'Britain, the dollar shortage and European integration, 1945–50', unpublished PhD thesis (University of Birmingham, 1982), 234–6.
23. Ibid., 231.
24. Milward, *The Reconstruction of Western Europe*, 203.
25. Scott Newton, 'Britain, the sterling area and European integration, 1945–50', *Journal of Imperial and Commonwealth History* XIII (1985), 171.
26. Newton, 'Britain, the dollar shortage and European integration', 213–16.
27. PRO T229/136, memorandum by R.W.B. Clarke, 15 July 1947; interview with Sir Austin Robinson, 5 June 1979.
28. Newton, 'Britain, the sterling area and European integration', 174.
29. PRO 134/222, EPC (49)73, memorandum by Cripps, 7 July 1949.
30. See Milward, *The Reconstruction of Western Europe*, 428–30.
31. Hoffman quoted in PRO FO 371/87137, UR3211/21, 7 February 1950.
32. See Newton, 'Britain, the dollar shortage and European integration', 312–13 and Milward, *The Reconstruction of Western Europe*, 334.

33. See Newton, 'Britain, the dollar shortage and European integration', 286.
34. Milward, *The Reconstruction of Western Europe*, 378–9.
35. Martin J. Dedman, *The Origins and Development of the European Union 1945–95* (London: Routledge, 1996), 60.
36. Ibid., 61–4.
37. Newton, 'Britain, the dollar shortage and European integration', 321.
38. Milward, *The Reconstruction of Western Europe*, 399.
39. *FRUS*, III (1950), memorandum by Acheson to President Truman, 16 February 1950, 834–5.

3

THE ROAD TO
CONVERTIBILITY, 1951–1958

◆ Economic Miracles

By the end of 1958 the dollar shortage had evaporated and, led by the British, EPU members embraced convertibility, formally bringing the institution to an end as they did so. With most restrictions on trade within the OEEC defunct and currency non-discrimination now covering most of the non-communist world, it seemed as if real progress had been made towards the open-door order envisaged by wartime planners. Yet the postwar structure of the world economy as it emerged by the end of the 1950s owed little to the IMF, the IBRD or the GATT, all seen by their Anglo-American creators as the guarantors of a reformed international capitalism. The advanced industrial economies of western Europe and Japan, which made up the core of the system had, with the backing of the United States, developed patterns of trade and payments whose first priority was not to fashion a liberal world economy but to sustain the economic miracles that were now bringing unprecedented prosperity to their populations (Table 3.1).

The figures show a spectacular economic expansion during the 1950s and 1960s. Perhaps yet more remarkable was the continuation of this boom, against all precedent, into the 1960s and beyond. Economists, journalists and politicians spoke of postwar Germany – which within eight years went from producing no cars for the international market to producing 34.8 per cent of all of them[1] – as having been transformed by an 'economic miracle'. But it soon became clear that the German experience was not unique. In Italy the post-1950 era was described as *il miracolo economico*; in France they talked about *les trente glorieux* (the 30 glorious years). Japan by the end of the 1970s had become the world's second economic superpower, the leading exporter of electronic goods, from hi-fi equipment and televisions to pocket calculators and cars. Rapid and sustained growth became the rule, not the exception, and even the United Kingdom, which failed to share the dramatically high rates of growth

TABLE 3.1: ANNUAL AVERAGE RATE OF GROWTH OF TOTAL OUTPUT IN SELECTED WESTERN EUROPEAN COUNTRIES, THE UNITED STATES, CANADA AND JAPAN, 1870–1969 (PERCENTAGES)

	1870–1913	1913–50	1950–59	1960–69
Belgium	2.7	1.0	2.9	3.3
Denmark	3.2	2.1	3.3	4.8
France	1.6	0.7	4.6	5.8
West Germany	2.9	1.2	7.8	4.8
Italy	1.4	1.3	5.8	5.7
Netherlands	2.2	2.1	5.7	5.1
Norway	2.2	2.7	3.2	5.0
Sweden	3.0	2.2	3.4	4.6
United Kingdom	2.2	1.7	2.7	2.8
Japan	2.4	1.8	9.5	10.5
United States	4.3	2.9	3.2	4.3
Canada	3.8	2.8	3.9	5.6

Source: derived from Van der Wee, *Prosperity and Upheaval: The World Economy 1945–1980* (London: Penguin, 1987), 50, Table 3

experienced by its main commercial rivals, enjoyed for over 20 years an average yearly increase in national income unmatched in its history. Throughout the advanced industrial world the years after 1950 were ones of plenty, characterized by full employment, social security and rising living standards. By the early 1970s millions were able to afford goods that, before the war, had been luxuries or at best restricted mainly to the middle class, such as motor cars, television sets, washing machines, refrigerators, telephones and foreign holidays. In Italy automobile ownership went from 750,000 in 1938 to 15 million by 1975, a trend common to all the west European economies. There were 270 million telephones in the world in 1970 (most in Europe and north America), with the number rising; and from the 1950s to the 1980s the number of tourists making for Spain rose from virtually zero to 54 million.[2]

These 'miracles' were driven by internal and external factors. The internal causes were, at root, twofold. First there was 'catch-up'. One feature that stands out from Table 3.1 is the relatively faster growth of the US economy up to 1950 and its relatively slower progress thereafter. This process reflects achievement of the 'sizeable but unrealized possibilities to accelerate growth'[3] in the industrial world outside North America after the Second World War. From the end of the Civil War in 1865, the United States had built a substantial economic lead over Europe and Japan, both of which were more heavily scarred by the impact of war and depression between 1914 and 1945. Now both were left with 'greater vacuums to fill'.[4] These opportunities existed both on the demand and on the supply side.

As far as demand was concerned, there was evidence that throughout the last third of the nineteenth century and up to 1914 this had been higher in the United States than in Europe and Japan. Workers in the United States had enjoyed higher real wages than their opposite numbers in other industrialized countries thanks to agricultural expansion, scarcity of labour and productivity improvement. Their relative affluence generated demand for the mass production of consumer goods and even luxuries. In industrializing Europe at the same time, despite the existence large and well-organized trades union movements in Britain, Germany, France and Italy, wage levels were relatively lower as a result of a labour surplus. Wage increases tended to be modest and, given the abundance of available workers, employers seeking to expand output in key industries (the British coal industry is a good example) did not need to spend money on labour-saving equipment, so that productivity levels were normally lower in Europe than in the USA. There was no radical change in this picture between the two world wars, largely because of the Depression, and it was only after 1950 that serious aspiration to American consumption levels could be realized. By this time the combination of self-confident trades unions with a scarcity of labour in western Europe was stimulating wage and salary rises, a process sustained year on year by full employment and by the expansionary impact of foreign trade between industrialized nations, which was facilitated byinternational co-operation in organizations such as the OEEC and the EPU. In consequence, wages and salaries took a growing share of national income, reaching historic highs during the 1950s (Table 3.2).

The rise in incomes after the Second World War ensured continuation of the boom stimulated by reconstruction. Investment in new machinery, transport, housing, energy and agriculture during the late 1940s and early 1950s had deliberately been driven to 20 per cent of the gross national product by governments anxious to make a new start (Table 3.3). They employed tax incentives for business, provided funds directly themselves, and used fiscal policy to restrict consumption in the early postwar years. Firms responded with ambitious plans, raising money through self-financing out of profits and borrowing from capital markets. The resulting high levels of capital spending (a key factor in the payments crisis of 1947, which led to Marshall Aid), together with generous welfare systems, had generated a dramatic increase in demand throughout the industrialized world. This could for a time be sustained by spending on more producer goods but by the early 1950s there was inevitably a diminishing need for these. On the other hand, it was possible to sustain investment activity, with its expansionary consequences, by focusing on the manufacturing of consumption goods designed to satisfy the material wants of the affluent worker

TABLE 3.2: WORKERS' AND EMPLOYEES' COMPENSATION AS
A SHARE OF NATIONAL INCOME: UNITED KINGDOM, FRANCE,
GERMANY AND THE UNITED STATES

	Share of national income (per cent)		
	Workers' and employees compensation	Income of entrepreneurs and self-employed	Income from assets
United Kingdom			
(i) 1860–69	47	17	36
(ii) 1905–14	47	16	37
(iii) 1920–29	59	15	26
(iv) 1954–60	70	9	21
France			
(i) 1853	36	46	18
(ii) 1911	44	32	24
(iii) 1913	45	33	22
(iv) 1920–29	50	29	21
(v) 1954–60	59	29	12
West Germany			
(i) 1895	39	45	16
(ii) 1913	47	35	18
(iii) 1913	48	33	19
(iv) 1925–29	64	26	10
(v) 1954–60	60	22	18
United States			
(i) 1899–1908	54	24	22
(ii) 1919–28	58	18	24
(iii) 1929	58	17	25
(iv) 1954–60	69	12	19

Source: derived from Kuznets, *Modern Economic Growth* (New Haven: Yale
University Press, 1966), 168–70

TABLE 3.3: TOTAL GROSS INVESTMENT AS A PROPORTION OF GNP
IN SELECTED WESTERN COUNTRIES

	Average for the periods				
	1900–13	1914–49	1950–60	1961–71	1972–82
Belgium	n.a.	n.a.	16.5	21.0	20.9
France	n.a.	n.a.	19.1	24.6	22.3
West Germany	n.a.	14.3	24.0	26.0	21.4
Italy	15.4	13.5	20.8	20.4	19.9
Japan	n.a.	n.a.	24.0	35.1	32.1
Netherlands	n.a.	n.a.	24.2	25.6	20.7
Norway	12.7	15.4	26.4	26.9	30.3
Sweden	12.3	15.5	21.3	23.0	20.4
United Kingdom	7.7	7.6	15.4	18.3	18.0
Canada	25.5	16.0	24.8	22.2	22.7
United States	20.6	14.7	19.1	16.8	18.2

Source: Van der Wee, *Prosperity and Upheaval: The World Economy 1945–1980*
(London: Penguin, 1987), 196, Table 23

for private comfort to complement the socialized security provided by the post-war state. From 1952 to 1953 the era of reconstruction gradually receded as the consumer society, pioneered in the United States during the first half of the century, came to western Europe and then Japan.

On the supply side there were special factors favouring the 'catching up' of the United States after 1945. For a start there was the high rate of investment, which more than matched the level reached in the United States and which was designed to renew economic sectors technologically backward compared to that country. Thus the French embarked on their efforts to modernize agriculture, the British strove with some success to introduce modern techniques of production into the coal industry, and the Dutch invested in the widening of their manufacturing base in order to reduce dependence on farm and market garden exports. These projects, typical of postwar Europe, were likely to enhance productivity and accelerate growth. Their impact was strengthened by wartime innovation. During the Second World War, significant technological advances had been made in electronics, radar, telecommunications, nuclear power, information technology, plastics, pharmaceuticals and aviation (the arrival of the jet aircraft). After the war there was no longer great military demand for these, but potential for civilian application existed, the development and refinement of the new technology transforming established industries such as civil aviation and creating new ones such as computing.

Both aspects of the postwar supply side revolution were supported by government in two fundamental ways. For a start, the state took responsibility for expenditure on new plant and equipment as well as on research and development devoted to new products and techniques, whether the sector undergoing modernization was nationalized (the British coal industry) or characterized by a strong commitment to private ownership (French agriculture). Beyond this, post-1945 governments showed a growing interest in educational programmes designed to create a workforce knowledgeable and skilled enough to work in the new industries. They raised the school leaving age so that the average number of years spent in full-time education by both sexes throughout the advanced industrial world rose from between five and seven years in 1913 to just under ten years by the 1970s and more than 11 years in the 1980s.[5] In addition, provision of technical education was commonly extended and access to higher education was widened, Britain, for example, embarking on a major expansion of its university system from the early 1960s.

The second key to postwar economic miracles was government policy, notably the Keynesian revolution. This made its strongest impact in the United States and the United Kingdom, but many of the central principles of what was known as 'Keynesianism' became commonplace in other advanced industrial countries such as France, Italy, Belgium, the Netherlands, Norway, Sweden, West Germany and Japan.

By the late 1950s all these countries were committed to managing the economy at levels of demand consistent with high or even full employment. This usually meant the use of contra-cyclical fiscal, monetary and public spending policies, raising taxes and interest rates, and reducing expenditures at times of excess demand (seen in inflation, external deficits and labour shortages), but increasing expenditures and cutting taxes and interest rates when unemployment threatened. The same formula applied to public spending projects. Generally, governments tended to boost investment in nationalized industries and in transport, energy, health and education when they were worried about lagging economic growth, and to scale down expenditure plans when concerned with what became known as 'overheating'. The policy succeeded in reducing the average annual level of unemployment in western Europe during the 1950s to 2.9 per cent of the working population, falling to 1.5 per cent during the 1960s.[6] These were levels of joblessness far below prewar norms; Angus Maddison, taking 16 advanced industrialized countries, calculated an average rate of 2.6 per cent unemployment between 1950 and 1973 against an average rate of 7.5 per cent for the period 1921–38.[7]

The adoption of Keynesianism by advanced industrial nations led to the development of a new kind of state, often called the 'mixed economy', characterized by a dramatic rise in the share of GNP taken by governments after

TABLE 3.4: TOTAL GOVERNMENT EXPENDITURE AS A PERCENTAGE OF GNP AT CURRENT PRICES, 1913–1973

	1913	1929	1938	1950	1973
France	8.9	12.4	23.2	27.6	38.8
Germany	17.7	30.6	42.4	30.4	42.0
Japan	14.2	18.8	30.3	19.8	22.9
Netherlands	8.2	11.2	21.7	26.8	45.5
UK	13.3	23.8	28.8	34.2	41.5
USA	8.0	10.0	19.8	21.4	31.1
Average	**11.7**	**17.8**	**27.7**	**26.7**	**37.0**

Source: Maddison, *Dynamic Forces in Capitalist Development* (Oxford: Oxford University Press, 1991), 77, Table 3.16

1945 compared with the prewar era (Table 3.4). In all mixed economies much enterprise still remained in private hands but the government took on responsibility for employment policy and welfare, and directly owned and ran a clutch of industries itself. In the Scandinavian economies, Britain and the Netherlands, these tended to have a service function, such as the public utilities and railways, although coal and steel featured as well. France followed the same pattern but nationalized Renault, one of its leading car manufacturers, and a large part of the financial sector. Italy had the IRI (*Instituto per la Ricostruzione Industriale*, originally established in 1933), which provided finance to firms and took shares in them in return. In the USA the federal government took on large responsibilities for economic development with the establishment of NASA (the National Space and Aeronautical Administration) in 1958 and the Inter-State Highway construction programme.

If it can be said that the postwar mixed economy had a 'mission', this was to create a society characterized by social justice, economic and social security, and rising living standards. This meant governments needed to deliver to their electorates full employment, an equitable distribution of wealth, generous social benefits, access to free health care and primary and secondary education, and yearly gains in personal prosperity for all. Achievement of these objectives required continuing high levels of investment spending as well as buoyant personal consumption. Striking this balance involved governments in arranging bargains between industry and organized labour that were designed to permit annual increases in wage and salary levels high enough to maintain demand but not so exorbitant as to eat into profits to the extent that planned investment targets would not be met. It followed that throughout the advanced industrial world governments tended to preside over institutionalized negotiations between capital and labour. This did not just mean centrally negotiated agreements on wage and salary increases but co-operation between both sides of industry and labour so that, in return for moderation over pay, workers gained security at their place of employment through recognition of trades union rights, health and safety reforms, pension arrangements and paid holidays. The pattern was closely followed in the FRG where the parties were called 'social partners'), the Netherlands, the Scandinavian economies, Italy and the United Kingdom. In Japan managers and union representatives co-operated in measures designed to enhance the profitability of their own companies while introducing a paternalistic regime designed to provide long-term job security for employees.[8]

Despite left/right political disagreements about levels of taxation and the extent of public ownership, the interventionist postwar mixed economy was accepted by most major parties as well as by industry and labour. This consensus was responsible for the appearance of a political and economic stability that had largely been absent during the prewar decades. Its existence now encouraged the continuation of high levels of investment, which, as Herman Van der Wee pointed out, took three separate channels. The first led to the manufacturing of consumer goods for the newly affluent workforce and to an expansion of the supporting infrastructure, notably of housing and the petrochemical industry; the second to the extension of both public and private services ranging all the way from health provision to the tourist industry; the third to expenditure on policies designed to revive long-depressed regions. These regional initiatives tended to be state led but with the aim of encouraging an autonomous process of growth. Thus the *Cassa per il Mezzogiorno* (Fund for the South), established in 1950 to stimulate social and economic development in southern Italy via road construction, drainage and the provision of essential services, had some success over the subsequent generation in modernizing agriculture and attracting industry to the area. NASA's expenditure on the US space programme helped to set off the 'moon boom' in southern states trapped in stagnation since the end of the Civil War. The same pattern could be seen in France, where the state invested in 'regional growth poles', Belgium, where policy focused on Flanders, and the United Kingdom, where governments worked to bring modern industry and employment to South Wales, north-east England and eastern Scotland.[9]

If 'catch-up' and the postwar mixed economy were central to the internal causes of the long boom, the external stimulus was provided by foreign trade, which expanded at a remarkable rate after 1950. Between 1951 and 1953 and 1969 and 1971 the volume of world trade in manufactured goods increased by 349 per cent. During these years exports from the advanced industrial world went up by 480 per cent. Unlike in the pre-1939 era most of these goods were sent not to underdeveloped nations to pay for imports of food and raw materials but to other industrialized states (the figure rose from 41.1 per cent in 1950 to 62.3 per cent in 1971)[10] and it was this exchange that accounted for the expansionary influence of international trade. Why did the old pattern alter?

The development was at root a reflection of the affluence caused by the catching up of the United States and by post-1945 policies. As the populations of western Europe and Japan became economically secure and increasingly prosperous, so their patterns of spending changed. Inevitably they devoted a relatively smaller proportion of income to expenditure on essential items such as food, clothing and medical treatment, and a relatively larger proportion to what Milward calls 'increasing ease of life',[11] namely cars and household gadgets. Not all of these would necessarily be purchased from domestic producers: the modern consumer, with an increasing variety of information at his or her disposal, thanks to television, radio and the press, was before long in a position to decide that in some areas imports might deliver this 'increasing ease of life'.

Consumer demand therefore stimulated foreign trade – and in so doing reinforced the trend to domestic growth and modernization. A good example is the impact of demand for cars. As incomes rose so did car ownership per head of the populations of the advanced industrial states, the product being regarded by consumers, manufacturers and governments as a symbol of the affluent society.[12] During the 1950s governments assisted the expansion of car production with tax concessions and (in France) direct support. They were aware of the strategic importance of this industry given its export potential, its impact on internal demand and its capacity to generate employment both directly and in related industries such as steel, electrical goods, synthetic textiles and petrochemicals. It was the West German car industry that emerged as the winner in international competition, the beneficiary of judicious fiscal incentives (for example, a tax rebate for car travel to work and a 20 per cent reduction in car tax) and of the economies of scale made possible by a Volkswagen plant that had the capacity to produce more cars than any European competitor. Demand grew at home as personal disposable income in West Germany increased by 33 per cent between 1952 and 1956, and this was compounded by orders from abroad, stimulated by the quality of the vehicle and, thanks to a 20 per cent fall in production costs over the same period, by a price that brought it within reach of an ever larger number of consumers. By 1960, West German car exports were dominating the European market and beginning to make headway in the United States. Yet the German success stimulated expenditure at home and turned the country into a magnet for consumer goods, machine tools and electrical equipment produced in France, Italy and the Netherlands in particular. The trade therefore was beneficial to modernization in western Europe and guaranteed that when the US economy dipped into recession as it did in 1952–3, and again in 1958, the growth and expansion of the continental economies continued.

◆ The External Environment

International economic issues during the 1950s were largely devoted to the creation of an external environment that would sustain the economic miracles.

One major stumbling block was the persistence of the dollar shortage, in other words the lack of hard currency reserves in the world outside North America. Up to 1951, the west Europeans had been able to reconcile their external deficits with the dollar zone with internal expansion via trade discrimination and Marshall Aid. But the European Recovery Programme was replaced by the Mutual Security Administration (MSA), established to merge defence aid with economic assistance. The MSA presided over a significant fall in dollar disbursements during its first year. By September 1952 there had been a net fall of $192 million in the supply of dollars to Europe compared with January–June 1950. This resulted from a $1.5 billion reduction in government grants and loans, a cut not fully balanced by a rise of $1361 million in US imports and in payments for military and other services.[13]

The difficulties created for the more dollar-dependent European economies such as Britain and France were compounded by the economic impact of the Korean War. Both countries embraced ambitious rearmament programmes. This led to an increase in imports from the dollar area. The French economy, for example, grew too fast for its own coal industry: the gap had to be filled with American supplies. In 1950 the sterling and franc areas had run dollar surpluses as a result of raw material stockpiling. But the stockpiling boom came to an end in 1951 and the independent members of the sterling area in particular used their hard currency earnings to import capital goods from the USA, so reversing their surpluses of the previous year. It all meant that neither the British nor French dollar deficits were offset by the performances of their currency zones, and both countries ran into external crisis. By February 1952 the sterling area gold and dollar reserves, which had stood at a healthy $3.8 billion in June 1951, had fallen to $1.8 billion and were expected to drop to $1.5 billion in March.[14]

This would have been bad enough but the position was made more acute by the appearance at the same time of large deficits with the EPU on the part of both countries. The deficits appeared following the OEEC decision, taken at the same time as the EPU began operations, to remove first 60 then 75 per cent of 1948 import quotas by February 1951. The overheating British economy sucked in imports from western Europe as well as the USA, and Britain's EPU account swung from a surplus of $52.8 million in the first quarter of 1951 to deficits of $171 million and $187.4 million in the third and fourth quarters respectively, setting off heavy gold payments to the Union. France's account with the Union deteriorated at the same time, from a surplus of $63.5 million in the third quarter of 1950 to a deficit of $95.2 million in the final quarter of 1951.[15] Both countries responded by reversing their OEEC trade liberalization: the French suspended it completely in April 1952 while the British retreated from 75 per cent to 61 per cent in November 1951 and to 46 per cent in February 1952. At the same time the sterling area tightened restrictions on dollar purchasing.[16]

The intensification of import restrictions by Britain and France followed the suspension of German liberalization in February 1951, a function of an import boom especially pronounced in food and raw materials. The episode demonstrated how lack of hard currency was liable to strangle trade within western Europe and its affiliated currency zones. It also suggested that continuing recovery could not be assured by welding all-round trade liberalization programmes within the OEEC to currency transferability within the EPU. On top of this, the external crises of 1951–2 confirmed to sceptics in the US Treasury, as well as in the British Treasury and Bank of England, that freedom of trade and payments in western Europe was not only unlikely in the absence of dollar assistance but not in any case the correct path to a world made safe for non-discrimination. On the other hand, leading continental European states such as France, the Benelux countries and West Germany argued that achievement of non-discrimination should be secondary to domestic growth – and they were supported in this view by the State Department throughout the 1950s. It all meant that there was, within the non-communist world, serious and prolonged argument about the shape of the world economy as it left behind the era of reconstruction.

At first sight the most surprising feature of this argument is the reversal of Anglo-American positions from those taken by London and Washington in the 1940s. At that time the British had consistently maintained that the liberalization of sterling as well as the removal of import quotas and the long-established imperial preference system would have to await a major injection of liquidity into the world economy, and a dramatic reduction of tariffs, on the part of the United States. By contrast the Americans had urged the British to take the lead in dismantling the systems of bilateral trade deals and exchange controls that had grown up in the non-dollar world during the 1940s. From the early 1950s, however, it was the British who pushed for early moves to currency convertibility above all, in the face of considerable American scepticism that such action would serve any useful economic purpose and that it might even be politically dangerous.

The shift in the British position followed a general election, held at the end of October 1951. This resulted in a narrow Conservative victory over the Labour Party that had been in power since 1945. Commercial interests rooted in the City of London, which prioritized Britain's historic role as a financial power, had long been influential in the Conservative Party. They had powerful support from within the state itself, in the shape of the Bank of England and the Overseas Finance section of the Treasury, which believed that the longer sterling inconvertibility lasted the more likely it was that governments, companies, banks and individuals would desert sterling for a currency they could use anywhere – in other words, the dollar.[17] Such an exodus from sterling would result in its relegation from use as a medium of exchange in worldwide trade, banking, insurance and investment to the status of a purely domestic currency. It would be a sad reflection on Britain's postwar position in the world and, in marginalizing London as an international financial centre, bring about significant losses to the invisible account of the balance of payments (the international use of sterling was contributing just under 10 per cent of all earnings in 1951).[18] The interest in sterling liberalization was backed by a middle class growing weary of rationing and controls, and keen to spend their rising incomes in a deregulated market.

The new government devoted much time and effort over the next three years to the restoration of sterling convertibility. Early in 1952, the Treasury and the Bank of England attempted to persuade the government that a unilateral dash to convertibility might be acceptable as long as the risk to reserves was minimized by a floating rate and the blocking of at least 80 per cent of the sterling balances. This plan, known as 'Operation Robot', was shelved out of anxiety about its impact on domestic prices and employment, but a modified version of it continued to dominate British financial diplomacy. Early in 1953, London adopted what it called the 'Collective Approach' to convertibility, by which sterling would be freed at a floating rate in return for a $2 billion credit from Washington. The reaction of the new, Republican, Eisenhower administration in Washington was, however, negative (it took the view that the British had received enough special treatment) and the 'Collective Approach' foundered in the absence of US backing.

Still the British worked for sterling convertibility. They saw this as the first and greatest step towards the removal of currency discrimination throughout the non-communist world. They were confident that other countries would follow, notably the Belgians, the Germans and perhaps even the French. As a result not only would sterling be returned to its elevated pre-1939 status in world finance, but there would also be a natural expansion of international trade. No longer (so it was argued) would trade be held back because creditors held foreign currency balances that could only be used in a regional payments unions such as the EPU; they would be able to deploy convertible balances freely to import from the United States, and the knowledge that this would be possible should, it was hoped, act as a stimulant to exports. Following up their convictions with action the British reopened the gold and foreign currency markets in London, and resumed trade liberalization within the OEEC. Restrictions on the use of sterling were gradually lifted so that by early 1955 all bilateral accounts had been terminated.

Yet the British failed to lead the non-dollar world into a new era of non-discrimination and expanding trade centred on the pound sterling. It is, of course, true that sterling convertibility was reintroduced, and this was followed by the replacement of the EPU by the European Monetary Agreement, where all settlements could be made in gold or dollars – but not until December 1958 and in circumstances very different from what London had imagined only a few years earlier. The fundamental problem was that the British plans held only limited attraction for other OEEC members, who were committed to upholding the discriminatory mechanisms of the EPU because its credit facilities were encouraging trade expansion. On convertibility, as the European Monetary Agreement demonstrated, these facilities would cease to be available except in a very limited capacity. Countries would only be able to sustain domestic expansion if they had access to plentiful reserves or healthy exports to other states whose currencies were convertible. In the absence of these preconditions convertibility was simply not compatible with the missions of the postwar mixed economies.

The British had no support in the EPU for an early return to convertibility. The French, as debtors on intra-European account, had no wish to lose the EPU's generous credit facilities. The Dutch argued against damaging an institution that had sustained growth in intra-European trade. Even EPU members with healthy surpluses were opposed to any action that would bring the institution to what they believed would be a premature end. Thus in 1952 the Belgians supported, against Britain, a two-year extension of the EPU rather than the one year favoured by London because 62 per cent of their exports went to members and this trade would be endangered by an early return to convertibility. The Germans, whose Finance Minister Ludwig Erhard was a staunch economic liberal, failed to support the British because they feared that any initiative that undermined the EPU would damage the flow of their exports to west European markets.[19]

The fundamental difference between the British and the continental Europeans was the latter's conviction that convertibility should be the facilitator of trade expansion. Whatever London said, all the evidence suggested that its introduction at any stage in the period 1952–5 would have had the reverse effect. However, EPU members, while resisting the pressure from London, did gradually increase the gold settlements ratio; by June 1954 it stood at 50 per cent and in July 1955 it was raised to 75 per cent. At the same time, the OEEC resumed its march to trade liberalization, with 89 per cent of all intra-trade being free by June 1956.[20]

It had become possible to harden the EPU arrangements and remove import quotas because of the steadily waning dollar shortage. The fading of the postwar disequilibrium partly reflected generous dollar disbursements, mostly for defence aid. But there was more to the coming of 'viability' to Europe than continual transfusions of dollars. The process was also a function of recovery, seen in the growth of industrial production. By 1955 this was 37 per cent above the 1950 level; by 1957 it was up by 47 per cent. The expansion of the European economies, and the commerce between them facilitated by the EPU, had led to a diminishing requirement for dollar goods and a growing ability on the part of the OEEC countries to meet each other's needs. Yet decontrol of foreign exchange arrangements lagged behind trade liberalization, with even the British losing enthusiasm after mid-1955. Grappling with rising inflationary pressures, a surge in imports and pressure on the reserves (all intensified by the 1956 Suez War), they also placed concern for domestic stability ahead of convertibility. It was not until 1958 that they were ready to take the plunge. By that time, with no dollar problem and booming activity in Europe, the subject of convertibility had become relatively uncontroversial. The timing was right for the EPU members whereas it had not been so in the 1952–5 period. The lateness of convertibility, from London's viewpoint, followed from the resistance of the Europeans and the Americans, and from Britain's own problems after 1955.

The willingness of all OEEC members to embrace convertibility did not mean they had been converted to the liberal aspirations of wartime planners. In reality, the motivations of many in this new international system had little connection with the ideals of non-discrimination. This applied most of all to the French, the Italians, the Benelux countries and West Germany. Throughout the period 1952–6 these countries (already collaborating in the Coal and Steel Community) had searched for an external environment that sustained the economic and social development of the post-1945 era.

The question was, what sort of environment? Clearly it could not be one based on the simple abolition of trade and exchange controls, since this would expose vulnerable sectors to the full impact of market forces, generating unemployment as a result. The key, as Alan Milward has noted, was the fusion of industrial (and agricultural) policy with commercial policy.[21] To put it more crudely, how would it be possible to reconcile the protection and modernization of the economy with the imperative of export expansion? In the west European context the answer to this question revolved around Germany. Germany had historically been the principal supplier of investment goods such as machinery, transport equipment and steel to the rest of Europe.[22] After the wartime and postwar hiatus it had started to resume this role in the late 1940s and early 1950s. As Marshall Aid started to fall away, so the west European states started to import heavily from the new FRG. At first, capital goods formed the major part of German exports, but during the 1950s these were joined by cars, then electronic equipment such as hi-fis and television sets. In return, German producers themselves began to import key materials such as machine tools, pumps, electrical machinery and textile machinery from other European states. By 1956–9, 80 per cent of all West Germany's electrical goods came from European suppliers, 21.5 per cent of them from the Netherlands alone, while the booming car industry sucked in steel from Belgium, Luxembourg and, above all, France.[23]

How could this symbiotic relationship between Germany and western Europe, critical to continuing economic growth, be maintained? The answer came in the form of an agreement – made in 1955 between the Benelux countries, the French, the Italians and the Germans – to form a common market. Talks began in 1956 and the participants signed the Treaty of Rome in 1957, with the new entity, known as the European Economic Community (EEC), starting operations at the beginning of the following year. A common market, which was allowed under GATT rules, worked by establishing free trade within its own borders but imposing a common tariff on all goods imported from outside. Its great merit for the six signatories was that it would sustain the expansionary pattern of intra-trade that had developed around their economic relationships with West Germany. Protection against the dollar zone could continue but liberalization within the six would guarantee Dutch access to French and German markets, and Belgian exports to the group, known as 'Little Europe'. For the French there was the attraction of continuing modernization, which the government concluded was best achieved by an expansion of exports, especially to Germany, even if this meant less protection for domestic industry.

Less protection for French industry did not mean that the EEC would adopt *laissez-faire* within its borders: members all agreed to work out a set of rules that would regulate competition through the harmonization of pay levels, regional policy to assist poor and less competitive areas, and a common policy to support agricultural production and farm incomes within the group. At the same time, the common market would join the ECSC as another institution that would contain Germany within a west European framework. Indeed, these strategic and diplomatic considerations were perhaps as crucial as the prospective economic benefits of the EEC to the FRG, and particularly to its Chancellor, Konrad Adenauer, who believed that there could be no security (and no prospect of reunification) outside an integrated western Europe. Politics and economics had combined to generate a novel, regulated pattern of international economic co-operation which, in underwriting the centrality of foreign trade to economic development, guaranteed that the new postwar states were able to protect the welfare of their electorates.

◆ The Eisenhower Administration and the Dollar Gap

The United States was unhelpful to the British campaign for convertibility but supportive of the common market project. Why were US governments during the 1950s prepared to put convertibility second to the achievement of European integration, and how did they propose to make the world safe for non-discrimination? The Cold War provides part of the answer to the first question. Ever since the Marshall Plan had been launched, Washington had been determined to ensure that the industrial capacity and potential military might of Germany be kept out of Soviet hands. In the circumstances of the time this had meant accepting that a divided Germany, whose western zones were irreversibly locked into the Atlantic alliance, was far preferable to a united Germany whose loyalties might either drift eastwards or gravitate towards the renewal of some mysterious *Sonderweg* that would once again threaten European, and indeed global, security. It followed that European integration became an American national interest: not only was this believed to be a precondition of economic recovery, it was also the only environment in which German revival could occur in safety. It is not surprising, then, that both Truman and Eisenhower supported all the initiatives designed to draw the western Europeans together, and gave special backing to the efforts of the six that had formed the ECSC to press on, first, with what proved an abortive attempt to establish a European Defence Community and, next, with the more successful EEC. In so far as British plans for sterling convertibility would have set back European integration as a result of their impact on the EPU, they flew in the face of US policy and could not be supported.

There were misgivings within the US Treasury about the apparent willingness of the State Department to live with a discriminatory west European bloc as long as the Cold War lasted, but this did not mean the Treasury opposed American aid to Europe or that it disagreed with the objective of European integration. It argued, however, that these should be seen as 'temporary measures which were necessary to establish Europe as an equal partner to the United States'.[24] Once Europe had reached this status there would be no need for continuing assistance, and the march towards a world order based on the open door could be resumed. This was the view of the Randall Commission, established in early 1953 to report to the President on foreign economic policy. Its first survey appeared in January 1954 and supported a gradual approach to convertibility, endorsed the role of the EPU and advised against its replacement in the foreseeable future. It noted that US gifts and loans to the rest of the world between 1946 and 1953 had totalled $33 billion (and this was exclusive of military items) but that the rest of the world still needed to discriminate against the dollar. The Commission advocated a range of measures which, it hoped, would expand the world's supply of dollars and so reduce the pressure for continuing controls. These included tax concessions for private overseas investment and some modest use of the IMF to support the reserves of other countries.[25]

The Commission pointed the way towards a non-discriminatory world for the Eisenhower administration, which over the next few years did indeed encourage the expansion of US private overseas investment and an increase in the world's supply of dollars. But the IMF did not take a leading role in this exercise: not until 1956 and after did this organization take on a high profile in the implementation of US foreign policy. The low-key role of the IMF in the first half of the 1950s was a function of the Eisenhower administration's political and ideological complexion. This reflected the increasingly dominant position in the US economy of large-scale corporate finance and industry. The American economists Paul Baran and Paul Sweezy argued that the USA had entered a new era, which they dubbed one of 'monopoly capital', a stage characterized by the tendency of increasing shares of business activity to be concentrated in fewer and fewer hands.[26] By 1957, 135 corporations owned 45 per cent of all the industrial assets in the United States.[27] When it came to voting, the executives who controlled these organizations were rather more likely to support the Republican than the Democratic Party. The former was ideologically much more sympathetic to free enterprise and low taxation than the latter, which had become identified, especially in the Roosevelt and Truman years (1933–53) with relatively high taxation, high levels of federal spending, state intervention in the economy, the extension of social welfare to underprivileged groups and sympathy for organized labour.

The moment was captured by the distinguished American sociologist, C. Wright Mills.[28] Writing in 1956 he noted the prominence in American life of large corporations, their directors and chief executives: 'Not great fortunes but great corporations are the important units of wealth, to which individuals of property are variously attached. The corporation is the source of wealth, and the basis of continued power and privilege of wealth.'[29]

Firms such as the Chase National Bank (later Chase Manhattan), American Telephone and Telegraph, New York Central Railroad, the Metropolitan Life Insurance Company, Du Pont, General Motors and Ford were well represented in the government of the day. Thus Winthrop W. Aldrich, Ambassador to the United Kingdom at the time, had held directorships in each of the first four in 1950. John Foster Dulles, the Secretary of State from 1953–9, was a partner in the Wall Street corporate lawyers Sullivan and Cromwell, who did business for Morgan and Rockefeller interests. His brother Allen, who was a member of the same firm, became Director of the Central Intelligence Agency (CIA) in 1953. George Humphrey at the Treasury was 'a director of a complex of over thirty corporations', and the Defense Secretary had been president of the largest producer of military equipment in the USA. Two other members of the Cabinet had held executive posts at General Motors.[30]

It was not that the corporate executives favoured a return to the fiercely competitive conditions of the late nineteenth century. Their ideal economy was one in which the government stepped back and left the market to be organized by large firms 'producing commodities which are more or less adequate substitutes for each other'[31] (this could apply, for example, to cars, cigarettes, household goods all the way from refrigerators to detergents, and petroleum products). The company overheads, on large plant, modern equipment, wages and salaries for qualified as well as semi-skilled staff, together with the costs of research and development on new product lines, led managers to eschew price competition. They tended instead to co-operate via cartels and informal agreements in which companies took it in turns to initiate price changes designed not to benefit one firm alone but to maximize the profits of the industry as a whole.[32]

The search of the corporation for stability in the market place was not confined to the territory of the United States. Even prior to the Second World War there had been firms that conducted substantial import and export trade, and owned foreign subsidiaries (the Rockefeller concern, Standard Oil of New Jersey, is an example). But there were few of these and, in fact, the direct foreign investments of US corporations fell from $7.5 billion to $7.2 billion between 1929 and 1946. However, there was a shift in the period from 1946–60 as the large US companies such as Ford, IBM and Westinghouse discovered that overseas earnings were booming and returns on investment abroad were often better than at home, largely a function of relatively lower costs and the high growth rates associated with reconstruction and the development of the consumer society. This was an incentive for the construction of factories, warehouses and distribution centres outside the USA as well as the purchase of foreign companies. The foreign direct investments of the US corporations shot up from $7.2 billion in 1946 to $40.6 billion in 1963. The process was accompanied by buoyant sales and profits for foreign branches and sub-sidiaries. Baran and Sweezy point out that in both relative and absolute terms the sales of foreign manufacturing affiliates, rising from $18.3 billion in 1957 to $28.2 billion in 1962, came to exceed the returns from merchandise exports (excluding foodstuffs), which stagnated over the same period, increasing only very slightly from $16.8 billion to $17.3 billion.[33] It followed that many large US businesses found this prosperity to be an indication that the best prospects for future growth were in overseas markets rather than at home.

Not surprisingly, the prominence of corporate interests in the Eisenhower administration influenced foreign economic policy. Only lip-service was paid to tariff reduction: the government was instead responsive to the protectionist lobbying of industrialists who had benefited from the expansion of demand generated by the rearmament programme of the early 1950s.[34] There was no great enthusiasm for Federal-funded overseas aid schemes on the scale of Marshall Aid since this might require tax increases. When it came to overseas investment the administration and its supporters looked to the private sector. In so far as it was willing to support the use of public funds, it favoured chan-nelling them through the US Export-Import Bank rather than the International Bank since the former would be more likely to support projects useful to American economic interests abroad (for example, in Latin America).[35] There was some backing for use of IMF assistance to countries whose reserves were running low, and the Fund was able to introduce a new facility, the stand-by credit, in 1952. However, very little use was made of this until the British suffered from external difficulties as a result of the Suez crisis in 1956, and the French balance of payments went dramatically into the red after an expan-sionary boom sucked in imports during 1956–7. The Fund's rather parsimo-nious attitude was largely a function of US Treasury anxiety that generous creation of credit for debtor economies might be inflationary. It was a fear that stretched all the way back to the reception of Keynes' Clearing Union scheme in 1942, and was a significant influence on the determination of the Treasury not to concede control over world liquidity to an international organization.

The interest in an expansion of private investment became central to the administration's view of how the United States could continue to assist recov-ery in Europe (and Japan) while deriving considerable benefits from it. It encouraged foreign direct investment by large firms, hoping that over time this would draw together the west European and American economies. The corpor-ations themselves actively supported this strategy. In May 1957 'some forty major American companies', including the 'Chase Manhattan Bank, Dupont, Ford Motor, Standard Oil of New Jersey, Westinghouse, etc' participated in a closed round-table discussion concerning the impact of the European common market on their own business.[36] The consensus was that the development would probably discourage US exports, partly because of its discriminatory nature and partly because of the likely improvements to European productivity that would result. This was not regarded as a tragedy but as an opportunity. US corporations could jump over the tariff wall and participate in a protected, fast-growing European market of 250 million increasingly affluent consumers unimpeded by internal trade barriers. Indeed 'some planning' was 'already under way on this basis'. The Ford representative at the meeting pointed out that 'the vast bulk' of the $1 billion sales made by the company in Europe came from production there and not from exports of vehicles made in the United States.[37] As companies followed the example of Ford so they would in turn draw together the American and European economies, side-stepping the effects of tariffs and quotas on income; it was a corporate version of the open door, which kept the dollars flowing and squared with the administration's concern that European economic integration harmonize with the 'major objectives of US foreign policy'.[38]

There was, however, a problem with relying on private investment as a means of bridging the dollar gap and preventing the emergence of anti-American economic blocs, even if the long-term prospects for this strategy were highly promising. The requirements of the non-dollar world for infrastructural funding were too extensive. In Europe it was not until 1957 and after that US direct investment really began to grow. In these circumstances, and given the disappearance of Marshall Aid and US reluctance to sanction more substantial IMF lending, the most significant source of hard currency for the non-dollar world during the first half of the 1950s turned out to be American military expenditure. This took the form of assistance for France and Britain, procurement in Germany and Japan and spending on goods and services by US forces stationed overseas in the multiplying number of bases established in Europe, the Middle East and the Far East. Policy-makers in the later years of the Truman presidency had been aware of the economic benefits that could follow from US defence spending and military assistance programmes[39] as far as the non-Soviet world was concerned, but the Eisenhower administration made far more extensive use of this tool. Moreover it did so knowing that the flow of funds would cover a substantial part of the US payments surplus with the rest of the world.[40] Indeed, there is no doubt that defence-related dollars were helpful to the west Europeans. Thus in 1952–4, the OEEC countries received $7.8 billion from the United States in the form of direct aid, funds for 'offshore procurement' (whereby, for example, they could purchase equipment from each other – but use dollars to do so) and spending by US personnel stationed abroad (Table 3.5).

◆ The Fading of the Dollar Shortage

The Japanese were also major beneficiaries of US military spending. Japan, like the states of western Europe, embarked on a reconstruction programme designed to provide postwar economic security. The chosen route lay through trade, but it was clear that the old prewar staple export of textiles could not be

TABLE 3.5: US EXTRAORDINARY EXPENDITURES IN WESTERN
EUROPE AND ITS AFFILIATED AREAS, 1952–1954 (MILLIONS
OF CURRENT DOLLARS)

Period	US government grants	Military expenditures	Total	Increase in Europe's dollar holdings and net purchase of gold from USA
1952 (Estimated)	1236	493	1729	322
1953 First half	726	592	1318	1121
Second half	573	716	1289	989
1954 First half	515	763	1278	799
Third quarter	532	810	1342	630
Total: 1952 to September 1954	3582	3374	6956	3869
Offshore purchases to the end of June 1954 (estimated)			800	
Total			**7756**	

Source: derived from United Nations, Economic Commission for Europe, *Economic Survey of Europe in 1954* (United Nations: Geneva, 1955), 107, Table 62

the foundation of full employment and prosperity. Governments therefore geared investment to future international demand, which they rightly expected to focus on sophisticated consumer goods. First, however, the country needed to construct a heavy industrial complex in which the predominant concerns were chemicals, iron and steel, metals and machinery. These could equip the newer industries, which would supply world markets.[41] Industrial output reached its 1938 level by 1950 and continued to rise throughout the decade, hitting 260 per cent in 1957.[42] This achievement was facilitated by an import surplus, just as it was in western Europe. The main supplier was, of course, the United States, which was an occupying power in the years after 1945.

Washington deemed Japanese recovery essential to the establishment of non-discrimination and peace in the Far East. It saw in a new, liberal Japan both a partner in the construction of a liberal-capitalist world and a strategic base that would assist in the containment of communism, a project which, after the successful Chinese revolution of 1949, had a Far Eastern as well as a European dimension. It is not surprising, then, that the Korean War of 1950–3, bringing the USA into open conflict with China, was a great opportunity for Japan. The country became a vast American base.[43] There were few problems with finan-cing the import sur-plus. Military operations both generated demand for the provision of goods and services by Japanese companies (paid for in dollars) and provided an extra stimu-lus to the heavy industries postwar governments had sought to develop.

By 1956 the products of the metal, machinery and chemical industries together totalled 38 per cent of all exports, outstripping textiles (34 per cent). They were indeed the foundation of an increasingly diverse economy, characterized by the growth of labour-intensive industries that produced consumer goods such as cameras, motor vehicles, television sets and transistor radios. The output of Japanese industry became famous throughout the world during the 1960s and 1970s, but the expansion of its export trade was obvious by the late 1950s. There was a problem, though: Japan's traditional markets were East Asian. Prior to the Second World War, 40 per cent of Japan's exports went to China and Korea, while 70 per cent of its imported soya beans and 40 per cent of its imported coal came from China. During the 1950s, trade with China contracted sharply. In 1957, Japan was buying 75 per cent of its imported coal and 90 per cent of its imported soya beans from the USA.[44] Dollars linked to the expansion of the American military machine could not be expected to cover these requirements indefinitely; Japan needed a trade network that would allow it to earn them.

This trade network needed to be characterized by convertible currencies and multilateral trade so that the proceeds of Japanese exports to non-dollar mar-kets could be used to finance imports from the United States. But as late as 1957 there was anxiety about the implications of convertibility throughout most of the non-dollar world, even in western Europe where significant reduc-tions were being made in the level of anti-dollar discrimination. Widespread concern remained that the world's supply of hard currency had not kept pace with the expansion of international trade.[45] It was true that the United States had 'taken on one role of a world central bank'[46] by creating international money through its provision of dollars to the rest of the world. Although the American trade surplus with the rest of the world was substantial until the end of the decade, its overall balance of payments with the rest of the world ran at an annual average deficit of $600 million between 1949 and 1959.[47] The expend-iture had certainly eased the pressure on the reserves of the non-dollar world, and had helped the OEEC countries and Japan to reduce discrimination without hav-ing to sacrifice expansion. It did not, however, silence those who were calling for a significant addition to the world's stock of reserves, and the annual meeting of the IMF in 1957 saw a call for increased quotas.

Washington's initial reaction was negative but it changed tack the following year. The new approach to international liquidity issues arose in the face of pressure from the Fund itself, but also from some of its more influential members such as the French, the British and the Canadians, the latter proposing a 50 per cent increase in quotas. Concerned about its own growing international unpopularity and a corresponding rise in Soviet aid to and trade with the developing world, the United States agreed,[48] paving the way for the introduction of convertibility throughout the advanced industrial world at the end of the year. By this time the gold and convertible currency reserves of western Europe and Japan had reached $22 billion out of a world total of $57 billion, having doubled since 1952.[49]

The fading of the dollar shortage and the introduction of convertibility at the end of the 1950s merged 'the two great monetary zones of the Western world' – the dollar bloc and the regional bloc based on the sterling area and the EPU – into one large multilateral payments area characterized by currency convertibility at fixed rates of exchange along with liberalized trade arrangements.[50] Yet it would be mistaken to argue that the era of discrimination and protection was over. As late as 1960 west European foreign trade was less liberalized than it had been in 1929.[51] The achievements of the OEEC had been concentrated on trade in manufactures; the agricultural sector in Europe and indeed throughout much of the world – including the United States – remained organized on protectionist lines, surrounded by trade barriers and generously subsidized by national governments. The advanced industrial states that comprised the core of this new system showed no inclination to deviate from their commitment to the postwar mixed economy variant of capitalism, which was helping to generate such unprecedented wealth and security for so many millions. The newly independent countries that were beginning to emerge from the western colonial empires meanwhile tended to follow state-led development programmes that prioritized import substitution rather than foreign trade (see Chapter 5). Nearly 15 years after the end of the Second World War the world economy was the product of nationalism, social democracy and socialism at least as much (if not more) as it was the creation of the American liberals who had dreamed of their own 'new order'.

◆ Notes

1. Alan S. Milward, *The European Rescue of the Nation-State*, 2nd edn. (London: Routledge, 2000), 368.
2. See Eric Hobsbawm, *Age of Extremes: The Short Twentieth Century* (London: Michael Joseph, 1994), 265–6.
3. Van der Wee, *Prosperity and Upheaval*, 51.
4. Ibid.
5. Angus Maddison, *Dynamic Forces in Capitalist Development* (Oxford: Oxford University Press, 1991), 64 and Van der Wee, *Prosperity and Upheaval*, 170, 536.
6. Van der Wee, *Prosperity and Upheaval*, 77.

7. Maddison, *Dynamic Forces in Capitalist Development*, 170–1, Table 6.2.
8. Van der Wee, *Prosperity and Upheaval*, 251.
9. Ibid., 55.
10. Philip Armstrong, Andrew Glyn and John Harrison, *Capitalism since 1945* (Oxford: Basil Blackwell, 1991), 153.
11. Milward, *The European Rescue of the Nation-State*, 129–30.
12. The argument here follows a case study in Milward, *The European Rescue of the Nation-State*, 367 ff.
13. United Nations, Economic Commission for Europe, *Economic Survey of Europe since the War* (Geneva: United Nations 1953), 129, Table 47.
14. Scott Newton, '"Operation Robot" and the political economy of sterling convertibility, 1951–1952', *EUI Working Paper* No. 86/256 (Florence: European University Institute, 1986), 1–2.
15. Milward, *The Reconstruction of Western Europe*, 456–9 and Newton, '"Operation Robot"', 2.
16. Jacob J. Kaplan and Gunther Schleiminger, *The European Payments Union: Financial Diplomacy in the 1950s* (Oxford: Oxford University Press, 1989), 140–1.
17. Newton, '"Operation Robot"', 13–15.
18. Milward, *The European Rescue of the Nation-State*, 389.
19. Ibid., 403.
20. Kaplan and Schleiminger, *The European Payments Union*, 372–3.
21. Milward, *The European Rescue of the Nation-State*, 130–1.
22. Ibid., 154–5.
23. Ibid., 166.
24. Van der Wee, *Prosperity and Upheaval*, 357.
25. Robert Solomon, *The International Monetary System, 1945–76* (New York: Harper & Rowe, 1977), 19–20.
26. Paul A. Baran and Paul Sweezy, *Monopoly Capital: An Essay on the American Economic and Social Order* (London: Penguin, 1966).
27. Ibid., 45.
28. C. Wright Mills, *The Power Elite* (New York: Oxford University Press, 1956).
29. Ibid., 116.
30. Ibid., 232.
31. Baran and Sweezy, *Monopoly Capital*, 66.
32. A similar argument is developed by John Kenneth Galbraith in *The Affluent Society* (London: Penguin, 1977), Ch. 8. *The Affluent Society* was first published in 1958.
33. Baran and Sweezy, *Monopoly Capital*, 197.
34. Block, *The Origins of International Monetary Disorder*, 119.
35. *FRUS 1955–57*, Vol. IX (Washington: United States Government Printing Office, 1987), memorandum from Henry C. Wallich to Clarence Randall, 22 April 1955, 331.

36. *FRUS* 1955–57, Vol. IV (Washington: United States Government Printing Office, 1986), report by Frank on 'Attitude to US business to common market and free trade area', 24 May 1957, 555–6.
37. Ibid.
38. *FRUS* 1955–57, Vol. IV, 'Report of the Subcommittee on Regional Economic Integration of the Council on Foreign Economic Policy', 15 November 1956, 485–6.
39. *FRUS* 1951, Vol. IV Part 1 (Washington: United States Government Printing Office, 1983), Conference of west European Ambassadors, Frankfurt, February 1951, 485–6.
40. Kaplan and Schleiminger, *The European Payments Union*, 177.
41. See Tom Kemp, *Industrialization in the Non-Western World* (Longman: London, 1983), 36–40.
42. United Nations, Economic Commission for Asia, *Economic Survey of Asia and the Far East in 1957* (Geneva, United Nations, 1958), 45.
43. Kemp, *Industrialization in the Non-Western World*, 38.
44. United Nations, *Economic Survey of Asia and the Far East 1957*, 59.
45. See G.D.A. Macdougall, *The World Dollar Problem: A Study in International Economics* (New York: St Martin's Press, 1957).
46. Solomon, *The International Monetary System*, 31.
47. Ibid.
48. Susan Strange, *International Monetary Relations* (Oxford: Royal Institute for International Affairs (RIIA), 1976), 102, in Andrew Shonfield (ed.), *International Economic Relations of the Western World 1959–1971* (London: Oxford University Press for RIIA, 1976), Vol. II.
49. Van der Wee, *Prosperity and Upheaval*, 451.
50. Ibid., 449.
51. Milward, *The European Rescue of the Nation-State*, 130.

4

THE FALL OF THE POSTWAR ORDER, 1958–1971

◆ **US Deficit**

The period from 1958 to 1971 was characterized in international monetary affairs by the hegemony of the dollar, the world's main international trading and reserve currency. Dollar reserves were convertible and could be used anywhere. Their value was guaranteed by the American commitment to exchange dollars for gold on demand at $35 an ounce (a price fixed in 1934). Sterling played a secondary role but it was confined to the sterling area, which itself continued to shrink during these years. The dollar was, however, held as a proportion of national reserves by most countries, including some in the Soviet bloc (who put their deposits in European, mainly London, banks, out of anxiety that they would be subject to political interference if left in New York). The dollar had been in demand in the early postwar era on account of the need for imports of capital goods and foodstuffs to sustain reconstruction. Now those days were over, but the dollar still remained attractive because of its universal acceptability and apparently unshakeable value.

In international trade policy these years were dominated by the struggle for liberalization, most of which occurred within the GATT. This was the forum for the 'Dillon' and 'Kennedy Rounds' of negotiations designed to reduce trade barriers. The Kennedy Round in particular revealed US concern that the world was not only one that fell short of the wartime hopes for an open door but was in danger of retreating even further away from it. These fears were not to prove misplaced. The postwar international economic order, based on the dollar's pre-eminence, convertible currencies, an Atlantic alliance, a united western Europe, trade liberalization and co-operation on currency issues between the industrialized countries, entered a deepening crisis during the 1960s and finally collapsed in 1971.

Throughout the period 1958–71 the foundations of the postwar order were being eaten away by the US balance of payments deficit. In one way this was good for the world economy since the US deficits were other nations' surpluses and so added to the volume of international reserves. The growth of these reserves encouraged the growth of trade and facilitated the credit expansion that helped to fuel the buoyant activity of the time. On the other hand, the net out-flow of dollars from the USA could not continue indefinitely since the resulting imbalance between the country's shrinking reserve assets and its reserve liabilities abroad would lead holders of dollars to fear for the value of their holdings. The danger was that there would not be enough gold in Fort Knox to permit auto-matic convertibility of dollars into gold at $35 per ounce. Therefore the price of gold would have to rise against the dollar; this would retain convertibility but mean that holders of dollar-denominated assets stood to lose a lot of money. If the deficits were eliminated, however, then the world would once again be short of liquidity, and the expansion of global trade and economic activity would no longer be sustainable. This was the 'Triffin paradox', named after the economist Lionel Triffin who identified it in the late 1950s. His answer was the creation of a new reserve asset under the control of the IMF, which would be empowered to use it so that what the sympathetic Fund insider Robert Solomon called 'the legitimate needs of an expanding world economy' could be met.[1]

The deficit itself was in large part a function of two significant developments. One was the decline of the United States relative to the West European economies, above all to the FRG, and to Japan. The other was the expansion of US govern-ment expenditure overseas. The first of these two was apparent in a declining share of world trade and in growing import penetration of the American market. Between 1958 and 1965 the US share of world manufacturing exports fell from 18.7 per cent to 15.8 per cent, while US corporations increased foreign direct investment 50 per cent more rapidly than investment in the United States, a clear indication of their views about where capital investment would achieve its best return.[2] The figures reflected a sluggish economic performance by the USA in the 1950s. Manufacturing investment was flat throughout the period from 1951 to 1955, and rose by just 8.2 per cent over the rest of the decade.

All this was consistent with the growing influence in the economy of the large corporations, which was noted in Chapter 3. These firms engaged in what econ-omists call 'oligopolistic competition', meaning that they enjoyed a protected internal market and managed their own environment through informal cartels and price collusion. The figures show that corporate investment strategy was conservative all the way through the 1950–8 period, spending on new plant growing on average each year by 1.1 per cent, while investment in equipment increased at an annual average rate of 2.2 per cent at the same time.[3] The extremely modest commitment to spending on plant reveals that large firms had collectively turned their backs on the construction of the new facilities that would have allowed them to expand market share with the aid of transformed production techniques and higher output. Instead, corporations preferred to hang on to their existing slice of the domestic market. There were two principle ways of achieving this. One was via the refinement of existing products; the other was through generous outlays on advertising, which rose from $10.3 billion in 1957 to $12 billion in 1962 (in both years, this figure represented just over 2 per cent of the American GNP).[4]

Why was oligopoly an inhibitor of corporate expansion in the home market? If a corporation wished to increase its market share at home it would have to break price agreements with other firms, fighting a price war with them and taking lower returns as a result. Modernization of plant was another road to increasing market share but the costs involved threatened profitability, especially if undertaken against a background of genuine price competition. Perhaps not surprisingly, therefore, a 1958 McGraw-Hill University Department of Economics survey found that 'less than one-third' of American business plant and equipment was 'modern, in the realistic sense of being new since 1950'.[5] There might have been more of an incentive for expansion by the private sector had demand been higher, but the cautious macroeconomic stance of the Eisenhower administration mitigated against this, and by the time the President stepped down in January 1961 unemployment had reached a postwar high of 6.7 per cent.

The FRG and Japan, by contrast with the USA, experienced strong growth during the 1950s and 1960s. German prosperity was in fact rooted in the trade expansion first seen in western Europe and which then spread throughout the industrialized world. German producers were encouraged to export by the federal government, which backed the spread of trade liberalization without at the same time following *laissez-faire* policies, despite the liberal reputation of its Finance Minister Ludwig Erhard. Thus the government borrowed money from industry and invested it in long-term projects through the *Kreditanstalt fur Wiederaufbau* (Bank for Reconstruction).[6] There were subsidies for exports and generous loans to promote them, as well as substantial tax allowances for depreciation. The unions observed wage restraint and, between 1950 and 1960, unit labour costs actually fell by 6 per cent relative to the USA, France and Italy. It was a climate conducive to the production of exports, and these grew by an annual average of 13.5 per cent throughout the 1950s. There was a pause in the early 1960s as the federal government damped down demand at home, concerned about the inflationary impact of expansionary taxation and expenditure policies. But from the middle of the decade a new boom was under way. Between 1965 and 1970 exports grew at an annual rate of 10 per cent, fuelled by domestic industrial rationalization, continuing income restraint and the impact of inflation in the USA, which increased the competitiveness of West German goods, especially cars, in the American market.[7]

The Japanese performance was even more spectacular. During the 1950s Japanese governments, as part of the drive to modernize the economy, had encouraged the import of innovation from abroad. Indeed Japanese manufactures acquired the reputation of being merely cheap copies of advanced western products. Yet this was unjust: during the 1960s the Japanese economy became highly innovative, improving the design and quality of its electronic equipment, cameras and vehicles. These products all sold well on the international market. The annual GNP responded to the combination of investment expenditure and export-led demand. Between 1966 and 1970 it was growing at an annual rate of 14.6 per cent, and the gap between west European and Japanese living standards, which had been notable during the 1950s, was starting to disappear.[8]

The increasing prosperity of Japan was not translated into inflation, with export prices in 1969 no higher than they were in 1959. This was central to the country's success in overseas markets and was assisted by successive governments, which provided tax incentives and presided over an interventionist industrial strategy designed to encourage continuous modernization. To this end the state operated an integrated industrial and foreign trade strategy through the Ministry for International Trade and Industry (MITI), which controlled the import and use of foreign goods and technology, rationed the availability of foreign exchange to domestic firms and conducted its own research and development programmes as well as financing those of private industry.[9] The ability of the Japanese economy to use innovation to enhance productivity and keep costs low ensured it a growing share of world markets while its competitors lost ground; Japan's share of the rest of the world's imports doubled between 1960 and 1970, by which time it was accounting for 15.5 per cent of all US imports.

The American trade surplus shrank under the impact of international competition (Table 4.1). Having dropped to $1.1 billion in 1959 it rose steadily up to 1964 when it reached $6.8 billion. Thereafter it fell back each year until, by 1968 and 1969, it was worth just $0.6 billion. For most of the postwar period the surplus had been substantial enough to outweigh other calls on the current account such as services, pensions, remittances and US government grants. But by the end of the decade it was too insignificant to do this; in 1968 the current balance, at

TABLE 4.1: THE US TRADE BALANCE WITH GERMANY, JAPAN AND THE WORLD ($ BILLION), 1963–1973

	1963	'64	'65	'66	'67	'68	'69	'70	'71	'72	'73
Japan	0.3	0.2	−0.5	−0.5	−0.3	−1.2	−1.6	−1.4	−3.3	−3.9	−1.3
Germany	0.6	0.4	0.3	−0.1	−0.25	−1.0	−0.5	−0.4	−0.8	−1.4	−1.6
Japan and Germany	0.9	0.6	0.2	−0.9	−0.55	−2.2	−2.1	−1.8	−4.1	−5.3	−2.9
World	5.2	6.8	4.9	3.8	3.8	0.63	0.61	2.6	−2.3	−6.4	0.9
Current account	4.4	6.8	5.4	3.0	2.6	0.61	0.39	2.3	−1.4	−5.8	2.3

Source: Brenner, 'The economics of global turbulence', *New Left Review* 229 (1998), 119

a negative $0.9 billion, went into the red for the first time since 1945. There was no improvement in 1969 and the gap widened to $1.6 billion. In 1971 merchandise imports, at $45.5 billion, exceeded exports, at $42.8 billion.[10] Until that year the merchandise trade balance had been positive every year since the end of the Second World War. The disappearing surplus on current account joined the longer-term trend to deficit on the capital account and meant that throughout the 1960s, especially in the years after 1964, there was a growing volume of dollars outside the USA, many in the banking systems of creditor countries such as the FRG and Japan. Meanwhile, those exporting to the USA continued to prosper given the relatively less competitive position of American manufacturers. The attraction of the American market was moreover enhanced by the willingness of the Johnson administration to sustain an expansionary domestic environment with low taxes and high federal spending to finance the Vietnam War and the 'Great Society' welfare programme. America's creditors were for the most part naturally anxious to preserve the export bonanza and accepted larger and larger piles of dollar balances, which were essentially loans to the USA so that it could carry on buying.

The impact of America's deteriorating trade position on the dollar outflow was strongly reinforced by government spending overseas. This included paying for the military machine, aid programmes and interest payments. The drain resulting from overseas military spending rose throughout the 1950s and reached a high point of $3.1 billion in 1958. The deficit fell by $1 billion over the next six years, largely as a result of economy measures, sales of military goods and 'offset' agreements by which foreign governments agreed to pay towards the costs of American bases on their soil (the West Germans were the most significant contributors under this heading).[11] After 1964, the cost of the Vietnam War pushed the figure back up and direct military spending rose steadily until it reached $4.8 billion in 1969. Offset agreements continued to offer some compensation as did sales of military goods, which rose from $300 million in 1958 to $1.5 billion in 1969. After allowing for these contributions, however, military commitments were still responsible for a loss of over $3.3 billion on government account.

Aid programmes represented another source of the dollar flow from the United States. Loans and grants, having fallen back from the levels achieved during the era of the Marshall Plan to just over $2 billion in 1954, started to rise as the Eisenhower administration became concerned about the success of the Soviet Union in forging ties with the developing world. By the end of the 1950s the figure had risen to $3 billion and the upward trend continued during the 1960s as the Democratic Kennedy and Johnson administrations used American money to encourage the growth of anti-communist, liberal nationalism in the Third World. By 1968, the aid programme was worth just under $5.4 billion – but it was countered by inflows of dollars from the sale of government-financed exports (many of which assisted infrastructural development) and from interest payments on loans. The result was a net loss to the United States of around $700 million each year during the 1960s.[12]

There was one more source of the drain of dollars on government account. This came under the heading of 'other government transactions' and was composed mostly of interest payments to foreign holders of US government liabilities, payments towards pensions and the provision of various (non-military) services. For most of the 1960s the outflow here amounted to very little until it suddenly exploded at the end of the decade. The development was a function of the rise in foreign dollar holdings, many of which had been invested in US government securities. Interest payments on these went from $489 million in 1965 to $1.8 billion in 1971; indeed, the net outflow from the 'other government transactions' account rose from $373 million in 1969 to $2.4 billion in 1971.[13]

The growing deficit and the consequent expansion of foreign dollar balances fuelled concern about the ability of the USA to honour dollar–gold convertibility, reflected in bouts of international currency speculation. Confidence could have been restored if Washington had taken steps to reduce the calls on its reserves, but this would have flown in the face of all its commitments and interests in the postwar world. For example, cuts in overseas military spending were hardly feasible given the determination to defend the client government of South Vietnam against the radical nationalists and communists of North Vietnam who were trying to unite the country. It was argued that withdrawal from Vietnam would mean defeat for the postwar strategy of containing communist expansion and would signal American weakness to the rest of the world.

Another option was the reduction of imports via deflation. This, though, would have exerted politically damaging pressures across the United States and its main trading partners, who would see their sales in the American market falling. Alternatively the introduction of protectionist measures at home could reduce the volume of imports without damaging domestic activity – but this would, once again, hit producers elsewhere. It would also threaten a worldwide return to the protectionism and discrimination of the 1930s. Both strategies therefore involved the rejection of the postwar commitment to building a US-led world economy characterized by falling barriers to trade and high levels of employment. As a result, neither was tried seriously during the 1960s.

By the start of the 1970s the US deficit and its implications for the future of international trade and for international currency stability was the leading item at economic summits involving the major industrial nations. The Kennedy–Johnson administrations had been unable to turn it around; the new Nixon regime seemed willing to allow it to accumulate. Serious questions were being asked about the future of the dollar. Was it realistic to expect it to continue playing the dominant role in the world economy as it had since 1945? Was it now time for fundamental international economic reform, for exchange rate adjustments, even for alternatives to the dollar? It certainly seemed as if corrective action by the United States was out of the question since every option contradicted American national and international interests as they had developed since 1945.

◆ The Multinational Firm and the Rise of the Eurodollar

The US deficit was both a product of the postwar international economic system and a threat to its future viability. But it was not the only development of the 1960s that provoked growing instability. Two other powerful forces surfaced at this time, making their own significant contributions to the increasing turbulence.

The first of these was the growth of the large firm into the 'multinational corporation'. This term was first used in 1960 to describe the increasingly obvious tendency of American corporations to invest in plant and equipment overseas, either through building from scratch or purchasing rival foreign companies. During the 1960s much of this expansionary activity occurred in western Europe. The concentration on investment in Europe was in part a response to market conditions, notably the contrast between its own economic miracles and the sluggish growth of the USA; but it was also a function of the rapid growth of international trade, which was such a notable feature of the postwar era. Of all the forms of trade it was the exchange of manufactured goods between industrialized countries that increased fastest. Within this category the most rapid growth occurred in the more advanced sectors such as chemicals, petrochemicals, detergents, electrical and electronic equipment, and cars, in which the large American corporation specialized, because these were most in demand throughout the affluent societies of the West.

Given the existence of the EEC tariff wall, relatively lower labour costs and rapid growth, it made more sense for the large firms to make the goods in Europe rather than send them across the Atlantic. By 1970, 31 per cent of US direct investment was located there as opposed to 15 per cent in 1955.[14] The result was that American firms became part of the European market, owning substantial shares in local industry (Table 4.2). By 1964, high-technology sales of US subsidiaries in Europe were running at four times the level of American exports to Europe. It all represented a major transfer of technology, knowledge and management techniques; Europe's technological deficit with the USA steadily closed during the 1960s. This process led the French journalist Jean-Jacques Servan-Schreiber to argue that the world's third industrial power was in the making – but that power was not the EEC so much as '*American industry in Europe*' (original emphasis).[15] Writing in 1968, he pointed out that US corporations in Europe now controlled 15 per cent of consumer goods' production; 50 per cent of semi-conductors' production; 80 per cent of computers; and 95 per cent of integrated circuits.[16]

The expansion of the multinational firm was at its most dramatic in Europe but it was not confined to that continent. Some affiliates and facilities were already established in less developed economies, especially those with plentiful oil reserves. From 1970 at the latest, as European wage costs rose, the corporations began to undertake increasing levels of direct investment in the less developed world. This generally flowed to those countries that were politically stable

TABLE 4.2: SHARE OF US AFFILIATES IN SALES OF MANUFACTURED
GOODS IN FOUR WEST EUROPEAN COUNTRIES, 1966

	UK	France	Germany	Benelux
Total manufacturing	10.5	5.9	5.7	10.3
Chemicals and allied products	17.6	9.5	5.3	28.5
Rubber	24.9	10.9	12.7	89.7
Machinery, except electrical	13.9	13.4	8.9	37.9
Electrical machinery	14.2	8.0	5.0	21.7
Transportation equipment	18.5	9.3	24.4	22.3
Instruments	35.8	13.5	18.6	45.0

Source: Dunning, 'Multinational enterprises, market structure, economic power and
industrial policy' (Reading University, January 1974), quoted in Andrew Shonfield
(ed.), *International Economic Relations of the Western World*, 139, footnote 36

(usually this meant, as with Indonesia, the Philippines, South Korea and most
Latin American states, that they were under the control of right-wing, anti-
communist dictatorships), could provide cheap labour, secure raw material supplies, and contained a relatively advanced transport infrastructure that ensured
easy and economical road, rail, sea and air links to the industrial world. Market
opportunities in the less developed world were more limited but did exist for
a limited range of goods such as transistor radios, aspirin, cigarettes and
powdered milk.

European corporations started to go down the multinational road in the second
half of the 1960s. They were driven by the gains to be made from exports of manufactures. The rich pickings of the period since 1950 had stimulated corporate
growth and economies of scale in western Europe. Increased size and higher overheads required generous returns and this implied not exposure to market forces
but market management. The 1960s had, for example, seen close co-operation
between Volkswagen and Daimler-Benz, rationalization in the French and Italian
chemical industries, and the fusion of national capitals into transnational concerns. Examples were mergers drawing together the West German and Dutch
steel industry, and the production of photographic materials and equipment in
West Germany and Belgium.[17] These large firms, now confronted with competition from US corporations within Europe, sought to maintain their own profitability via a search for global markets. Just as the US multinational firm sought
to control its costs by reproducing itself within overseas markets, so European
firms now started to do the same. British firms had long been able to exploit the
legacy of Empire and the worldwide financial links of the City of London. Their

expansion was now matched by overseas investment on the part of German, Japanese and Italian corporations.[18] Initially a good part of this was in southern Europe and Latin America, but it spread to the USA, the Far East and even to newly independent states in Africa, where German capital was challenging the traditional hegemony of British firms in former colonies such as Nigeria and Kenya. In 1969 West German foreign direct investment outstripped foreign direct investment in West Germany.

The growth of the multinational firm led to the increasing internationalization of production. By the early 1960s US multinational firms were responsible 'for over three quarters of their country's exports and almost half its imports'.[19] These figures disguised the reality that what appeared to be sets of national trade statistics were partly records of *trade within a single corporation*. Thus American car producers such as General Motors imported into the USA their own range of models, built in British or German or Canadian or Japanese factories.[20] Or, given the ability of the multinational to assign production to where costs are lowest it was possible to manufacture the components of a product in different locations, characteristically ones where the expenses of building and maintaining plant and equipment, and raw material prices and labour were all cheap, before bringing them together at an assembly plant in another country. By the late 1960s intra-company transactions accounted for 20 per cent of British and 25 per cent of American exports.[21] Shonfield reported that by 1971 the total value of international production, defined as 'the output of firms owned or controlled by parent organizations outside the country where production occurred', amounted to $330 billion and exceeded the total value of world exports, which reached $310 billion. Foreign affiliates of multinationals were responsible for 33 per cent of all international trade.[22] The ability of the multinational to operate this pattern of trade, simultaneously *free and planned*, reinforced the trend to concentration. It was estimated that as early as 1960, 17 per cent of the world's product could be accounted for by the sales of the 200 largest firms; by 1984 this proportion had increased to 26 per cent.[23]

The rise of the multinational and the consequent trend to internationalization of production posed a threat to the stability of the postwar order. For a start, it presented a challenge to the ability of national governments to manage internal demand. The problem was that multinationals were not dependent on finance whose availability was subject to changes in domestic monetary policy. They were able to raise money from within; indeed, between 1960 and 1967, US multinationals were able to use their own cash flow to meet 75 per cent of all their financial requirements.[24] Thus they could circumvent the credit policy of national governments – for example, thwarting a credit squeeze simply by drawing on funds hitherto at the disposal of subsidiaries in countries where the monetary regime was relaxed.

In addition, the multinationals were in part responsible for the revival of a liberal international capital market after a long period during which it had been subject to controls imposed by national governments and largely inactive.

Corporations did not tend to repatriate their overseas earnings; instead they either placed them in banks where they could be drawn on for reinvestment or they moved them from one financial centre to another in search of a good rate of return, dependent on interest rate variations and alterations to exchange rates. About 50 per cent of the foreign assets of the multinationals were subject to speculative movements of this kind. The banks that handled these assets tended to fall into three categories. They were either foreign (often Swiss or British), or US financial institutions operating in Europe, or they had been established by the multinationals themselves. The funds placed with them could be moved freely across state borders, escaping the jurisdiction of the monetary authority in the country where the subsidiary operated, and became a significant source of footloose capital. They fed, and were fed by, the remarkable growth of the 'Eurodollar market', the second major international economic development of the 1960s to contribute to the increasing turbulence of the time.

The 'Eurodollar market' was so called because the greater part of the market was in Europe and most of the transactions within it were made in dollars. It was not new for banks outside the USA to hold dollar balances: some, based in London, had done so prior to 1939. At the end of the 1950s this dollar business received a shot in the arm from the arrival of convertibility, as a result of which European banks could trade freely in dollars and invest them anywhere. Once again it was good business for the City of London banks. They were not subject to US tax and banking regulations (notably Regulation Q, which placed a ceiling on interest payments derived from long-term deposit accounts). A side-effect of the rule was that no member of the US Federal Reserve banking system could offer the level of interest payments that were available in Europe. As a result European banks, and particularly those in London that had a long tradition of large-scale international dealing, attracted dollars from US corporations with European subsidiaries and from smaller private investors.

A further stimulus derived from the efforts of the Kennedy–Johnson administrations to control the outflow of capital overseas, known as 'Operation Twist'. One important measure was the Interest Equalization Tax (1963), which was designed to stop the large-scale purchasing of foreign securities by American citizens through the simple expedient of imposing a tax on these transactions. In July 1965 the tax was extended to cover credits provided by US banks to customers abroad. Other steps included restrictions on private investment abroad. At first (1965) this was voluntary and took the form of guidelines for commercial banks, pension funds, insurance companies and companies with subsidiaries abroad, but in January 1968 the Johnson administration made the programme compulsory.

These controls reinforced the influence of Regulation Q. In order to avoid being subject to the taxes and capital controls being introduced in the USA, corporations allowed their profits to accumulate as dollar balances in foreign banks. In doing so they fuelled the growing supply of dollars in the banking systems of west European states, which was the obverse side of the US payments deficit.

These deposits became the centre of a rapidly expanding international financial market beyond the control of any single nation state. Mary Kaldor provides the example of a cheque for $1000, drawn on an account in the Chase Manhattan Bank in New York and deposited by a multinational in a London bank. The London bank would treat this deposit as an asset and use it as collateral for a credit, in dollars, worth as much as 90 per cent of the original holding.[25] The bank or corporation that took up what was now a loan of $900 could of course follow suit and turn it into a credit of $810, and so on. This process could continue indefinitely. It was encouraged by the growth of London subsidiaries of New York banks at the end of the 1960s. These issued transferable dollar certificates of deposit, which could be traded freely in the market. All this meant that the Eurodollar market was able to grow uncontrollably and nobody could be sure how large it was. Estimates suggest that it expanded from very little in the late 1950s to $16 billion in 1966 and to $145 billion in 1971, with the trend rising sharply.[26] Over time it earned the name 'Eurocurrency market', as it became not just a market for expatriate dollars but for European and Japanese firms, as well as for the financial surpluses of the oil-producing and exporting states seeking to enjoy the freedom to move money at will throughout this alternative, private international financial system.

The Eurodollar market facilitated the expansion of American multinational firms in western Europe since these corporations were able to borrow from it to finance the purchase of local companies and use it as an alternative or supplement to their own resources when undertaking programmes of investment in plant and equipment. As early as 1965, 55 per cent of the $4 billion used by American firms for direct investment in Europe came from borrowing Euro-issues on the European capital market and from direct bank credits.[27] Some loans to individual corporations ran into hundreds of millions of dollars and the packages could only be put together by international consortia of banks, which developed an increasingly refined set of tools, such as Eurobonds (bonds denominated in more than one currency) and syndicated dollar credits.

The growth of the Eurodollar market led to a substantial increase in world reserves and this no doubt assisted in the expansion of economic activity that was shared by so many states in the 1960s. Yet there were serious drawbacks to this new bounty of international credit. First of all, to the extent that Eurodollar credits represented loans to US banks and multinationals they represented an increase in US dollar liabilities. By the end of May 1968, US gold reserves stood at $10.7 billion, while dollar assets in the hands of foreigners were $31.5 billion. Three years later these figures were, respectively, $13.9 billion against $67.8 billion.[28] Second, the rise of a genuinely international credit system in the Eurodollar market left operators commanding a massive volume of liquidity, which could move anywhere in response to speculative hopes of gain.

The internationalization of finance, marching alongside the internationalization of production, threatened the economic sovereignty of national governments which had been central to the successful administration of the postwar mixed economies. The power of the markets to generate destabilization was revealed in the 1960s and early 1970s when the footloose funds boosted speculation first against the pound and then against the dollar, precipitating the devaluation of both and the collapse of the gold–dollar standard. It represented a reassertion of market forces in the international economy and was accompanied by a revival of enthusiasm for liberal, even *laissez-faire*, economics, not just in the banks but in a growing number of (initially) American universities. The multinational firm and the Eurodollar were at the cutting edge of a challenge to the postwar order that was simultaneously material and ideological.

◆ The Liberal Strategy and its Outcome, 1961–1967

Government anxiety about the implications of an American deficit for the dollar's role as an international currency had begun to surface during the last years of the Eisenhower presidency. The administration initiated a new round of trade liberalization talks in the GATT with the aim of opening export markets to US producers, and in January 1960 authorized a programme of public spending increases, designed to stimulate domestic economic activity.

Neither of these moves achieved distinguished results. The spending programme had been left too late to make inroads into unemployment by the time Eisenhower left office a year later. The trade discussions, known as the 'Dillon Round' after the Under-Secretary of State Douglas Dillon (a director of the investment bankers Dillon Read and of Chase Manhattan), who led the US delegation in Geneva, were hampered from the start by a protectionist attitude on the part of the American administration. It limited to a very restricted list the commodities that would be subject to discussion (they were mainly manufactured goods). Dillon was authorized to offer tariff concessions on only 18 per cent of total US imports. Delegations from the EEC and the UK had approached the negotiations in a rather more adventurous spirit, but when the round ended in 1962 the upshot was, according to one expert, an agreement that might have reduced the unweighted average tariff on manufactured goods by 1 per cent.[29]

The Kennedy administration, which took over in January 1961, was determined to reverse the dollar deficit without major reductions in US overseas military commitments or aid and without deflation at home. One of its first initiatives was the 'gold pool', proposed by Treasury Secretary Robert Roosa. This arose from the experience of fighting a large-scale move out of dollars in the autumn of 1960. The panic was caused by anxiety on the part of European bankers that a Kennedy administration would revalue gold against the dollar. It led to gold selling on the London market at $40 per ounce. In order to guarantee continuing ability to honour dollar–gold convertibility at the established rate of $35 per ounce it became necessary to intervene in the London gold market. At first, the arrangement was an Anglo-American affair, with the United States providing the funds and the Bank of England acting as agent. Other central banks meanwhile agreed to refrain from buying gold, and this moratorium lasted for the rest of the year. The price dropped and stayed below $36.50 per ounce. The gold pool formalized this international co-operation: its members (the USA, the Bank of England and the central banks of the FRG, France, Switzerland, Italy, Belgium, the Netherlands and Luxembourg) agreed to operate what was in effect a sales consortium to prevent the market price of gold from exceeding US$35.20 per ounce, buying gold as the price dipped and selling as the price rose.

The gold pool was one of a number of what were called 'ad hocceries', invented by the Kennedy administration and designed to reinforce international confidence in the dollar. Other measures included 'Roosa bonds' (non-transferable US Treasury Securities issued to foreign governments) and the 'swap' arrangements. The swap arrangements were introduced after the dollar had come under pressure in 1961 as a result of deutschmark and Dutch guilder revaluations. The idea was for the Federal Reserve Bank to establish mutual short-term credit facilities with other central banks, which could be opened in order to counteract speculative flows of money out of one currency and into others. The lenders were to be repaid at the end of a three-month period and they were given a guarantee that their money would be refunded at the same exchange rate as had been used when the initial transactions had been made. By the end of 1962 the Federal Reserve had organized a network of 'swap lines', administered by the Bank for International Settlements in Basle, Switzerland, and worth $900 million. Originally established to support the dollar, the swap arrangements, known as the Basle Agreements, were also used to help other currencies, notably sterling on several occasions, but also the Italian lira in 1964 and the French franc in 1968. These facilities reinforced the General Agreement to Borrow (GAB) agreed by the International Monetary Fund at the end of 1961, whereby the world's ten wealthiest states (called the Group of Ten, and comprising the USA, Canada, Japan, the UK, France, Italy, the FRG, Sweden, the Netherlands and Belgium, with Switzerland as an observer) agreed to make an extra $6 billion available to the Fund so that its resources could be used to support significant British and American withdrawals made to protect sterling and the dollar respectively. The GAB made its debut in late 1964 when the UK took out a large IMF loan.[30]

These 'ad hocceries', which included Operation Twist and the campaign to restrict the export of capital from the USA, were one of four sets of measures undertaken by the Kennedy and subsequent Johnson administrations to preserve the international position of the dollar within the context of an open world economy. The others were a Keynesian programme of domestic economic expansion, the federal government playing a significant role with anti-poverty programmes and tax reductions; a new round of trade negotiations in GATT; and reform of the international monetary system. Each one was consistent with the coalition that had brought the new, Democratic administration to power.

The domestic agenda followed from the 'New Dealing' tradition of F.D. Roosevelt. It addressed the concerns both of an organized labour movement worried about high unemployment and pressure on wages, and a significant constituency of liberal professionals opposed to racial discrimination and the existence of what J.K. Galbraith had identified in his 1958 book, *The Affluent Society*, as 'private affluence and public squalor'. The international strategy reflected the traditional Democratic Party leaning to free trade, and the Atlanticist interests of the liberal, East Coast financial establishment, some of whose members were influential Kennedy advisers and Cabinet members. In the first category came Robert Lovett, Defense Secretary from 1951–3 and a career banker with Brown Brothers Harriman and Company; in the second came Douglas Dillon, who continued to be part of the government (Treasury Secretary) after Eisenhower's departure, and Averell Harriman, who was first Assistant Secretary of State for Far Eastern Affairs and then (from early 1963) Under-Secretary of State for Political Affairs.[31]

The package reconciled limited state intervention at home with trade liberalization abroad. The administration believed in activism both in domestic and international affairs, and embarked on what has been called 'the Kennedy offensive'.[32] This was created as a response to the challenges now facing the postwar American project to build a liberal-capitalist international order. First, there was the balance of payments deficit. Second, came the rise of the EEC. This development had been regarded with equanimity by the Eisenhower administration. Kennedy certainly welcomed the creation of the Common Market, but at the same time feared its potential to turn into a protectionist trade bloc and fracture the postwar unity of the Atlantic alliance in the process. A State Department paper of 4 October 1961 questioned whether 'the newly created preferential trading area will draw the ... EEC and its overseas associates into a separate political force'.[33] Third, there was the need to improve the US position in the developing world where the USSR, offering aid and preferential trade deals, had recently been making progress.

These challenges called for an integrated response. To begin with, the dollar deficit could be cured with an expansion of exports, generated by a modernized, fast-growing US economy. In order to guarantee markets for these it would be necessary to pursue a trade liberalization programme that undermined the discriminatory impact of the EEC tariff system, a strategy that would also reinforce Atlantic unity. International monetary reform did mean conceding influence to the IMF, something previous administrations had not encouraged, but this could help solve the Triffin paradox by ensuring that the continuing expansion of international trade was not made dependent on a spiralling American deficit. At the same time the enlargement of international credit facilities, allied to generous overseas aid from the USA and the opening up of market opportunities in the industrialized world, would draw the developing countries away from the Soviet bloc and towards the West.

The Kennedy offensive achieved some successes but, overall, fell a long way short of its objectives. The expansionary domestic macroeconomic policy did generate higher growth, which ran at an annual average level of 4.6 per cent between 1961 and 1965. Manufacturing output rose at a rate of 6.55 per cent a year over the same period, while profitability, boosted by a fall in real wage costs between 1958 and 1960, rose rapidly enough to fuel a 15.6 per cent increase in investment from 1961 to 1965.[34] The US trade surplus grew during the first half of the 1960s, rising from a modest $3 billion in 1958 to over $6.8 billion in 1964. The prestigious think-tank, the Brookings Institution, even predicted a return to dollar scarcity. By 1967–8 the economic impact both of the Vietnam War and of overseas competition on the USA was making this exercise in futurology look absurd.

Meanwhile the attempt to strengthen the Atlantic alliance and liberalize world trade also ran into trouble. The first stage of this programme had been the expansion – on the suggestion of the USA – of the OEEC into the OECD (Organization for Economic Co-operation and Development, based in Paris). The OECD was intended to bring together not just the nations of western Europe but all the advanced capitalist powers, so that it included the USA and Canada from September 1961 and Japan from 1964. The second stage was the Trade Expansion Act, passed in 1962. It was an ambitious piece of legislation, aiming at a 50 per cent reduction in all tariffs, while under the Act's 'dominant supplier provision' tariffs on goods in which the USA plus its trade partner accounted for 80 per cent or more of world trade were to be eliminated. The dominant supplier provision was directed mainly at the EEC, then involved in negotiations about admitting the United Kingdom. The administration calculated that given the volume of US commerce with an enlarged EEC it would be possible to use the Trade Expansion Act to build a single Atlantic Free Trade Area, so removing the application of the common external tariff to American exports; but the plan failed when President de Gaulle of France vetoed the British application early in 1963. There was to be no enlargement, and talks under the heading of the dominant supplier provision only succeeded in two areas where the USA and the UK between them accounted for 80 per cent of world trade: margarine and aircraft.[35]

The campaign to reduce trade barriers around the world led to the 'Kennedy Round' of talks in GATT, following from the disappointing Dillon Round. The achievements of the Kennedy Round were limited. It did achieve weighted tariff cuts of 25 per cent on manufactured goods but these did not apply to the chemical industry, where American protectionists prevented concessions, nor to industrial problem areas, while the results in agriculture were minimal. The US had hoped that it would be possible to introduce non-discriminatory tariffs that could be negotiated away in stages in the same way as tariffs on manufactured goods. It was particularly keen to achieve markets for its agricultural sector in the EEC, and had promised the traditionally protectionist American farmer that lower tariffs in the USA would be more than matched by export opportunities abroad. However, the EEC was in the process of establishing its own Common Agricultural Policy (CAP), designed to safeguard farmers' living standards. Under the CAP a variable levy was imposed on foreign farm imports into the EEC. This was based on the difference between the world price and the European price, and the proceeds from it were channelled into agricultural modernization and price support, so that if a farmer could not sell produce at the 'target' price designated for it then the Community would step in and purchase the surplus at an 'intervention price', after which it would be stored or exported at subsidized prices. It was a scheme that gave great advantages to Dutch and French producers, allowing them to displace the farm exports of efficient agricultural exporters outside the EEC such as the Danes – or the Americans, who were estimated to have lost between $150 million and $200 million of agricultural exports as a result of Common Market agricultural policy between 1958 and 1966.[36] The determination of the six to stick by the CAP was what wrecked the Kennedy Round when it came to agriculture, and when the talks concluded in 1967 no progress had been made in waiving the common external tariff or the agricultural levy. From 1953 to 1972, EEC agricultural imports subject to the variable levy fell by 33 per cent.[37]

The failure of the Trade Expansion Act and the arguments in the Kennedy Round between the EEC and the USA if anything widened the gap in the Atlantic alliance. The diplomatic frustration of the US initiative owed a good deal to the French who, under President de Gaulle, pursued their own vision of what the international order should be. De Gaulle did not share US aspirations in foreign economic policy nor in East–West relations. He won the support of the protectionist Right and the radical Left in France when he argued that the US deficit was allowing American corporations to buy up the continent with dollars borrowed from the Europeans, who were only lending them because they were notionally convertible into gold. In fact (the French argued), the dollar's position as an international reserve currency was merely a licence to print money. The aim of US foreign policy was to undermine all that distinguished the EEC, above all its common external tariff and its industrial and agricultural base, and transform it into a free trade area that had much the same relationship with the USA as Canada. Against this, de Gaulle waved the banner of an independent Europe, free from American anti-communism (anachronistic after the death of Stalin) and so a force for détente in the Cold War and willing to work on development projects with radical nationalist regimes in the developing world. From such a perspective it made sense to block British entry into the EEC given the dependence of the British nuclear deterrent on the American Polaris missile system and London's support for Kennedy's trade liberalization agenda. British membership of the EEC had been pivotal to the Kennedy's liberal strategy. The French veto was a severe rebuff.

French willingness to challenge American leadership in the western world embraced international monetary policy as well as trade issues. Convinced that the dollar's domination of the world's monetary system was assisting American economic imperialism, and at the same time encouraging creditor countries to build up assets whose value could never be redeemed, the French supported enhancing the use of gold as an international medium of exchange. From 1963 they were converting their dollar reserves into gold at a rate of 30 tons per month and in 1965 announced that there would be an immediate conversion of $150 million with all future accumulations of dollars subject to immediate conversion into gold. In 1967, France walked out of the gold pool.

The attempt to rehabilitate gold as a medium of exchange was defeated by the USA. Washington frustrated France's call for a new international asset, the Collective Reserve Unit (CRU), which would be controlled by the Group of Ten and allocated throughout the world according to the size of national gold reserves. The CRU itself would be transferable and would have a fixed link to gold. The initiative threatened the dollar in two ways. First, all CRU recipients would be required to keep a portion of their reserves in gold, obviously reducing the incentive to hold dollars; and, second, given the use of the CRU to settle international payments, deficit countries would inevitably lose gold. The implications for the United States were obvious: unless it was prepared to see its reserves disappear, and with them the worldwide role of the dollar, it would have to take corrective action.[38]

The USA argued that the French proposal would restrict national and international economic expansion. Developing countries supported the American position, fearing that a CRU-based system would restrict their access to liquidity. In 1967–8, the French position hardened and Paris suggested a full-blown return to the gold standard. This attempt to roll back the years was a total failure and left France isolated in both the Group of Ten, where there had been some sympathy for the CRU initiative, and the IMF. The French position was finally wrecked by domestic economic and political crisis in 1968–9, which ended with the resignation of de Gaulle and a devaluation of the franc. This effectively drew a line under the French challenge to US hegemony, a development reflected by agreement within the Fund on the creation of a new international reserve currency, to be known as the 'Special Drawing Right' (SDR). The provision of SDRs was to be managed by the Fund, with the result that it would no longer confine its activities to the extension of credit but now had the authority to generate international reserves, with the governors meeting every five years to decide how large the volume of available SDRs should be. They were expected to base their judgements on the level of demand for liquidity in the world and on expected changes, whether up or down, on the size of international reserves. The first issue of SDRs followed in September 1969. It ran to $49 billion, starting from 1 January 1970 and spread over three years.[39]

At first blush the creation of the SDR looks like the least compromised triumph of the Kennedy offensive. It was a way of enlarging the world's liquidity without adding to the global surplus of dollars and provided a good example of co-operation on reforming the world economic system. Yet it failed to sustain the postwar order. As it happened, SDRs were not used in very significant amounts and despite all that had gone before in the negotiations that led to their creation, not many made their way to the developing world[40] even though they would have been welcome there. The fundamental problem was that by the time the SDR was introduced, the advanced industrial states that dominated world trade and finance needed no extra fund of liquidity since they were grappling with a mounting surplus of reserves arising from the US deficit and the Eurodollar market.

The liberal approach to turning around the balance of payments had failed. It had not proved possible to transform America's economic performance relative to West Germany and Japan. The trade liberalization programme had been derailed. Now the campaign for international monetary reform had ended in anticlimax. It had been overtaken by events so that by the late 1960s the main items on the agenda were how to adjust to the large surpluses and deficits that characterized the deutschmark and the yen on one side and sterling and the dollar on the other, along with the speculative flows of capital that were responses to these disequilibria. Would it be possible to stabilize the movement of money? Would a major exchange-rate adjustment be required affecting all the advanced industrial states?

◆ The Decline and Fall of the Dollar

Apart from the flurry of speculation surrounding the price of gold in 1960–1, it was sterling that first bore the brunt of the growing international economic turbulence. The British tendency to run into balance of payments deficits whenever governments embarked on expansionary economic programmes encouraged speculative attacks on sterling in the foreign exchange markets. The first of these had occurred in 1961 when support under the Basle agreements had helped Britain through a sterling crisis.

By late 1964 sterling was under pressure again. In 1963, the Conservative government had launched a 'dash for growth', which certainly delivered rapid expansion but also, in 1964, a growing payments deficit. This external problem, compounded by the sterling balances, or liabilities, of £4 billion, was inherited by a Labour administration under Harold Wilson, which had been elected with a mandate to modernize the economy. The balances were three or four times larger than the gold reserves and were mainly in the hands of private creditors or foreign monetary authorities. These creditors and authorities were beyond the control of the British government yet their accumulation of sterling reflected the official encouragement given by administrations of the 1950s to the re-establishment of London as an international financial centre.[41] The discrepancy between reserves and liabilities, and the vulnerability of sterling to international market operations conducted through the City of London generated a growing unease about the future of the currency on the part of foreign exchange dealers, bankers and speculators. Their concern was exaggerated by fear that Labour's ambitious domestic programme would suck in imports and put more pressure on the reserves. How much longer would Britain have the resources to maintain the exchange rate of £1 = $2.80, which had held since 1949? This jittery climate encouraged speculators to sell sterling whenever a poor set of trade figures was announced.

Theoretically it would have been possible for Wilson to have reinforced the reserves via deflation or by devaluation. But the first involved a repudiation of everything the government stood for, while the Prime Minister violently opposed the second. He feared it would be the first stage in international currency chaos, with the dollar likely to come under attack by the markets after a sterling depreciation. Wilson therefore played on the Anglo-American 'special relationship', and Britain received IMF assistance as well as large-scale loans organized by the USA in return for stringent wage and price controls. Wilson's conviction that the dollar would follow sterling down the road of devaluation if the speculators were allowed to have their way was shared in Washington, and the Johnson administration was keen to help sustain the sterling parity.[42] All the same there were sterling crises each year from 1965 to 1967, the last of these provoked by the Six-Day Arab-Israeli war of that year. The Suez Canal was shut and a significant exodus from sterling by Middle Eastern holders was anticipated. This was bad enough, but the *coup de grâce* was administered by a poor set of trade figures, which led to uncontrollable selling of sterling. On 18 November, the government bowed to the inevitable and announced a 14.3 per cent devaluation, lowering the rate against the dollar to £1 = $2.40.

The attack on the dollar followed, as had been foreseen. Just as the international financial community had felt that Britain's international economic position was too weak to support the old sterling–dollar rate so it concluded that the US deficit made the dollar a poor investment. The first target was the gold pool, which became the centre of hectic activity in late 1967 and early 1968. A wave of gold buying occurred, putting upward pressure on the price. Members responded by selling gold to keep the price down and in the process they lost about one-eighth of their reserves.[43] Indeed, in November 1967, the pool had to sell $800 million and the US Air Force had to fly gold into London to meet the demand.[44] The episode reached its climax in March 1968. At this point the old gold pool was scrapped and a two-tier price was established for gold. The free-market price was disconnected from the official price. Central banks agreed to limit their gold market activities to dealing with each other. They would abstain from the free market, and the United States announced that it would no longer honour the commitment to sell gold to private parties at $35 per ounce.[45] The measure amounted to a significant move away from automatic dollar–gold convertibility, but it appeared to be the only way to protect members' reserves from the impact of fluctuations in the free market supply of and demand for gold.

In retrospect, it is clear that the changes to the operation of the gold pool marked the beginning of the end for the dollar and the postwar system. It is easier to recognize this now than it was at the time because, for a while, some stability returned to the markets. In the USA Johnson and the Federal Reserve acted to rein in domestic expansion with a programme of tax and interest rate increases. Meanwhile the Germans responded to a large capital inflow with a revaluation of the deutschmark. These measures were followed by an improvement in the US balance of payments, with surpluses in 1968 and 1969. The improvement was not, however, a function of economic performance – the trade position continued to deteriorate – but of capital inflows caused by US bank borrowing on the Eurodollar market. This was in fact a recipe for more turbulence because the funds were moving in response to differences in interest rates between the USA and western Europe. In 1968–9, US rates tended to be higher, but what would happen if the position was reversed?

The arrival of a quiet interlude did not lead to complacency. Indeed, the problems affecting sterling and the dollar stimulated growing interest throughout the advanced industrial world in reform of the international monetary system. It was obvious that the fixed exchange relationships against the dollar, which had been established for a decade, were under great pressure. For a long time America's creditors had connived at the growth of the deficit because it was good for their exports. The Germans in particular began to lose patience in 1968 because the inflow of dollars was not only putting unwelcome upward pressure on the national currency but importing inflation into the economy. The incoming dollars made their way into the banking system where they were used to underwrite credit expansion; with exports booming and a rapidly growing home market there was a risk that demand in the economy could not be absorbed by production. Germany had already undertaken a reluctant revaluation of the deutschmark but now argued for a US initiative. Within the IMF Robert Solomon canvassed in favour of exchange rate 'flexibility'. This could operate through acceptance of wider margins for exchange rates around parity, or through what was called the 'crawling peg', in which currencies were fixed against each other but with parities open to frequent readjustment. Others suggested that the current volatility of the markets could only be managed by floating rates. The proponents of flexibility and floating rates argued that, if undertaken in conjunction with more use of interest rates, their strategy for bringing order back to the currency markets stood a better chance of success than continued reliance on fixed rates bolstered by exchange controls, which now could be circumvented by the footloose Eurocurrency billions.[46]

In the circumstances of the time these measures would have led to some revaluation of European currencies against the dollar. But there was resistance to this within the EEC based on a conviction, particularly strong in the FRG, that as a result European exports would suffer while the USA would not need to make fundamental adjustments to correct its own deficit. Instead the EEC Council of Ministers approved the Werner Report (1970), which called for a European Monetary Union (EMU). The reception accorded to the Werner Report showed preference for a system of stable exchange rates – but one in which the national currencies of EEC members would be replaced by a fixed currency bloc commanding enough resources to manage speculative capital movements, and powerful enough to press the USA into appropriate corrective action. It was a proposal that reflected the eclipse of France and the economic dominance of the FRG within the Six; in future any plan for a 'European Europe' would have to be based on this reality.

What followed in 1970–1 suggested that the advocates of some 'flexibility' were more realistic about how the international monetary system could be changed than those who argued for fixed rates based on corrective action by the USA. The Republican President Nixon, having started in 1969 with a deflationary package, began in 1970 to worry about a sluggish domestic economy. Taxes were reduced and there was a cut in the American interest rate. The European economies, concerned to keep inflationary pressures under control, did not follow suit. As a result the US banks that had borrowed so heavily on the Eurodollar market in 1968 now engaged in massive repayments. The flow of dollars was reinforced by a trade deficit, and the overall US balance of payments for 1970 went $9.8 billion into the red,[47] rising to $30 billion the following year. There was a growth of 18 per cent and then of 32 per cent in world reserves.[48] The expansion of these funds was reflected in the shrinking of US gold reserves relative to the country's liabilities, and led to a renewal of international anxiety about the dollar parity. This was expressed in the traditional form of uncontrollable speculation in favour of other currencies, notably the deutschmark and the yen. The West Germans and the Dutch both decided to float against the dollar as did the Belgians, though for financial, not trade, transactions, and there were Swiss and Austrian revaluations against the dollar.

These radical steps could not stop the speculation, especially after the appearance of an OECD report which argued that there was now a 'fundamental disequilibrium' in the world economy that only exchange-rate adjustments could solve. Speculative capital moved into France and Belgium, and continued to enter West Germany. In August 1971, the dollar price of gold rose to $44 per ounce. All this was evidence of a widespread understanding that the dollar was overvalued. The Nixon administration finally embraced corrective action but its actions on 15 August came as a shock to the international community. Instead of deflation or drastic cuts in overseas spending, Nixon decided to suspend the convertibility of the dollar into gold. At the same time the administration introduced a 10 per cent import tax, a 90-day wages and prices freeze to hold back domestic demand, and called on the IMF to produce a set of proposals for a new international monetary system. The ending of gold–dollar convertibility caused anger outside the United States. The Americans were attacked for resorting to economic nationalism and for taking unilateral action to tackle a problem that was the legitimate concern of the international community.

There is no doubt that American policy did reflect economic nationalism. The Treasury Secretary, John Connally, was a lawyer from Texas well connected to the booming south-western oil and construction industries, which had been prominent supporters of the Nixon presidential campaign in 1968. These sectors of the economy were not as integrated into the world economy as the eastern financial establishment (several of whose members in the administration resigned in protest against the decision to suspend dollar–gold convertibility)[49] but would have been damaged by an austerity package designed to rescue the dollar. In common with most postwar governments throughout the world,

Nixon decided to put the achievement of external equilibrium second to domestic growth. 'I am a Keynesian,' he announced[50] and when in the following year an adviser tried to raise the issue of speculation against the lira, Nixon replied that he didn't 'give a [expletive deleted] for' it.[51] Yet it would be wrong to argue that the administration had turned its back on a collective approach to the problem of the dollar's relationship with the rest of the western world. The point was that it refused to accept sole responsibility for correcting the dollar deficit, which after all had facilitated global expansion since the 1950s. The August measures were intended to draw a recognition from creditor countries that there was an onus on them to revalue against the dollar so that a reformed international economic system could be developed on the foundation of a new set of currency relationships.

In December 1971, it seemed as if progress had been made. At this point the Group of Ten, meeting in Washington, concluded the Smithsonian agreement, which saw the revaluation of other currencies against the dollar: the DM by 13.5 per cent and the yen by 16.88 per cent. The dollar was devalued against gold by 7.89 per cent. But the Smithsonian agreement was not the opening of a new era of international economic stability – it was really the epilogue to the decisions of 15 August. For a start there was some feeling in the USA that the revaluations against the dollar had not gone far enough, while agreement on a new dollar price for gold was academic since convertibility remained in suspension.

The end of dollar–gold convertibility was an acknowledgement that the United States did not have the power to lead the world towards an open international economic order. The Triffin paradox of the late 1950s and early 1960s had been superseded by new problems, generated by the relative economic decline of the United States, the appearance of powerful economic rivals and the expansion of footloose international capital. Now the world economy was awash with liquidity and characterized by vast payments imbalances. With the United States itself obviously unenthusiastic about multilateralism, a weakened Atlantic alliance and a stalled international trade liberalization programme, the future of postwar capitalism was uncertain. How could the universal commitment to sustained growth be reconciled with external disequilibria and, at the same time, remain compatible with an 'international market system'[52] characterized by fixed exchange rates? Events had seemed to show that there was no answer.

◆ Notes

1. Solomon, *The International Monetary System, 1945–1976*, 32.
2. Robert Brenner, 'The economics of global turbulence', *New Left Review* 229 (1998), 62.
3. Figures are from Brenner, 'The economics of global turbulence', 51–2.
4. Baran and Sweezy, *Monopoly Capital*, 123 and 374, Table 22.

5. Quoted in Baran and Sweezy, *Monopoly Capital*, 102.
6. Van der Wee, *Prosperity and Upheaval*, 308.
7. Brenner, 'The economics of global turbulence', 115.
8. Hobsbawm, *Age of Extremes*, 276.
9. Scott Newton and Dilwyn Porter, *Modernization Frustrated: The Politics of Industrial Decline in Britain since 1900* (London: Unwin Hyman, 1988), 208–9.
10. Van der Wee, *Prosperity and Upheaval*, 451, Table 37.
11. Fred Block, *The Origins of International Monetary Disorder*, 143.
12. Ibid.
13. Block, *The Origins of International Monetary Disorder*, 144.
14. Philip Armstrong, Andrew Glyn and John Harrison, *Capitalism since 1945*, 160.
15. Jean-Jacques Servan-Schreiber, *The American Challenge* (London: Hamish Hamilton, 1968), 3.
16. Ibid., 10.
17. Ernest Mandel, 'International capitalism and supranationality', in Hugo Radice (ed.), *International Firms and Modern Imperialism* (London: Penguin, 1975), 144–5.
18. Bob Rowthorne, 'Imperialism in the 1970s – unity or rivalry?', in Radice (ed.), *International Firms and Modern Imperialism*, 169–70.
19. Hobsbawm, *Age of Extremes*, 279.
20. John Kenneth Galbraith, *Economics and the Public Purpose* (London: Penguin, 1975), 184–5.
21. Andrew Shonfield, 'International economic relations: an overall view', in Andrew Shonfield (ed.) *International Economic Relations of the Western World, 1959–1971. I: Politics and Trade* (London: Oxford University Press for the RIIA, 1976), 116.
22. Andrew Shonfield, 'International economic relations: an overall view', 115.
23. Hobsbawm, *Age of Extremes*, 279.
24. Stuart Holland, *The Socialist Challenge* (London: Quartet Books, 1975), 80–1.
25. Mary Kaldor, *The Disintegrating West* (London: Penguin, 1979), 20.
26. Susan Strange, *International Economic Relations of the Western World, 1959–1971. Volume II. International Monetary Relations*, ed. Andrew Shonfield (London: Oxford University Press for the RIIA, 1976), 182 and Jerry Coakley and Laurence Harris, *The City of Capital: London's Role as an International Financial Centre* (Oxford: Basil Blackwell, 1983), 52, Table 3.1.
27. Servan-Schreiber, *The American Challenge*, 11.
28. Brett, *The World Economy since the War*, 119 and Harry Magdoff, *The Age of Imperialism* (New York and London: Monthly Review Press, 1969), 108.
29. Gerard and Victoria Curzon, 'Trade liberalization in the 1960s', in Shonfield (ed.), *International Economic Relations of the Western World*, Vol. I, 174.

30. Van der Wee, *Prosperity and Upheaval*, 460–1.
31. Kees van der Pijl, *The Making of an Atlantic Ruling Class* (London: Verso, 1984), 198.
32. Kees Van der Pijl, *The Making of an Atlantic Ruling Class* (London: Verso, 1984), Ch. 7.
33. *FRUS 1961–1963. Vol. IX*, Section 11, Document 224.
34. Brenner, *The Economics of Global Turbulence*, 58.
35. Kaldor, *The Disintegrating West*, 95.
36. Milward, *The European Rescue of the Nation-State*, 315.
37. Kaldor, *The Disintegrating West*, 102.
38. See Van der Wee, *Prosperity and Upheaval*, 464–6.
39. Ibid.
40. Michael Stewart, *Keynes and After*, 2nd edn. (London: Penguin, 1975), 273.
41. Susan Strange, *International Economic Relations of the Western World*, ed. Andrew Shonfield, Vol. II, 120–1.
42. *FRUS 1963–1968, Vol. VIII*, Document 65, Ball to Fowler, 28 July 1965.
43. Van der Wee, *Prosperity and Upheaval*, 474.
44. Solomon, *The International Monetary System*, 117.
45. Brenner, 'The economics of global turbulence', 120.
46. This debate is summarized in Solomon, *The International Monetary System*, 168 ff.
47. Solomon, *The International Monetary System*, 177.
48. Brenner, 'The economics of global turbulence', 121.
49. Van der Pijl, *The Making of an Atlantic Ruling Class*, 257.
50. Stewart, *Keynes and After*, 287.
51. James Foreman-Peck, *A History of the World Economy: International Economic Relations since 1850* (Brighton: Harvester, 1983), 346.
52. The phrase is Van der Wee's, in *Prosperity and Upheaval*, 478.

5

THE QUEST FOR A NEW INTERNATIONAL ECONOMIC ORDER, 1971–1980

◆ Prologue

The period from 1971 to 1980, framed by the ending of dollar–gold convertibility and a surge in the price of oil, was the most turbulent yet in the history of the international economy since 1945. It was characterized by international monetary disorder, highly erratic growth and inflation. The industrialized and the developing nations attempted to construct a new order that would reconcile the changes in the world economy since the late 1950s with the historic commitment to full employment and economic security. Success in this endeavour would have built a world safe for social democracy; failure opened the door to a revival of economic liberalism.

◆ Floating Rates and the Failure of International Monetary Reform

The vast payments imbalance between the USA and the rest of the world, which had led to the abandonment of dollar–gold convertibility, continued into the first half of the 1970s. Yet the dollar remained the world's main international trading and reserve currency and the Nixon administration made no serious effort to reduce the outflow of dollars that continued to accumulate in the hands of America's creditors. Long-term outflows of capital from the USA, having fallen from $7 billion in 1971 to $1.6 billion in 1972, rose to $7.9 billion (a record level) in 1973.[1] The US authorities generally pinned their hopes of reducing the external deficit on encouraging exports. For this reason the Smithsonian agreement was not regarded with much enthusiasm in Washington, where it was seen as having failed to deliver an exchange rate adjustment large enough to give America the chance to turn its economy around while sustaining high employment and growth. In consequence the US authorities first encouraged international monetary reform and then became increasingly comfortable with a floating exchange rate for the dollar, especially since this tended to move downwards (by mid-1973 the dollar stood 19 per cent below its external value three years earlier).[2] By pursuing this policy Washington began to achieve the correction it had long wanted: the current account swung from a deficit of $9.8 billion in 1972 to surpluses of $7.1 billion and $4.9 billion in 1973 and 1974. This transformation was accompanied by a surge in exports that more than doubled from $48.8 billion in 1972 to $98.3 billion in 1974.[3]

From a European perspective it looked as if Washington was happy to leave its creditors holding onto significant dollar balances of dubious value. This was not an attractive option, and in 1972 the EEC determined to press ahead with the implementation of the Werner Report of 1970. It established the famous currency 'snake' by which all members established a system of mutual fixed parities, which then were allowed a variation of just 1.125 per cent above or below the dollar parity established for them in the Smithsonian agreement. Yet the snake was a failure; the will to create a stable European currency bloc could not prevail against different national priorities concerning growth, employment policy and inflation throughout the EEC, about to take in the UK, the Irish Republic and Denmark. Indeed the three new members quickly dropped out while two non-members, Norway and Sweden, joined in – a development that turned the snake into a deutschmark-dominated zone. The British Conservative government of Edward Heath meanwhile allowed sterling to float, not just against the snake but against all other currencies, having come to the conclusion that fixed rates were not compatible with the sustained economic expansion it was attempting to generate.

The failure of the snake had two important effects. First, it led to the end of the sterling area. The 1967 devaluation and then the floating of the currency in the early 1970s was not an incentive to foreigners to hold the currency and, in any case, most of the London banks that had handled sterling now made more money out of the Eurodollar business. Heath did not come under the pressure to 'save sterling' endured by his predecessor. By the time Britain left the snake only 12 nations linked their currencies to sterling and several of these abandoned it in the following years. There was a tendency throughout what was left of the sterling area to diversify into other currencies, and this process culminated in the Basle agreement of July 1977, when the Bank of England agreed with the central banks of eight industrialized countries to arrange for the orderly liquidation of remaining foreign sterling balances.

The second significant effect of the snake's failure was a general move to floating exchange rates. After the floating of sterling and the termination of the sterling area, the last attempts to preserve some kind of international monetary order collapsed. US trade figures had shown a worse than expected deficit. Neither the Europeans nor the Japanese were keen to hold more dollar balances. There was a surge of speculation against the dollar and in February 1973 a new devaluation of the dollar in terms of its gold price was announced – from $38 per ounce to $42.2. However, the new arrangements failed to halt continuing activity against the dollar, which was allowed to sink by the US authorities. These were now committed to the policy of 'benign neglect', in other words of minimal intervention, out of the conviction that depreciation would ultimately correct the US deficit. The continuing decline in the value of the dollar was balanced by massive speculation in favour of the deutschmark, so that in March 1973, with domestic monetary management increasingly difficult in the face of the capital inflow, this currency was floated.

The international monetary disorder of the period took place against a background of discussions concerning international monetary reform. At first the US attitude was negative. Under the influence of Connally the US Treasury showed no interest in the British Barber Plan, which envisaged the replacement of the dollar as a trading and reserve currency by the SDR. This would be placed under the control of the IMF, which would be able to apply sanctions to persistent creditors who refused to reflate. Exchange-rate parities would be fixed but more easily adjustable than hitherto in the postwar era.

The question of international monetary reform was taken more seriously by his successor from April 1972, George Schultz. Schultz turned to his Under-Secretary of State, Paul Volcker, whose background included the Chase Manhattan Bank. This led Volcker to be more of an economic internationalist than his previous master and he now had the chance to display these credentials in his own initiative. The resulting Volcker Plan, first discussed at length at the annual IMF meeting in September 1972, was in fact similar to the British scheme launched the year before. It called for fixed rates but with wide bands to allow for some flexibility – or, as an alternative, a system of managed floating. The dollar would return to convertibility but only on condition, first, that US balance of payments improve and, second, that conversion be into SDRs only. All countries with dollar balances would be permitted to present for conversion only a fixed allocation of them. The SDR would thereby replace gold and its reserve role would be enhanced dramatically.[4]

The Volcker Plan went beyond the question of reserves to deal with the issue of adjustment to disequilibrium. The central international monetary problem of the past decade had been the massive imbalance between surplus and deficit countries, and the unwillingness of either to act on this. To sort this out Volcker proposed a Reserve Indicator test – each country would be set a basic level of holdings of international reserves. If they grew beyond this then reflation would be required; if they sank below it then deflation would result – all on a sliding scale of intensity. Finally there would be multicurrency intervention to replace the old dollar intervention. A surplus nation whose exchange rate with a deficit country was at the top of the permitted band would be required to buy that nation's currency, which could then be converted into SDRs or just held. It all meant, as did the Barber Plan, that IMF authority would have to increase.

The problem was that the main participants in the talks each had different national interests and in the end it was not possible for these to be made compatible. For the British and the Americans the benefit of the Barber and Volcker Plans was that they reconciled multilateralism with expansion: external crises would not be allowed to undermine growth. There was some sympathy for this in the developing states, which also favoured an expansion of SDRs, although they wanted these to be distributed by reference to developmental needs as established by agreement between international agencies such as the World Bank and the IMF rather than according to the size of their very small quotas. But the Europeans and the Japanese, while not dissenting from the Keynesian principles behind the Plans, were worried about how they would work in the international circumstances of the time. First, the French and the smaller European states preferred more rigid exchange rates than the Americans; second, all feared that given the continuing US deficit the Reserve Indicator test would more likely force them into untimely expansionary policies that, given the existence of buoyant growth, would boost inflation. They argued that a deflationary adjustment from the US was still more appropriate.

The whole attempt at reform foundered amid these disagreements. And with the downward float of the dollar sustaining expansion by generating export-led growth, the USA lost interest in the idea of international monetary reform: the floating rate effectively forced the adjustment it wanted between debtor and creditor. Once the need for international monetary reform had faded there was little to be said, from Washington's viewpoint, for a new deal in which the dollar would be replaced as the world's main international trading and reserve currency by an IMF-controlled SDR currency.[5] Such a development would rob the USA of its ability to use the dollar's status as a means of financing the external deficits generated by its role as world policeman and by its relative industrial decline in comparison with Japan and the EEC.

The era of floating rates was unfriendly to international Keynesianism but proved compatible with continuing commitment to the Keynesian-inspired domestic growth policies that most of the advanced capitalist world had followed since 1945. The period 1970–3 was one of expansion. Government and private spending rose (the latter encouraged by low interest rates and reductions in taxation), stimulating rapid growth. This was synchronized, in the sense that it occurred in all the leading capitalist economies at the same time.[6] Between 1 July 1972 and 30 June 1973 real GNP throughout the OECD rose by 7.5 per cent and industrial production increased, in real terms, by 10 per cent. But there were mounting problems beneath the surface prosperity. The expansion generated increasing demand for raw materials and foodstuffs: in 1972–3 primary product prices (excluding energy) rose by 63 per cent. Over the period 1971–4 they increased by 159 per cent. There was growing speculation in property (encouraged in some nations, like the UK, by a liberalization of banking regulations) and an explosion of demand for gold.[7] During the second half of 1973 governments became worried about what economists called 'overheating' – in other words, a level of demand so high that it was generating inflation. They began to announce reductions in planned public spending programmes, along with tax increases and rises in interest rates.

◆ The OPEC Shock

The macroeconomic climate was turning cool in late 1973, but what really brought this expansionist phase to a dramatic end was the behaviour of the oil-producing states, grouped together in a producer's cartel known as the Organization of Petroleum Exporting Countries (OPEC). In the last months of 1973, OPEC quadrupled the price of oil. It was an action that simultaneously drew a line under the longest period of sustained economic expansion in modern history, brought the problem of dollar balances to an end and threatened to overturn the rules of the international economic system as they had developed since the 1950s.

The price increase came as a counterstroke against a series of developments that had prevented the OPEC states from sharing the prosperity of the industrial nations even though this could not have occurred without oil. First there was the impact of cheap oil at the start of the 1970s. This resulted in large part from the activities of the major oil corporations such as Exxon, Mobil, Royal Dutch Shell, British Petroleum, Texaco and Gulf Oil, which had entered into long-term agreements and joint ventures with host governments designed to guarantee a continuous and steady flow of fuel to the industrial world. As a result there was an abundance of supply by the late 1960s, reflected in the price. A barrel of imported crude oil in the USA was, at $3, the same price as it had been in 1957 – but in real terms its value had fallen given low but steady inflation in the developed world during the 1960s. Second, the OPEC states suffered from the falling dollar since most of the world's oil was traded in dollars, not in the local currency of the producers. Finally, OPEC incomes had been adversely affected by the increasing prices for food and industrial imports that followed from the economic spurt of the early 1970s. It all meant that the terms of trade for OPEC had barely improved at all since 1957 (125.2 against 123.5, with 1970 = 100).[8] There were therefore good reasons why OPEC members should have wanted a new deal and, with Arab oil producers leading the way, they took advantage of the Yom Kippur Middle Eastern war of October 1973 to impose embargoes on states suspected of supporting Israel, and push through a sharp increase in the price of crude oil. By early 1974 a barrel of imported crude in the USA cost $10.

The jump in the oil price was followed by a sharp fall in demand throughout the industrialized world and the international economy lurched into a deep recession that lasted until 1976. In the wake of the oil price increase there were actual falls in output and in the volume of international trade all over the developed capitalist world. Output in 1975 was just below the level it reached in 1973 – the first time this had happened since 1929–31. It all occurred because governments were struggling with huge import bills as well as with inflationary pressures, which were given a push by the oil price increase. With some exceptions – notably the British Labour administration elected in 1974 – the first response of governments was to intensify the deflationary cuts in spending and increases in interest rates first introduced to rein in the rapid expansion of 1972–3. The impact of macroeconomic policy was reinforced by developments in the private sector. In 1974–5 profits dropped sharply (Table 5.1) in response not just to wage demands but to the higher cost of raw materials, oil being the largest item on this bill. The result was a fall in investment expenditure. The cumulative result of these developments was revealed in mounting factory closures and job losses. By the autumn of 1975 about 11 per cent of fixed capital in the advanced industrial economies lay idle while unemployment rose from 8 million in 1973 to 15 million in 1975. It looked like the end of the 'golden age'.[9]

At the same time, the oil revenues flowing to the OPEC nations grew from $33 billion in 1973 to $108 billion in 1974. This represented a dramatic transfer of wealth and, since the OPEC states were unable to spend it all on goods produced in the industrialized world, they accumulated large payments surpluses, which reached $55 billion in 1974. These were counterbalanced by the

TABLE 5.1a: BUSINESS PROFIT RATES, 1968–1975 (PERCENTAGES)

	OECD	USA	Europe	Japan
1968	19.3	17.1	18.1	30.8
1973	15.4	13.2	16.0	21.6
1975	11.7	11.0	11.4	14.5

TABLE 5.1b: MANUFACTURING PROFIT RATES, 1968–1975 (PERCENTAGES)

	OECD	USA	Europe	Japan
1968	26.8	28.8	17.4	52.8
1973	21.9	22.0	15.4	38.8
1975	13.1	16.2	8.8	15.2

Source: Armstrong, Glyn and Harrison, *Capitalism since 1945* (Oxford: Basil Blackwell, 1991), 229, Tables 13.1 and 13.2

appearance of equally significant deficits both in the western industrial world and in the non-oil primary producing countries, which needed to import energy supplies to fuel their own economic development. With the local OPEC currencies insignificant, gold convertibility suspended and, still, a relative scarcity of SDRs, it was only the dollar that could finance the large payments deficits. The dollar value of commodity imports including fuel rose dramatically and the overhang disappeared. The doubling of world reserves that had occurred by the start of the 1970s and which was reflected in the expansion of dollar balances from the early 1960s onwards actually ensured that the demand for liquidity caused by inflation and the oil crisis could be met.

The accumulated dollar balances were central to the financing of the oil deficits in 1974 and after. Not only did they represent the main method of payment for oil, they were recycled partly as loans by the OPEC states to western countries and partly in the form of credit arrangements established by the IMF to help oil importers. Yet the larger share of what became known as 'petrodollars' were channelled back to the industrialized world through the agency of the private sector. Large-scale OPEC deposits were made in the Eurocurrency market and these became the basis of loans to western governments. The trade led to a bonanza for the London Eurocurrency market and stimulated an increase in lending on the part of American banks, free from restrictions on the provision of credit to foreigners since the start of 1974 and now anxious to benefit from the demand for dollars (Table 5.2).

TABLE 5.2: FINANCING THE OPEC SURPLUS, 1974–1975 ($ BILLIONS)

	1974	1975
Financial surplus	55.0	31.7
Investments in US	12.0	10.0
Investments in UK	7.2	0.2
Eurocurrency banks deposits plus domestic currency deposits (excluding USA and UK)	22.7	9.1
International organizations	4.0	2.9
Grants and loans to developing countries	2.5	4.0
Direct loans to developed countries (excluding USA and UK)	4.5	2.0
Other net capital flows	2.1	3.5
	−55.0	−31.7

Source: Scammell, *The International Economy since 1945* (London: Macmillan, 1983), 198, Table 12.3

Most fundamentally, the OPEC action represented a challenge to an international economic order dominated by the industrialized states that had enjoyed such rapid economic growth after 1945. It suggested that if developing countries took collective action they could transform the terms of trade to their advantage. It followed that the success of the OPEC nations concentrated the mind of the industrial states on the search for a new international economic order that simultaneously generated the wealth of the postwar system and ensured that what President Roosevelt had called 'freedom from want' was extended to all humanity, not merely the richest portion of it. By what rules would such a system run? Were they at all compatible with liberal capitalism or with a more socialistic, or at least social-democratic, order in which interventionist agencies, discrimination and planning sought to guarantee rising living standards and job security in the developing world?

◆ The 'Third World'

The search for a new international economic order did not start in 1974. The subject had been discussed inside and outside the United Nations since the early 1960s, but the oil price rise acted as a catalyst: willingness to talk was now backed by a commitment to action on the part of the developed and less developed world. For a time it seemed as if this might succeed in the most radical restructuring of the world economy since the 1940s.

The impetus for change came from the developing countries that had either been colonies of the great industrial powers (such as India, Pakistan, Burma, South Korea, Indonesia or most of the African continent and the Caribbean) or their satellites (the nominally free republics of Latin America, which had been informal colonies of the British Empire up to 1914 and thereafter of the United States). This group of nations, often called the Third World or the Less Developed Countries (LDCs), was attracted by socialist ideas since these were identified with liberation from simultaneous colonial and capitalist oppression. It equated the open door with the injustices of the market and looked to a system of protectionism, preferences and planned international trade that would guarantee outlets to LDC producers and jobs to LDC populations.

The overriding aim of the LDCs was development. This was focused on industrialization, which was seen by all LDCs as the escape route from dependence on production of primary products. This pattern of production had been of no help in the Depression, when commodity prices had collapsed, depriving the producing countries of their export revenues and causing widespread poverty and unemployment. With political independence came a determination to secure economic sovereignty, an aspiration that could only be achieved with the construction of an indigenous industrial base. Just as industrialization in the nineteenth century had liberated what had become the advanced capitalist economies from subjection to the climate and the soil, so it would now bring an end to what Hobsbawm called 'agrarian backwardness' in the developing world,[10] free the new state from reliance on imports of manufactures, and generate an economic surplus that could be used to finance universal health care and education to secondary level.

The LDCs' development strategy allied state power to the creation of import substitution industries. The extent of government intervention varied according to circumstances and ideology. In some nations, especially in East Asia and Latin America, there was enough private capital for the state to concentrate on promoting economic transformation through the provision of monopoly positions in the domestic market to private firms, which were directly subsidized and granted privileged access to foreign currency for imported inputs. In others, where private capital was scarce, such as India, there was more concentration on state ownership and enterprise. Yet other LDCs, such as Ghana (after 1957) and Indonesia (at least until 1965 when the Leftist Sukarno was replaced by General Suharto in a pro-American coup), which were politically radical, also pursued the statist model out of a distrust for capitalism and capitalists. Whatever the differences in approach to the use of state power, however, all LDCs shunned economic liberalism when it came to trade and financial policy. Customs barriers were established to shield infant industries from competition, while foreign exchange controls (currencies were generally inconvertible) were imposed to prevent outflows of capital. This was protectionist but not isolationist, for governments encouraged the inflow of capital, whether in the form of grants and credits from the rich countries and from international agencies such as the World Bank and the United Nations, or in the form of direct investment on the part of western multinational firms, which were offered favourable terms for the repatriation of profits.[11] The whole package was known as 'import substitution industrialization' (ISI).

The ISI strategy delivered reasonable, if uneven, growth during the 1950s and 1960s. The World Bank reported that between 1960 and 1970 the low-income LDCs grew by 3.6 per cent, while the middle-income countries expanded at a rate of 5.7 per cent each year. This compared favourably with the industrialized nations, which enjoyed growth of 4.7 per cent per annum on average during these years.[12] A trend to industrial growth was marked and, as a result, between 1960 and 1975, industry increased its share of exports from 1 per cent to 8 per cent of exports in low-income countries and from 5 per cent to 17 per cent of exports in middle-income countries.[13] With the postwar boom in the industrialized world feeding demand overall, LDC export earnings rose by 6.6 per cent between 1960 and 1969. Manufactured exports led the way with an expansion of 15 per cent, which was more rapid than the growth in world trade in manufactures, while earnings from primary product exports lagged.[14] The export performance could not, however, prevent constant pressure on the balance of payments, unsurprising given the need to import capital goods. However, the deficits were covered by official development aid (worth $86 billion between 1956 and 1970) and private long-term foreign investment (amounting to $57.6 billion between 1956 and 1970)[15] so that no general external crisis occurred.

The economic performance of most LDCs during the 1950s and 1960s was impressive when set against their past experience and against the record of the developed nations when they were industrializing. Yet it was not good enough to satisfy the aspirations of governments in the postcolonial world in terms of improving living standards. One problem was that growth barely kept pace with a rapid post-1945 increase in population. This meant that per capita food production hardly increased at all. The result was growing reliance, especially in Africa, on imported food (about half of this was grain), and frequent undernourishment and malnutrition, estimated by the Food and Agriculture Organization (FAO) of the UN to be afflicting 1 billion people by the 1970s.[16] At the same time wealth per head in the LDCs generally failed to exceed between 7 and 8 per cent of that in the developed economies. The developing nations could not generate a surplus large enough to provide their growing workforces with increasing capital and infrastructure. All they could manage was to supply them with more equipment without improving the capital stock, so that productivity improvements would come from extra work rather than from modernization. The net result was that over the period between 1950 and 1974 the LDCs in fact experienced relative *decline* compared with the advanced countries – their economic growth was simply not fast enough to prevent the gap between GNP per head in the rich and the poor worlds growing from $2.2 billion in 1950 to $4.8 billion in 1974.[17]

The increasing inequality between rich and poor nations was not counteracted by the world trade system. Primary exports ran into the regimes of agricultural protection established in the USA and the EEC. The GATT was of little help and acquired a reputation for being 'a rich nation's club'. It focused on liberalizing trade in goods exchanged between advanced countries, mainly manufactures, rather than in agricultural goods or in the labour-intensive output of light industries such as textiles, both significant contributors to LDC output.[18] In any case initiatives such as the Kennedy Round offered little to the LDCs since they revolved around reciprocal tariff concessions. The poor countries were keen to protect their nascent industries rather than open them up to foreign competition.

Frustration with the widening gap in living standards between the developed and the developing world, and with the trade relationships that seemed to discriminate against the poorer countries, led the LDCs to organize and begin a campaign for change. By the start of the 1960s many of them had gathered together under the umbrella of the 'non-aligned movement', in other words a neutral position between the USA and the USSR in the Cold War, and had started to co-operate in a project to transform the international economy with a new set of rules that would protect living standards and promote industrialization. The position of these nations in the UN was steadily reinforced by decolonization in the late 1950s and the 1960s. Indeed by the start of the 1960s their prominence led the UN in 1961 to designate the 1960s as the 'Decade of Development', focusing on the expansion of trade as the key.

The issue of trade expansion was debated under the auspices of the UNCTAD (United Nations Conference on Trade and Development), which convened first in 1964 and was then transformed into a permanent body. The greater part of its early deliberations concerned the Prebisch Report, which called for co-operation between the rich and poor countries of the world. The headlines were: preferential agreements that guaranteed markets in the wealthy nations to the industrial exports of the developing states; guaranteed prices for raw materials and agricultural goods; compensation to Third World producers if the terms of trade shifted against them; and lower tariffs and quotas on tropical and subtropical crops. Although the first UNCTAD gathering succeeded in drawing attention to the problems of the developing world, it did not achieve much outside this public relations coup and in order to give more weight to the campaign for development UNCTAD members formed themselves into a pressure group, the 'Group of Seventy-Seven'. Under this guise they met to debate a more radical manifesto, in Algiers in 1967, producing the Algiers Charter in the process.

The Charter was highly critical of the developed world. It pointed out that while the developed countries were adding approximately $60 to the per capita income of each citizen every year, the annual increase in per capita income in the developing world was just $2. The share of world trade taken by the developing nations had fallen from 27 per cent in 1963 to just 19.3 per cent in 1966. At the same time the terms of trade had shifted against them so that for a given volume of exports they could only buy 90 per cent of the imports they had been able to afford with revenues from the same volume of exports ten years earlier. The purchasing power of the developing world had fallen steadily during the 1960s so that there was now a growing problem of international indebtedness. Debt transfers were worth $4 billion each year and threatened to offset the transfer of resources from the rich countries by the end of the decade. On top of this the activities of the multinational firms were generating resentment. This centred first on the monopolization of patents, which was restricting the transfer of technology to Third World states. It was a practice that both held back development by protecting the multinationals from local competition and ensured that they produced an increasing volume of the exports as well as the imports of the LDCs. Second, there was the issue of 'transfer pricing', by which a multinational firm charged artificial prices for goods transferred within the corporation but across national boundaries in order to manipulate the accounts of its different components so it was able to avoid taxation in its host countries. It was time for the industrial countries of the world to make real concessions, and the Group of Seventy-Seven agreed to 'maintain and further strengthen' their unity and solidarity to this end.[19]

The problem was that the rich countries had no incentive to act. They expected reciprocity when they made concessions but there was nothing that the developing world could give them. It followed that although the Group of Seventy-Seven continued to meet, little progress was made in designing a new international economic order that recognized the need to distribute the world's wealth more widely. The Group of Seventy-Seven adopted increasingly confrontational tactics as a result and these finally bore fruit after the oil embargo of November 1973. Now the industrial nations were prepared to discuss the Group of Seventy-Seven's programme for change, published under UN auspices, and officially known as the 'New International Economic Order' (NIEO).

The NIEO became the subject of extensive discussions within the General Assembly in the 1970s. By 1974–5 the Group of Seventy-Seven were taking an increasingly radical line. They argued that developing states had the right to nationalize natural resources, foreign properties and local subsidiaries of multinational firms, with compensation to be determined by national governments rather than by international law. The Group wanted a new deal in international trade, arguing that producers of staple goods were particularly in need of this and should organize themselves into cartels on the OPEC model. It called for the diversification of exports from developing countries, international debt relief and the creation of buffer stocks so that exporters of primary goods would be protected from the consequences of oversupply for their foreign exchange revenues. The reformed system would be financed by a common fund that would guarantee a steady stream of earnings to exporters of staple commodities.

The new deal was not intended to limit itself to primary products: the Group of Seventy-Seven demanded the 'global redistribution of world industry'. To this end it proposed technology transfer to the developing world from the industrialized countries, revolving around a code that would allow LDCs to use patented processes in return for payment of nominal charges.[20] It repeated the call of the Prebisch Report for preferences (not to be reciprocated) within the markets of the advanced industrial states for manufactures from the developing nations. Governments in the rich nations would then adopt industrial readjustment policies to compensate local producers for losses resulting from LDC competition, and encourage them to invest in new product lines or even new industries. It all amounted to an ambitious plan to redesign the world economy so that international trade and finance were once again subject to the intervention that had been characteristic of the immediate postwar era. This time, however, the idea was not to build an environment compatible with reconstruction in the developed world, but a global order that would institutionalize in the LDCs the economic and social rights the populations of the wealthy nations had enjoyed for so long.

The solidarity of the LDCs throughout the UNCTAD meetings of the mid-1970s impressed and disturbed the industrialized countries, whose economies had all been upset by the oil price rise introduced by OPEC. Yet the agenda of the Group of Seventy-Seven did not square with the interests of many in the developed world. The call for preferences not only flew in the face of the whole trend of postwar negotiations in GATT but was unpopular with governments and industry. Multinationals, responsible for 75 per cent of the technology transfers to Third World countries,[21] were, not surprisingly, uncomfortable with the proposals under that heading. None of these groups had any enthusiasm for the willingness of the Group of Seventy-Seven to extend nationalization or to form commodity producer cartels on the OPEC model. The question then became: how could the rich nations, and the powerful industrial and financial groups within them, frustrate the radicalism of the Group's plans while at the same time avoiding further confrontations? Third World solidarity was now demonstrating real muscle. The slow-growing and inflation-prone advanced economies were not well positioned to take another show of strength from the LDCs without more severe shocks to their economies and to living standards. The joint US and European response, when it came, was therefore conciliatory. In 1974 the Club of Rome released a report chaired by the economist Jan Tinbergen, called *Reshaping the International Order*. It appeared amid a growing consensus in favour of a 'North–South' dialogue, so called to reflect the geographical distinction between most of the industrialized world and the majority of the poor and developing countries.

The dialogue became reality with the Conference on International Economic Co-operation (CIEC), an 18-month assembly of 27 nations held in Paris in 1976–8. Despite the goodwill on both sides with which the North–South talks started, at the end of the day there was not much to show for all the effort. The talks failed to engage with the growing problem of international debt. No progress was made with the 'global redistribution of world industry'. The question of the common fund was only addressed in outline. The most notable achievements of the CIEC were agreement on a $1 billion package of special measures to help the poorest nations, acceptance in principle of commodity price stabilization, and a willingness to keep the North–South dialogue in business.[22]

If the CIEC was something of a disappointment, more progress towards North–South partnership was made with the Lome Convention. Lome followed from the Yaounde Conferences of 1964 and 1970, which had resulted in a preferential deal between the six nations that then made up the EEC and the former African dependencies of Belgium and France. British, Irish and Danish membership of the EEC in 1973 made it necessary to revise the Yaounde arrangements so that they were extended to cover developing countries in the British Commonwealth. Lome was the result and covered the economic relationship of the ACP (46 African, Pacific and Caribbean countries – most of them former dependencies of EEC members) with the EEC. It allowed the ACP group preferences in the European Community and provided for industrial co-operation whereby the EEC would assist with technology transfer, aid for small and medium-sized enterprises and for industrialization programmes, and with the marketing and promotion of ACP exports. The Convention also resulted in the Integrated Programme for Staple Products, otherwise known as STABEX, a fund paid into by the EEC nine to compensate producers when export income dropped below a minimum level. Initially this covered 12 commodities; on Lome's renewal in 1980 it was extended to another 44. Lome was hailed by its European supporters as a real step towards a new world economic order, and the stabilization scheme was accepted in UNCTAD as a system that should be applied to an increasingly wide range of goods produced in developing countries. To this end, discussions started within UNCTAD in 1976 and international agreements were reached for cocoa, sugar and tin. In 1979 the scheme was extended to coffee, tea, cotton, rubber, jute, hand textile fibres, copper, rice, bananas, wheat, wool, bauxite and iron ore.

With the Lome Convention the EEC established itself as the world's largest source of official development aid for the less developed countries. Yet the EEC only made modest sums available for STABEX – about £190 million in 1975, spread over five annual instalments – and the positive impact of Lome was further reduced by the two recessions of 1975 and 1979–81, which owed a lot to the rise in the price of oil. Yet Lome was probably the most positive result of the campaign for a new international economic order, which had started in the late 1960s. It went through four revisions between 1975 and 1989. Despite its limitations it did appear to point towards a future when trade relations between the rich and the poor countries would be managed with the intention of encouraging development and protecting living standards in the developing world.

◆ The Brandt Report

The last major initiative in the campaign for a New International Economic Order owed much to the North–South dialogues. Chaired by the former West German Chancellor Willy Brandt it was actually called *North–South: A Programme for Survival*. The Brandt Report sought reform in the interests of the poorer nations and represented an attempt to build a global system based on the social-democratic principles that had guided the postwar mixed economies.

The recommendations in the Brandt Report embraced development, trade, aid and international monetary relations. Under the first of these headings it supported industrialization in the developing world, notably through migration of labour-intensive industries and technology transfer from the advanced industrial states. Local needs would be met by the traditional sector with the support of 'simple applied technology', while the industrializing sector would focus on production for the export market. The multinational corporation was to be encouraged to continue its expansion into the developing world – but under strict regulations regarding cartels, patents and labour standards. A system of international co-operation between governments was proposed as the means by which transfer pricing could be brought under control.

Trade relations between the developing and the industrial worlds were to be reformed in favour of the former. The report supported the long-standing campaign for the granting of preferences to LDC industrial exports and investment by the wealthy nations in the commercial infrastructures of the poorer. As far as commodities were concerned, the Brandt Report backed the campaign for a common fund that would finance international commodity agreements, stabilize prices 'at remunerative levels' and finance the holding of stocks. It called for compensation to offset shortfalls in real earnings from the export of commodities.

New rules governing international trade would not protect living standards in the short term, and the authors of the report were aware that an ambitious aid programme was necessary to tackle poverty and famine, and to assist the poorer developing states with their efforts to establish basic health care and educational provision. To this end, the Brandt Report argued that official aid from the wealthy countries should be increased as a proportion of GNP to 0.7 per cent in 1985 and to 1 per cent by the end of the century.

Finally, the report called for a reformed international monetary order, the changes much in line with proposals made over the years by the Group of Seventy-Seven. The key alteration was to be the replacement of national currencies as international reserves by the SDR, and that developing countries with large adjustment difficulties should be allocated generous liquidity. Debtors should not be required to take deflationary action by the Fund. At the same time the World Bank would be transformed by an increase in its borrowing capacity. Its capital had recently been doubled to $40 billion, but its rules allowed a borrowing-to-capital ratio of 1:1. The report wanted this altered to 2:1 in order to release a significant flow of funds into the developing world. Clearly, however, giving more money to the IMF and the World Bank would not be enough to effect the 'massive transfer' of resources favoured by the Report. The private banks had a role to play, and this was to facilitate the recycling of financial surpluses – notably those that had accumulated after the oil price shock. Brandt acknowledged that this process had already started, but argued that the flow of lending from the commercial banks could be enhanced if the World Bank was willing to supplement their activities with joint initiatives, guarantees, and by the provision of 'concessional' finance characterized by long repayment periods at interest rates well below the market level.

The authors of the report appealed to altruism and self-interest. They claimed that their proposals could provide the framework of a campaign to end destitution (the World Bank estimated that about 800 million people, just under 20 per cent of the world's population, lived in this state), assist development and transform living standards in the Third World, all through the recognition that the fates of the rich North and poor South were connected. This was 'one world', not in the economists' sense of being a single unified free market but because it was a mutually dependent society. Recognizing that the prospect of material benefit was also a powerful incentive to action, Brandt pointed out that a redistribution of global wealth would actually help to stimulate growth in the industrialized states. The report referred to a European Commission paper which had shown how the refusal of developing countries to follow the example of the rich and deflate in response to the oil price rise of 1973–4 had softened the recession. Figures for 1975 were especially striking since they showed a fall of 17 per cent in European Community exports to the USA but an increase of 25 per cent in exports to the developing world and one of 33 per cent to the ACP alone.

If developing countries had cut public and private spending to meet the larger oil bill 'there would have been three million more unemployed in the OECD countries'.[23] This showed the importance of the markets of the South to the northern economies: the Brandt recommendations, if implemented, would be the foundation of an external environment that sustained the prosperity of the postwar era. The report's simultaneous expansionism and internationalism, within a framework regulated by governments and international institutions, made it a true successor to Keynes' visionary schemes of the 1940s.

◆ The NIEO Frustrated I: The Third World

The high hopes of the mid-1970s that a new international economic order would be established on the ruins of the old were to be frustrated. There were essentially two sets of reasons. To begin with, Third World solidarity began to weaken under the impact of economic change. Second, there was an ideological shift in favour of economic liberalism at the heart of the advanced industrial world.

The Brandt Report was well received in the UN and subject to considerable discussion throughout the developed and developing world. Speakers took its message to 'churches, civic organizations, conferences, non-governmental organizations, and national and international agencies'. More than three-quarters of the world's nations endorsed the Brandt proposals at the 35th and 36th sessions of the United Nations General Assembly. But the timing was wrong.[24]

The development of the LDCs had always been an uneven process, but this feature was made more obvious in the later 1970s as the expansion of world trade began to slow down dramatically. Exports grew by just 1.5 per cent in 1981 and declined by an estimated 2 per cent in 1982; only a few developing countries managed to increase exports, mainly of manufactured goods, in this climate.[25] The industrialized countries suffered from balance of payments problems and after 1979 tended to react to these with deflationary measures that inevitably slowed growth and therefore reduced demand for some Third World products. At the same time the developing countries were rocked by a rise in the fuel bill, pushing their external accounts into the red. In order to try and salvage their development plans, Third World governments sought to make up for the shortfall of foreign exchange through the negotiation of large credit agreements with western banks.

The credit agreements were part of an increasing flow of resources into the developing world during the 1970s. For a start there were direct payments from the oil-importing industrialized world to the OPEC countries. These rose with the aid of the 1973 oil price increase from $35 billion per annum to $140 billion per annum in 1978. Some of the gains to be made from the oil price boost were lost because the price of imports into the OPEC states went up but it was still calculated that the terms of trade enjoyed by OPEC countries improved,

TABLE 5.3: PRIVATE TRANSFERS TO LDCS,
1971–1982 ($ BILLIONS)

	1971	1982
Direct investment	3.31	11
Bank lending	3.30	29
Export credits	2.71	9
Total	9.32	49

Source: Brett, *The World Economy since the War: The Politics of Uneven Development* (London: Macmillan, 1985), 216–17

from a baseline of 100 in 1973 to 110 in 1978, a level commensurate with a net transfer to the oil producers from the western industrialized world of $40 billion.[26] Transfers were also composed of aid, which rose from $9.14 billion in 1971 to $37.33 billion in 1980 and of contributions, made by the OPEC states arising from their new wealth, rising from $2.03 billion in 1973 to $8.75 billion in 1980. There was also significant private investment (Table 5.3). These different forms of finance helped developing countries increase spending on investment by 10.7 per cent per year between 1973 and 1979, and over the same period the share of global investment occupied by the LDCs grew from 16.5 per cent to 23.3 per cent.[27]

The capital was not spread evenly, however. Quite apart from the bonanza enjoyed by the OPEC countries, much of it tended to flow to middle-income LDCs, which had already achieved partial industrialization and were producing goods for the export markets. These nations, known as the Newly Industrializing Countries (NICs), ranged from the larger Latin American economies such as Brazil to fast-growing East Asian states such as South Korea, Taiwan and Singapore. In the 1980s they were to be joined by Malaysia and Indonesia. They had all followed the ISI model of industrialization and to that end had collaborated with multinational firms, welcoming the foreign companies' money, skills and technology. During the 1970s the lion's share of foreign investment went to the NICs and became increasingly concerned with production for export markets. The multinationals were attracted by government concessions and low wage costs,[28] especially in the labour-intensive trades such as textiles and footwear. However, by the end of the 1970s states like South Korea, Taiwan and Malaysia were being used as bases by corporations such as ITT for the production of transistors and television sets, and as far as the first two were concerned, ships (the Far Eastern share of world ship production rose from 37.8 per cent in 1969 to 60.4 per cent in 1982).[29] Brett records that between 1970 and 1979 the manufactured exports from the top 10 NICs increased by 26 per cent each year and the exports of the next 16 by 37 per cent each year,[30] South Korea and Taiwan leading the way.

Differentiation within the Group of Seventy-Seven was reinforced by the oil price rise of 1973 and another increase, albeit short-lived, of 100 per cent, in 1979–80. By the end of the 1970s it was possible to argue that the Group did not exist in reality but had been transformed into three classes of less developed state: the oil rich ones, notably the gulf states, which were now so prosperous that they had become international creditors; then the second level, of states where development had already started but which needed to import oil (countries like Brazil, the Philippines and South Korea); and finally the third (increasingly known as the 'Fourth World'), of countries where industrialization had made virtually no progress, and which were heavily dependent on overseas aid and international credit. These divisions put an end to the co-ordinated action of the 1970s. The OPEC nations became increasingly integrated into the existing international economic order. The NICs became more interested in investment and markets than in the terms of trade facing primary producers. Solidarity declined and the campaign for an integrated programme of measures leading to the creation of a new international economic order now gave way to painstaking discussions in the UN designed to produce piecemeal reforms such as the linking of raw material to industrial prices and the regulation of multinational companies. The integrated approach to international economic reform, favoured for so long by the Group of Seventy-Seven and championed by the Brandt Report, was abandoned in practice, the favourable and high-profile publicity the document received notwithstanding.

◆ The NIEO Frustrated II: Inflation and the Rise of Neo-liberalism

Brandt provoked enthusiasm in centre and centre-left parties throughout Europe and Latin America, and some support from the American Democratic Party. But on the right there was scepticism and in the end the proposals were not followed by the creation of a new international economic order. It proved impossible to gain a consensus for concerted action in the UN, the IMF and the World Bank. The IMF did increase quotas, from 39 billion SDRs in 1978 to 90 billion in 1983, and enlarged the General Agreement to Borrow from 6.4 billion SDRs to 17 billion SDRs in 1983. Outside the expansion of the SDR the Fund provided additional credit to states with external difficulties – but despite the strictures of the Brandt Report this aid was generally conditional on the adoption of deflationary policies by the recipients.

Some governments did increase spending on overseas aid; others (such as the UK) actually reduced it. The essential problem was that the Report's appearance coincided with a turn to the Right in the advanced industrial economies (France was an exception to the trend), and in Britain and the USA especially.

This resulted in a tendency to deflationary macroeconomic policies, even in centre-left governments such as that of West Germany, in the face of pressures from inflation and the 1979 oil price rise. In other words, these countries chose to follow the reverse of the expansionary approach advised by Brandt so that demand fell and world trade slowed. In so far as money continued to flow in significant volume to the Third World it did so more and more through the mechanism of the private banking system, leading to an accumulation of debt that was not easy to pay off in view of the slowdown in the West.

The right turn in the industrialized world came after a three-year period during which governments had attempted to recreate the conditions for growth following the 1974–5 recession. Between 1976 and 1979 the USA, Japan, France, West Germany, the UK and Italy were all run by centrist or centre-left administrations. In keeping with their political complexion they all deployed the techniques of the Keynesian era to support mildly expansionary policies designed to increase output and reduce unemployment. Inflationary pressures were held in check by incomes policies, and wage and price freezes, while trade controls and subsidies were introduced not just in response to external deficits but to protect jobs and industries threatened by international competition.

The use of interventionist measures in the foreign trade sector led commentators to talk about an era of 'neo-mercantilism'. Thus the USA established a system of 'voluntary restraint' with its trading partners relating to export volume (for example, concerning television sets from Japan or footwear from Taiwan and South Korea). In 1978 the Democratic administration of Jimmy Carter, responding to anxiety in the trades unions, unveiled the Solomon Plan, which safeguarded the steel industry (mainly against Japanese competition) through the imposition of import duties. The trend to protectionism was not confined to the USA: in 1978 the EEC, having established a European Steel Cartel, introduced anti-dumping taxes. All this happened despite the efforts of GATT negotiators who took six years to complete the latest set of tariff reductions, concluding the Tokyo Round in 1979. Although the Tokyo Round did achieve a package of tariff reductions worth 33 per cent it could not by definition have any impact on the spread of non-tariff barriers. An example was the international textile trade. This had been regulated since 1970 by the Multifibre Agreement by which developing countries were committed to voluntary restraint on their exports of cotton materials to industrialized nations. The period 1978–82 saw these restrictions being tightened.

The drift to economic nationalism, a reaction against the impact of the multinational corporations and footloose capital on the international economy at the end of the 1960s and in the early 1970s, however, was not universal. In international monetary affairs, where it had taken the form of the floating rates established after 1973, it was reversed. Late in 1978 the Carter administration abandoned the policy of 'benign neglect' of the dollar and took steps to stabilize it on the international markets. These included an increase in interest rates, the establishment of an intervention fund, and a doubling of existing swap arrangements with West Germany, Japan and Switzerland. It was the prelude to a new effort at returning order to the currency markets, to be based, so the hope went, on a system of 'managed floating' designed to prevent competitive downward drifting of rates but with enough flexibility to allow for easy adjustments to disequilibria. The turnaround resulted from anxiety in the USA about inflation and from a conviction that its adjustment was by now complete given the reappearance of equilibrium to the external accounts. In 1979, for the first time in the postwar era, both the US current and capital accounts were in the black.[31]

The mix of mild expansionism, 'neo-mercantilism' and increasing international monetary co-operation facilitated a recovery in the industrialized world. US growth was especially strong in 1976 and 1977 (6 per cent and 5 per cent respectively) but all the OECD economies performed well by comparison with the period 1973–5 (Table 5.4). Unemployment fell steadily. Yet there was one serious problem. This was inflation, which affected all countries (though not to the same extent). Its growth had become increasingly obvious since the mid-1960s. In 1965 consumer prices had risen at an annual average rate of 3 per cent in the advanced industrial nations. By 1973 the figure was 7.8 per cent. Between 1974 and the first half of 1977 the average annual rate across the

TABLE 5.4: GROWTH OF OUTPUT OF INDUSTRIALIZED COUNTRIES, 1975–1979 (% CHANGE OF GNP FROM PREVIOUS YEAR)

Country	Average 1963–72	1975	1976	1977	1978	1979
USA	4.0	−1.1	5.4	5.5	4.8	3.2
Canada	5.5	1.2	5.5	2.1	3.6	2.9
Japan	9.8	2.8	5.0	5.3	5.1	5.2
France*	5.5	0.2	5.2	3.1	3.8	3.3
Germany	4.5	−1.8	5.3	2.8	3.6	4.4
Italy*	4.6	−3.6	5.9	1.9	2.7	4.9
UK*	3.0	−1.1	2.8	2.2	3.7	1.9
All industrial countries	4.7	−0.5	4.9	4.0	4.0	3.6

*GDP at market prices
Source: derived from Scammell, *The International Economy since 1945* (London: Macmillan, 1983), 215, Table 14.1

OECD as a whole hit 10 per cent before settling back to 9 per cent; in the UK during the course of 1975 it exceeded 20 per cent for a brief period.

The impact of inflation was disturbing. It put pressure on profits, which employers could only release by passing on rising costs to consumers. It encouraged class confrontation over the distribution of the employer's profits between wages, dividends and investment. This provoked worker–employer disputes that frequently escalated into strikes. The period 1968–70 saw bitter industrial disputes all over western Europe. There was a three-week general strike in France in May–June 1968. Italy experienced what became known as the 'hot autumn' in 1969; in the UK, days lost to strike action increased from 7 million in 1969 to 11 million in 1970. In 1974 the efforts of the Conservative Prime Minister Edward Heath to bring an end to a miners' strike by calling a general election on the theme of 'Who governs?' resulted in the defeat of the government at the polls. Thus inflation ate away at the stability of the mixed economy by removing the foundations of the social partnership between labour, capital and the state, which had been one of the conditions of the high investment of the 1950s and 1960s. Yet rising prices did more than generate industrial strife – they eroded the value of savings, a particular concern for those living on pensions and fixed incomes, and reduced the confidence of the financial markets in the currencies of nations suffering from accelerating inflation. Given the large volume of mobile international capital in the system the consequences of such disapproval could be devastating. Not only did the markets undermine the stability of the dollar in the early 1970s, they also sparked an exodus from sterling in 1976 even though by this time the government had mastered the pressures that had driven the cost of living so high in 1974 and 1975. The British Labour administration was forced into negotiating support from the IMF.

Economists argued about the causes of inflation.[32] Some, led by the American economist Milton Friedman, blamed lax control over the money supply by governments. Friedman argued that there is a relationship between the level of national income (measured in current prices) and the stock of money. This means that there is a strong correlation between the rate at which the national income grows and the rate at which the stock of money expands. Given that national income tends to grow at a trend rate a more rapid increase in the money supply may well raise the level of demand and hence economic activity in the short term. But once economic growth reverts to its historic level the continuation of a monetary expansion in excess of the real increase in national income will generate inflation, or the phenomenon of 'too much money chasing too few goods'.

The Friedmanite theory (known as 'monetarism') found support among economists and bankers who believed it could be applied to the experience of the western economies during the late 1960s and 1970s. There seemed to be a correlation between the monetary expansion followed by the Heath government and British inflation after 1973. It was also suggested by Otmar Etminger, then a Director of the West German central bank (the Bundesbank), that the US deficit had played its part by causing large-scale capital flows, the money being banked in creditor countries where it was used to underwrite expansions of credit that could not be absorbed by local production. So it could be argued that European countries and Japan started to 'import' inflation.

Economists sympathetic to Keynesian ideas, such as Robert Solomon, challenged this view. Solomon could not find much evidence for imported inflation. He pointed out that wholesale prices in the FRG rose at a rate of just 2.8 per cent per annum in the first three quarters of 1972 even though reserves had increased by $10 billion in 1970–1. Moreover the pressure of German domestic demand varied. It was high in 1969 but slack in 1970–1. When it recovered in the second half of 1972 it was stimulated by export orders despite an expansionary monetary stance during the previous year. Meanwhile, Japanese reserves quadrupled from mid-1969 until the end of 1972 – and wholesale prices rose at just 1 per cent a year.[33] There was no obvious link between monetary expansion as a result of the US deficit and inflation. On the other hand there did seem to be a genuine connection between inflation rates, which accelerated throughout the OECD in 1972–3, and the interaction of the rising commodity prices of the time with wage settlements designed to cover the cost of living. A variation on this argument was developed by J.K. Galbraith, who maintained in *Economics and the Public Purpose* (1975) that the monopolistic corporations pushed inflation upwards by passing wage and other cost increases on to the public, which then responded by agitating for higher levels of pay.

Another possibility apart from lax control of the money supply and 'cost–push' pressures was the willingness of the banking system to provide credit for investment and consumption at a time when profit levels were under pressure from rising wage and raw material costs. When prices were raised to offset the effect of wage increases on an employer's bill there was likely to be pressure on overall profit levels unless people were still able to buy the goods at the higher prices. This they could do if the banking system was prepared to advance the credit – and so the price rises were sustained.[34] Moreover, the abundance of credit available through the Eurodollar market allowed businesses to borrow in order to continue investment programmes in response to the prevailing conditions of high demand (Table 5.5). This in turn led to higher raw material and commodity prices. These pressures all started working together in the late 1960s and early 1970s and were reinforced by trades union pay demands.

Although there was no consensus within the economic profession about the causes of inflation, the one explanation that began to make headway with governments, especially in the USA and the UK, and within international institutions, was monetarism. Its success was not based on empirical evidence, which offered no clear support, but on politico-economic developments in the West that generated a powerful coalition of interests in favour of rolling back the state and reversing the Keynesian revolution.

Perhaps the key change was what Van der Pijl calls the 'resurgence of money capital' in the 1970s.[35] European and American banks found that the financing of external deficits was good business, the opportunities of this commerce

TABLE 5.5: BUSINESS BORROWING AS A PROPORTION OF FIXED INVESTMENT

	USA	Japan	France	Germany	UK
1962–67	15.4	n.a	32.3	31.9	n.a
1968–72	27.2	29.4	31.8	33.8	5.2
1973	36.1	39.2	40.8	41.2	8.3

Source: OECD, *National Accounts* (1981), Vol. II

growing rapidly in the aftermath of the OPEC shock. At the same time, the multinationals continued to diversify into banking, a trend already visible by the start of the 1970s, and their readiness to engage in financial dealing was enhanced by the floating rate system. This had made the multinational vulnerable to exchange risk on long-term investments and on its short-term trade. The way around the problem was to establish foreign exchange subsidiaries. Some of these handled significant volumes of cash. For example, in 1982 it was estimated that BP's currency trading turnover exceeded that of the Bank of England and that there were another 20 or 30 large multinationals powerful enough to alter individual exchange rates through their activities in the market.[36]

The international banks and corporations that became so wealthy during the 1970s disliked inflation, and their sentiments grew in strength as their financial activities multiplied. Inflation left them holding on to monetary assets of decreasing real value and they became increasingly averse to investing in countries where it was not under control. But how was inflation to be controlled? The combination of incomes, policies, price controls and restrictions on the expansion of bank deposits (known as 'the corset') favoured by the mixed economies throughout most of the 1970s was not popular since it interfered with the freedom of capital. On the other hand, a counter-inflation strategy that revolved around reducing government spending was attractive since it meant, in addition, reducing the role of the state and its tendency to intervene in economic life. Ultimately, the only approach that was compatible with the ability to move money around the world without impediment was one that rolled back the frontiers of the state. This was not simply a function of distrust for interventionism per se but because the welfare states of the postwar era, all (in western Europe) investing over 40 per cent of the GNP in the public sector, were believed by monetarists to be inflationary by their very nature. Their commitment to supporting welfare, employment and key industries ensured that those governments that did not maintain the infrastructure and protect jobs would be punished by electorates. The self-interest of governments in their own re-election was a guarantee that the mixed economies were programmed to lose control over the money supply. Monetarism therefore not only won the support of transnational finance but inevitably implied a revival for the free market political economy of pre-Keynesian days.

The *laissez-faire* reaction against Keynesianism had been led unswervingly since the 1940s by the London-based Austrian political economist F.A. von Hayek. Hayek's most famous book was *The Road to Serfdom* (1944) and he had long been an advocate of the small state, directly responsible only for the maintenance of law and order and for monetary stability. The economy should be left to the free play of market forces, subject to a legal framework that guaranteed free competition. Trades unions were labour monopolies that extorted unsustainable wage rises from employers. In a free market, firms that could not afford their wages bill would have to close down or at least cut what they paid their workers, either by reducing salaries or by losing jobs, or through a combination of both. But now the willingness of the state to finance the pay settlements either by printing money (if the workers were in the public sector) or by an overgenerous credit policy (if they were in the private sector) protected the unions from the consequences of this abuse of power.

It followed that the revival of what became known as 'neo-liberalism' attracted not only finance but a coalition of interests that had turned against the postwar state. This also included managers anxious to regain authority on the shop floor and multinational executives who saw the nation state as an obstacle to the growth of their own corporation. In addition, throughout many of the postwar mixed economies there had developed a prosperous middle class, keen to spend its money on the latest consumer goods, and an affluent working class with disposable income. Now these groups had begun to resent the tax bills that arose from the need to pay for all the services of the modern state, and listened sympathetically to politicians whose radical agenda was legitimized by attacks on 'waste' and 'bureaucracy'. Inflation therefore generated support for those political parties that claimed they could bring a halt to rising prices through reductions in public spending and taxation. In the UK and the USA this led to the election, in 1979 and 1980 of administrations, led respectively by Prime Minister Margaret Thatcher and President Ronald Reagan, which identified not full employment but low (or even zero) inflation as the central target of macroeconomic policy. In both countries there was a steady flow of anti-union measures that ran in parallel with steps to deregulate the economy, the most dramatic example perhaps being Britain's abolition of exchange controls in the autumn of 1979.

The neo-liberal counter-revolution was fatal to the prospects of the Brandt Report and the cause of a new international economic order. The Reagan administration maintained that the way to development lay through free trade, unrestricted private foreign investment and open capital markets. It argued that the postwar decades had been characterized by a steady flow of aid to socialistic Third World governments which had (since they were socialistic) used it in pursuit of ill-judged and wasteful plans. Their enthusiasm for import substitution, exchange controls and state trading had pushed up the cost of consumer goods, while the enforcement of collectivization and the suppression of private economic initiatives in favour of co-operatives and state enterprises had undermined prospects for growth. Some of the world's poorest nations were those where these 'dysfunctional policies' had been tried – for example, Tanzania, Zaire, Ethiopia, Somalia, Burma and Mozambique. Thus the USA supported use of the World Bank and the IMF to deliver assistance to countries in need of aid and in external deficit – but on strict terms that involved the retreat of the state from the development strategy and its replacement by the market. Indeed, the USA rejected the whole distributivist ethos of the Brandt Report – arguing that this merely subsidized the misguided policies of developing countries – and set out its own free market agenda at the Cancun summit of 1982. This was followed up in February 1982 by a programme for Central America and the Caribbean basin based on free trade, aid mainly in support of the private sector, technical assistance and investment. It was supported by the Conservative Thatcher administration in the UK, which had argued that the British government 'believes strongly in the merits of the present world economic system, with its wide reliance on open markets for trade and financial flows'.[37]

The Brandt Report was launched just as the neo-liberal counter-revolution was gathering steam, and into a world crisis sparked off by the Soviet invasion of Afghanistan and rising tension in Europe over nuclear missiles. The international agenda was suddenly once more being dominated by the East–West rather than the North–South crisis. All this occurred against the backdrop of the worst recession to hit the western world since the war, triggered by another sharp rise in oil prices, and it meant that western leaders lost sight of the views of the Brandt Commission on how to generate world recovery and bring an end to world hunger and poverty. With no unanimous backing from the developed world the Brandt Report became the subject of debate but not of action.

There was to be no 'New International Economic Order' recognizable to its proponents in the Third World and among the supporters of the Brandt Report. The sidelining of this document meant that the world economy of the 1980s was likely to be more market-oriented than at any time since the start of the Second World War. The collapse of the postwar order in 1971 had been followed by a genuine international effort to build a reformed and extended version of the old Keynesian consensus. The discussions on international monetary reform and on the NIEO that culminated in the Brandt Report had all been attempts to respond to the major economic changes of the 1960s – increasing integration in global trade and finance, volatile capital markets, and the rise of the Third World – while consolidating the post-1945 social-democratic commitment to national economic sovereignty, full employment and growth. But the attempt to build a world system on the principles of international social democracy could not survive the weakening of Third World solidarity and the fallout from inflation in the mixed economies. The *coup de grâce* for this campaign was delivered by the USA: its turn to neo-liberalism after 1980 undermined any prospect that there could be an international consensus behind Brandt or that the resources essential to the transfer of wealth it proposed would be found.[38] The failure of the search for a new international economic order marked the end of the Keynesian era. The Anglo-American lack of faith in the ability of interventionist international agencies to improve living standards in the Third World coincided with, and shared the same roots as, loss of belief in the nation state's ability to deliver economic security. Although the endurance of the Lome Convention, a regional effort at laying the foundations of a new system, showed that the crisis of confidence in the old ways was by no means shared universally, it was to make the macroeconomic weather during the following decade.

◆ Notes

1. Van der Wee, *Prosperity and Upheaval*, 452–3, Table 37.
2. W.M. Scammell, *The International Economy since 1945* (London: Macmillan, 1983), 190.
3. Van der Wee, *Prosperity and Upheaval*, 452–3, Table 37.
4. Ibid. and Solomon, *The International Monetary System, 1945–1976*, 225–6.
5. Van der Wee, *Prosperity and Upheaval*, 489.
6. Armstrong, Glyn and Harrison, *Capitalism since 1945*, 215.
7. Van der Wee, *Prosperity and Upheaval*, 83.
8. Ibid., 133.
9. Armstrong, Glyn and Harrison, *Capitalism since 1945*, 228–9.
10. Hobsbawm, *Age of Extremes*, 350.
11. Brett, *The World Economy since the War*, 184–5.
12. Ibid., 186.
13. Ibid., 287, footnote 10.
14. I.M.D. Little, *Economic Development* (New York: Basic Books, 1982), 281.
15. Brett, *The World Economy since the War*, 186.
16. Van der Wee, *Prosperity and Upheaval*, 104.
17. Brett, *The World Economy since the War*, 187.
18. Scammell, *The International Economy since 1945*, 167.
19. See 'First Ministerial Meeting of the Group of 77: Charter of Algiers' (Algiers, 10–25 October 1967).
20. Ankie M.M. Hoogvelt, *The Third World in Global Development* (London: Macmillan, 1982), 85.
21. Ibid.
22. Scammell, *The International Economy since 1945*, 177.
23. Brandt Commission, *North–South: A Programme for Survival* (London: Pan Books, 1980), 238.
24. See 'The Brandt equation: 21st century blueprint for the new global economy', at http://www.brandt21forum.info/2aFirstCrisis.htm.
25. Brett, *The World Economy since the War*, 214.

26. Hoogvelt, *The Third World in Global Development*, 46.
27. Armstrong, Glyn and Harrison, *Capitalism since 1945*, 285.
28. Ibid., 289.
29. See http://www.coltoncompany.com/shipbldg/statistics/world.htm.
30. Brett, *The World Economy since the War*, 197.
31. Van der Wee, *Prosperity and Upheaval*, 452.
32. There is an interesting discussion of the competing theories in Susan Strange, *Casino Capitalism*, 2nd edn. (Manchester: Manchester University Press, 1997), 75 ff.
33. Solomon, *The International Monetary System 1945–1976*, 273.
34. Armstrong, Glyn and Harrison, *Capitalism since 1945*, 266.
35. Van der Pijl, *The Making of an Atlantic Ruling Class*, 262–71.
36. Coakley and Harris, *The City of Capital*, 180.
37. Leonard Downie, 'Economic Talks Stalled 6 Months After Brandt Group's Plea', *Washington Post*, 19 July 1980.
38. See also Strange, *Casino Capitalism*, 153–5.

6

THE LIBERAL REVIVAL, 1981–1990

◆ The New Macroeconomics

The period 1981–90 saw a consolidation and then an acceleration of the neo-liberal revolution, and its extension into the less developed world. There was a decisive turn away from the interventionism of the period since 1945. This occurred with the enthusiastic support of the governments in Washington and London above all, with the backing of the international institutions established in the 1940s (the IMF, the World Bank and the GATT), and with the encouragement of the international financial markets as well as the multinational corporations.[1] The revolution did not appear to generate the greatest good for the greatest number, as liberal apologists claimed that it would, but it greatly strengthened the forces that had been working for international economic integration since the end of the 1950s.

The decade started with monetarism in vogue in the USA and the UK, and with a major international recession sparked by the sharp rise in the price of oil that followed the replacement of the Shah of Iran by an Islamic Republic. Governments throughout the advanced industrial world, even those not well disposed to neo-liberalism, reacted to large external deficits with cuts in public spending and interest rate rises to reduce the growth of consumer demand. In the USA and the UK this contractionary stance was reinforced by a deliberate exercise in monetarist economics. Interest rates were kept high, with the intention of restricting the growth of credit so that it did not keep pace with inflation, and in Britain, in the teeth of the recession, the Thatcher government defied all Keynesian teaching by actually reducing public expenditure, its budgetary squeeze of 1979–81 reducing demand by 5 per cent of GDP.

The consequences were spectacular. Unemployment rose to 12 per cent of the workforce by 1981; manufacturing output dropped by 15 per cent in the single year from December 1979 to December 1980; even in the 1930s the largest fall in a single year had been a comparatively modest 5.5 per cent. The combination of a high value for sterling (pushed up by the tight monetary policy and the proceeds of North Sea oil) and deflation produced the worst of two worlds: an import surge (by the start of 1983 imports of manufactured goods were 24 per cent up on 1979 while exports were 16 per cent down) and an industrial crash. In the USA the combination of high interest rates, exceeding 5 per cent in real terms, unprecedented in the US experience, and the high dollar reduced the competitiveness of US manufacturing by 20 per cent. Industrial production fell by 8 per cent in 1982 while unemployment exceeded 10 per cent, a postwar high.[2] With bankruptcies at a record level and the stability of the banking system threatened by the onset of an international debt crisis, the experiment in 'pure monetarism' had run into the buffers.

One advanced industrial state to buck the trend to monetarist and neo-liberal policies was France. François Mitterrand was elected president in 1981 at the head of a socialist administration determined to use a combination of economic planning, extensions of public ownership and Keynesian demand management to stimulate the French economy out of the post-1979 recession. In response the economy expanded at a rate of 2.5 per cent in 1982, a marked contrast with the contraction elsewhere in the industrialized world. On the other hand, the current account deficit doubled, to $12.1 billion, and there was a flight of capital. The external problems led to a steady fall in the exchange rate and by 1984 the franc was worth 13 per cent less than it had been in 1981. It was a slide that disturbed the markets and led to pressure on domestic prices at the same time. Inflation, which had been running at an annual rate of 14 per cent when Mitterrand was elected, was still almost 10 per cent in 1983, while by now it had dropped well into single figures throughout most of western Europe. In West Germany it was just under 4 per cent.[3] There was growing trades union discontent, although the government was able to contain this by indexing pay increases to the cost of living.

It was pointed out that Mitterrand's experiment had run into trouble because it had followed an expansionist path at a time when no other OECD nation was doing so. In these circumstances it was inevitable that French imports, fuelled by high internal demand, would outpace exports, hit by recession in the rest of the industrial world. This was unfair. As late as July 1981 the OECD was forecasting that the advanced countries would show a growth rate of 2 per cent in 1982; the actual outcome of 0.4 per cent, which was indeed damaging to French interests, was not expected when Mitterrand's presidency started. All the same it was clear by the end of 1983 that the socialist programme was not sustainable in the absence of extensive controls on prices, imports and capital movements, a course rejected by the Prime Minister, Pierre Mauroy and one quite possibly counter to French obligations under the Treaty of Rome. The prevailing deflationary orthodoxy outside France ultimately pushed the government into its own strategy of 'rigour', based on a series of austere budgets introducing tax increases and spending reductions designed to bring about a fall in inflation, public borrowing and the external deficit. This was accompanied by a determination to win the support of private industry, reflected in a turn to fashionable deregulatory policies, which were applied to financial and foreign exchange markets. It was an exchange of growth for price stability: inflation fell back to 2.5 per cent by 1986 (helped by a drop in the price of oil) and the franc appreciated on the international markets, while unemployment rose to 10.5 per cent of the workforce in 1987.

The about-turn in macroeconomic policy was also fuelled by anxiety about French isolation. From the time of the Schuman Plan in 1950 France had been committed to European economic and political integration, based on an unshakeable Franco-German alliance, to safeguard its own economic growth and national security. It began to appear in 1982–3 that the Mitterrand experiment was incompatible with this strategy, not just in terms of its implications for foreign trade and exchange policy but also because of the dangers it presented to the creation of a single European currency. In Paris this was now seen as a precondition of ever closer political co-operation within the EC. The objective, set out by the Werner Report in 1970, had seemed to fade during the era of floating rates in the 1970s. But it was revived by Roy Jenkins, President of the European Commission, in 1978. The first step towards monetary union was to be the establishment of a European Monetary System (EMS) by which member currencies were pegged against each other but which was adjustable when it became clear that there was a serious deviation between official and market rates. Given both the discrepancy between inflation in France and the rest of the European Community (only in Italy was it higher) and the falling franc after 1982 it was not clear how continuation of the Mitterrand experiment could be squared with membership of the EMS. It therefore became apparent that in order to protect the national interest France had to commit itself to measures that would strengthen the EMS not weaken it. This was why the policy of 'rigour' became inescapable. It was aimed at delivering French and German economic convergence, defined in terms of a stable franc, pegged against the deutschmark (le franc fort), and similar inflation and interest rates. Given that the Christian Democrats in West Germany had themselves followed a deflationary course in order to minimize inflationary pressures since coming to power in 1982 this could only mean French macroeconomic contraction.[4]

It was not therefore France or any European state that was able to produce a workable expansionary alternative to monetarism in the advanced industrial world. Yet one did emerge, and ironically it was developed by the United States itself. The recipe was called Reaganomics and made its first appearance in the pit of the recession of 1979–82. Reaganomics delivered an old-fashioned stimulus to the US economy via tax cuts and a rise in federal expenditure, notably on defence. It was called 'military Keynesianism' and signalled the weakening grip of monetarist orthodoxy, although this lingered for a time in the use of high interest rates to slow down demand for credit. In 1983–5 real interest rates were fluctuating between 7 and 8 per cent, but they lacked the impact they had made in the early 1980s because they were accompanied by a brisk rise in federal spending and by tax cuts. Together, the tax cuts and the spending increases injected demand equivalent to about 3.5 per cent of GDP into the US economy.

This somewhat eclectic macroeconomic policy had three fundamental results. First, it generated a significant federal deficit, which increased from 1.8 per cent of GDP in 1980 to 3.6 per cent in 1984, stimulating spending and employment (the latter after 1983). Between 1982 and 1989 output grew by almost 4 per cent per annum while unemployment fell back to 5.4 per cent of the workforce.[5] Second, the high interest rates drove up the dollar. This reduced inflationary pressures inside the USA and encouraged an expanding inflow of goods and capital from Europe, Latin America and East Asia. Japanese and German exports in particular flourished and by the mid-1980s were expanding at annual average rates, respectively, of 7.7 per cent and 7.9 per cent.[6] Third, the sustained expansion helped to revive growth in the industrialized world. US government consumption expenditure rose at an annual rate of 50 per cent between 1979 and 1989, and this compensated for cuts under the same heading in other leading industrial countries such as France, Germany and Japan. Here there were falls, respectively, of 33 per cent, 47 per cent and 57 per cent.[7]

◆ Deregulation I: The Domestic Economy

Although the expansion of the post-1982 period was driven, in classic Keynesian style, by the increase in US federal expenditure, it had a peculiarly liberal twist that was lacking from the growth-oriented macroeconomic strategies of the golden age. This was the emphasis on tax cuts and financial deregulation in the domestic economy and trade liberalization in the international economy. All of these were especially notable in the USA, the UK and even Japan during the 1980s.

The federal deficits of the Reagan era pushed up output and in the process generated a sharp rise in profits. With profitability up, taxes down and, after 1985, lower interest rates, it was easy to purchase assets. This was the background to a wave of speculation in the USA, whose most overt manifestation was in a wave of mergers, sometimes referred to as 'corporate downsizing'. These were frequently financed by debt (junk bonds and leveraged buyouts), which produced high rates of return, usually as a function of mass layoffs, wage reductions and fierce productivity drives. What became unprecedented levels of borrowing, largely by one corporation in order to gain a controlling interest in another, led to a growth in interest payments as a proportion of profits from 15 per cent (1973–9) to 35 per cent (1982–90).

The neo-liberals explained all this away as the price of regenerating the US economy. Unable to hold its own in international competition it needed to purge itself of uneconomic plant and equipment and unproductive labour, and focus on modernizing the fast-growing sectors (computing) and the most profitable and efficient plant. There certainly was a major shake-up in the US economy, with over 30,000 mergers worth a total value of $1.34 trillion, a figure equivalent to 33 per cent of the amount spent on non-residential investment,[8] during the decade between 1980 and 1989. Yet much of the merger activity and corporate expansion that did occur during the Reagan years was devoted to finance, insurance and real estate (FIRE). Indeed, between 1982 and 1990 this sector absorbed 25 per cent of all new investment in plant and equipment in the private business economy and used 35 per cent of the net stock of computing, office and accounting equipment used in the US economy as a whole, whereas the share taken by manufacturing was just 25 per cent.[9] Employment in manufacturing fell by 1.1 million between 1979 and 1990 but rose by 20 million in the service sector over the same period, much of the work in property and financial services and in low-paid trades such as hotels and catering and sales, both wholesale and retail.[10]

The intensity of the merger wave was also characteristic of a stock market bubble in which investors borrowed heavily in the expectation that rapidly rising prices would allow them to sell their shares and so both pay off debt and reap handsome profits. In the first eight months of 1987 stock prices as measured by the Dow Jones industrial average on Wall Street increased by 40 per cent, but the trend came to a sudden halt on 19 October 1987 when they fell by 23 per cent in a single day ('Black Monday'). The crash appeared to have been set off by rising long-term interest rates, caused by market expectations of a fall in the dollar. The increase in interest rates both ate into corporate profits and encouraged investors to buy bonds because they were starting to yield more than shares; these were good reasons for an investor to sell stock as fast as possible before prospective profits were wiped out by prospective indebtedness. The collapse on Wall Street was followed by falls in other stock markets throughout the industrial world and there were fears that it was the prelude to a recession. Yet the crash had no long-term impact on the expansion of the Reagan era. The neo-liberal revolution was able to continue, ironically thanks largely to Washington's persistent Keynesianism. The USA and the UK both pursued loose monetary policies in the wake of the crash and there was no effort to rein in the federal deficit. The climate remained conducive to growth and by 1989 stock prices were back where they had been in late 1989.[11]

The US experience was paralleled in the UK. Competition between banks and building societies was encouraged, hire purchase controls were abolished, tax cuts were introduced and, from 1983, the government set about privatizing the nationalized industries at low prices. Yet perhaps the most dramatic act of deregulation was the abolition of exchange controls by the Thatcher administration in the UK (see Chapter 5). Its impact was mainly threefold. First, it facilitated the exodus of portfolio capital from Britain. Armstrong, Glyn and Harrison noted that British financial institutions increased their holdings of shares and bonds overseas by $75 billion between 1979 and 1988. Second, the move ensured that any time interest rates failed to reflect expectations in the financial markets about the future level of the exchange rate there would be large-scale outflows (if depreciation seemed likely) or inflows (if appreciation were forecast) of capital likely to destabilize the government's efforts to manage money, credit, inflation and growth. The domestic economy's last major barrier against disruption by externally driven crises had been removed; Britain was more integrated into the international economy than at any time since its departure from the gold standard in 1931.

The third major result of abolishing exchange controls was to add to the pressure towards the internationalization of financial markets arising from the falling costs of communication and information worldwide, thanks to computers, the telex machine and the fax. By the 1980s financial transactions represented the fastest-growing area of international economic activity, with daily foreign exchange dealings in New York rising from $18 billion in 1980 to $192 billion in 1992,[12] while it was estimated that each day in 1987 an average of $420 billion crossed the world's foreign exchanges, 90 per cent of this related to financial business not to trade and investment.[13] Determination on the part of the City of London and a friendly Conservative administration to take a large share of this business and remain (with New York and Tokyo) a leading international centre of financial trading led to the liberalization of the financial markets. Examples of deregulation were the removal of fixed commissions on share dealings and the ending of limits on foreign ownership of British stockbroking firms (this was known as the 'Big Bang' and arrived in 1986). By the late 1980s half the shares traded in London were foreign, most of them being either German or Japanese.[14]

The liberal climate encouraged a boom in which expenditure grew on consumer goods, share ownership and financial services, as well as houses and other forms of property. The spending spree generated an annual average expansion of 3.4 per cent after 1983. As in the USA this turned into a speculative bubble, which burst in October 1987, although economic growth remained buoyant for another two years. Again, as in the USA there was a trend to the expansion of the service sector and away from manufacturing; in 1983 Britain ran a deficit in manufactured goods for the first time since the Industrial Revolution. Turning its back on industry Britain still attempted to exploit the advantages of its long history as an international financial intermediary.[15]

The same pattern was visible in Japan. Here the government sought to stimulate the economy through a cheap money policy designed to encourage the purchasing of land and shares. The expansionary monetary policy was supplemented by financial liberalization, encouraged by the US Treasury. The idea was partly that Japanese financial institutions should take advantage of the massive expansion of international capital flows that had developed during the previous 15 to 20 years and make profits by competing with their counterparts in the trade in financial instruments. It was also believed, though, that deregulation, in terms of the removal of government-imposed ceilings on interest rates, freedom for domestic commercial banks to attract various types of deposits, and freedom for firms to borrow abroad from banks and securities markets, would stimulate the speculative climate and sustain the rising price of shares.[16]

The policy worked, and corporate wealth expanded on the basis of high-value company stock and expensive real estate (many corporations had for years owned prime sites in Tokyo). The state-backed windfall financed a wave of investment in plant and equipment by as much as 10.5 per cent a year between 1986 and 1990. The economy was stimulated by the expenditure and grew at a rate of 4.6 per cent per annum over the same period. Yet there was increasing evidence that demand for shares was being fuelled more by rising property prices, which led large companies to anticipate generous capital gains, than by profits from productive activity. Indeed Japanese companies failed to raise profit levels despite massive accumulation of capital stock, inventories and investment after 1985. At the same time share values by the end of the 1980s amounted to as much as 75 per cent of underlying corporate assets.[17] This, too, was a bubble and by early 1990 it seemed to be on the point of bursting. Concern at the level of speculation led the government, in 1989, to increase interest rates. This started an appreciation of the yen and increased corporate debt burdens. Share prices on the Nikkei stock exchange in Tokyo reacted by falling 30 per cent in the first quarter of the year. Falling share values and stagnant profits would not leave companies with a surplus to spend on the Nikkei or on further property acquisitions and development. The downward path of the stock exchange and land values meant a reversal of the capital gains enjoyed after 1985 and so eroded the liquidity needed by the corporate sector to service its debts to the banks. Deregulation seemed to be leading the most successful of all postwar economies towards falling profitability and a financial crisis.

◆ Deregulation II: Trade Liberalization

The drive to promote another round of trade liberalization via the GATT began at the prompting of the USA in 1982. It was supported by the World Economic Forum, originally formed in 1971 to bring together the chief executives of large European companies. Over the subsequent decade its membership had expanded to include government representatives and heads of international organizations such as the IMF and the World Bank. Other enthusiasts were the US Business Round Table and the European Round Table of Industrialists (ERT). The first of these had been formed in 1972 and was composed of the chief executives of leading firms such as Alcoa and General Electric. The second was more recent, having been established in 1983. Its membership was composed of the heads of multinational corporations such as British Petroleum, Daimler-Benz, Fiat, ICI, Nestlé, Philips and Unilever. It had quickly established itself as a major influence on the development of the European Community, pushing (in the end with success) for the removal of all restrictions and barriers remaining within it, and their replacement with a single market.[18]

Proponents of liberalization expressed particular concern about the need to reduce barriers to trade in agriculture, and in investment and services. Although the call for a new GATT round was justified given the importance of opening western markets to LDC producers, the particular agenda developed by its US and European sponsors reflected the interests of American farmers and multinational corporations from both sides of the Atlantic and Japan (drawn together into the Trilateral Commission established by David Rockefeller, chairman of the Chase Manhattan Bank in 1973). The US farm sector was regularly producing surpluses and was eager to penetrate protected markets in Europe and East Asia. At the same time the large corporations, backed by their national governments, sought to exploit the growing market in services that was developing out of the deregulation and privatizations being undertaken in the advanced industrial states. There was already an obvious move to increase foreign investment in this sector, which included construction, finance and legal services, telecommunications and transport (these accounting for approaching 66 per cent of the growth in foreign investment during the 1980s as a whole).[19]

Many of the existing regulations concerning foreign investment were to be found in the LDCs, where governments had attempted to link it to their national development strategies. As a result it was normal to find criteria for investment setting a limit on foreign equity ownership; regulations specifying that there had to be a set amount of local material used in the manufacture of products; and requirements that multinationals export some or all of their production. Public utilities tended to be nationalized, with governments unwilling to turn them over to private ownership. It followed that most misgivings about using the GATT to push ahead with the liberalization of services came from the LDCs. With the OECD and corporate lobbies such as the ERT and the US Business Round Table all pushing the same way, however, it was agreed at a ministerial meeting of GATT members held in 1986 at Punta del Este in Uruguay, to start a new round, which became known as the Uruguay Round.

The agricultural negotiations stalled but some progress was made with the drive to deregulate trade in investment and services. These talks were organized under the collective umbrella of Trade Related Investment Measures (TRIMs). Throughout the TRIMs discussions, the GATT Secretary-General, Arthur Dunkel, called for concessions by the LDCs that would decouple foreign investment from national development strategies, notably by repealing provisions concerning local content and export requirements (no mention was made of transfer pricing, a practice that allowed the multinationals to circumvent local tax regulations). Although the parties failed to reach an early consensus, Dunkel proposed a draft agreement on services which established the principal of 'national treatment', in other words of ensuring that foreign investors and suppliers of services were given the same treatment by national and local governments in the LDCs as those from within the host nation.

By the end of the 1980s the Uruguay Round talks were still a long way from resolution. Many issues, not just TRIMs but also those concerning Trade-Related Intellectual Property Rights (TRIPS) remained controversial. But there was no mistaking the trajectory of international trade policy or the identity of those responsible for driving it. These were the advanced economies, their governments working in alliance with those sectors, in finance and industry, which were already most integrated into the international economy. The direction was towards one world, characterized by a set of rules that institutionalized non-discrimination in trade and finance, and created a global environment safe for the simultaneously free and planned economies of the multinational corporations.

◆ Growth and Development in the International Economy

Apologists for international trade liberalization argued that it would generate faster growth throughout the world economy. Yet the pre-Uruguay regime was one in which international economic growth remained buoyant, with the most rapid progress being made by the newly industrialized East Asian countries (known as the 'Tiger economies') deploying state-led development strategies. These were beneficiaries of the Japanese turn to Asian markets in the wake of the 1985 Plaza Accords.

The Plaza Accords realigned exchange rates in response to a mounting American current account deficit, balanced by record German and Japanese surpluses, all this being a function of the high dollar and the buoyant US economy. The dollar was allowed to fall, the interest rate prop being removed. Just as there had been in the 1970s, there was a sharp decline in the value of the dollar while the yen and the deutschmark appreciated on the international markets. There was an expansion of American exports, while German and Japanese exports suffered, in a reversal of the conditions that had prevailed between 1982 and 1985.

The Plaza Accords helped to provide international expansion with a new direction. The effect of the high dollar had been to stimulate Japanese exports, which had grown at an annual rate of 23 per cent from 1982 to 1986. This strengthened the dependence of the Japanese economy on exports which, by 1985, represented 14.5 per cent of GDP, having been worth 11.1 per cent in 1979.[20] Investment tended to concentrate on advanced products such as computers, personal organizers, sophisticated cameras and semiconductors – all seen as part of the next wave after cars, television sets and domestic consumables. Indeed, high-tech and mixed high-tech and capital-intensive production accounted by the end of the decade for 85 per cent of all manufacturing output.[21]

Japanese governments in the mid- to late 1980s were keen both not to lose ground in overseas markets and to ensure that the economy remained innovative. The fall in the value of the dollar was a problem in these circumstances, but the Japanese were able to offset the difficulties of exporting to the USA (the US share of Japanese exports fell from 40 per cent in 1986 to 31.6 per cent in 1990)[22] by expanding the European share of their exports (by 168 per cent in dollar terms between 1985 and 1990) and above all by reorienting to East Asia. There was a surge in direct investment in the region as Asia's share of all

Japanese direct investment increased from 12 per cent in 1985 to 24 per cent in 1994.

Japan's foreign trade and investment strategy had two objectives. The first was to use direct investment in the lower-cost economies of East Asia as a springboard for continuing, albeit indirect, penetration of the American market. The second was to use the dynamism of these economies as a source of demand for Japanese production. Japanese producers supplied the Asian NICs with capital and intermediate goods (usually via intra-industry trade), most of which could be used to manufacture textiles and cars in the 1980s but which, in the 1990s, could also be employed in the manufacture of electronics and information technology exports for the US and Asian markets. The concentration on the East Asian market showed up in the figures: Japanese exports to East Asia rose as a percentage of all Japanese exports from 18.7 per cent to 28.9 per cent between 1985 and 1990.[23] During the same period $15 billion of Japanese investment flowed into East Asia, especially Indonesia, South Korea, Singapore, Thailand and Malaysia, and helped to stimulate high, or at least buoyant, rates of growth in these countries during the subsequent decade.

It was a logical strategy since, despite some difficulties with international debts, the East Asian economies were less disturbed by the shock of the 1979–82 recession than most others in the developed and less developed worlds. Malaysia, for example, pursued a development strategy more in the tradition of the ISI than along the free market lines now fashionable in Washington and London. Its trade policy was protectionist while the state guided and assisted investment in key sectors it identified as most responsive to international demand in the developed world, such as the car industry. At the same time, it encouraged the inflow of foreign direct investment. Solomon noted that it accounted for over 50 per cent of total investment by the early 1990s, the highest proportion in any East Asian economy apart from Singapore.[24] In the 1980s this foreign direct investment was a key foundation for rapid industrialization, with manufactures advancing from occupying 18.8 per cent of all exports (1980) to 70 per cent by 1992. Cars, disk drives, semiconductors and other electronic goods featured prominently. Between 1986 and 1992 the country experienced an average annual growth rate of 8 per cent.

It is true that both Indonesia and Thailand needed assistance from the Fund and the Bank in the 1980s, but both countries frequently ignored the advice they were given to deregulate and cut back the role of the state. Indeed, liberalization in Indonesia was limited. Regulations continued to govern the inflow of foreign capital, production was dominated by monopolies and, as in Malaysia, the country's foreign trade strategy remained protectionist. The growth of the Indonesian economy cannot therefore be attributed to neo-liberal policies, but it can be correlated with the inflow of Japanese money (worth almost $4 billion between 1985 and 1990) as well as the provision of generous loans from Tokyo at the start of the 1980s when the external accounts began to appear unhealthy.

As far as Thailand is concerned, the government refused to dismantle its controls on imports. It did prioritize production for the export market, largely using tax incentives, but this was accompanied after 1985 by increasing investment in import substitution. The maintenance of this dominant position for the state, with its controls over trade and capital flows, preserved Thailand from external crisis – but did not discourage Japanese investment. Indeed Japanese car manufacturers exploited the protected Thai market and by the early 1990s were responsible for 50 per cent of automobile production there. Large corporations such as Toyota and Mitsubishi figured prominently, encouraged by regulations that supported foreign direct investment on condition that 80 per cent of production was for export. The high levels of industrial investment stimulated domestic expansion and there was an annual average growth of GDP between 1986 and 1996 to 9.1 per cent. The net result of Japanese investment, buoyant international demand and state-guided development was to sustain the industrialization of the East Asian NICs even as stagnation and recession afflicted the Latin American states that had appeared poised for take-off in the 1970s. The four leading Tiger economies – Singapore, South Korea, Malaysia and Indonesia – increased their combined share of world exports from 1.2 per cent to 6.4 per cent between 1965 and 1990.[25]

The experience of the international economy in the 1980s was clearly mixed. After 1982, trade continued to expand. As before, the driving force was the exchange of industrial goods between the advanced nations, which consumed 71 per cent of their own exports in 1980 and 75 per cent of them in 1992.[26] This trade continued to grow at a rate comparable with the golden age.[27] Products enjoying the more rapid increases in output tended to be either those where increasing demand followed from rising incomes or those characterized by expensive and sophisticated capital investment programmes, usually undertaken by the large corporations. Machinery, electronic equipment and chemicals all tended to fall into these categories, and production of such commodities tended to be concentrated in the advanced industrial world, although there was the increasing contribution of the East Asian NICs. The only significant exception to this rule concerned clothing and textiles, where the location of production shifted towards the lower-wage economies (Table 6.1).[28] Although it was the NICs that enjoyed the most rapid growth rates during the 1980s, the performance of the OECD members was a distinct improvement on the previous decade: between 1973 and 1981 the average annual growth rate was 1.9 per cent; from 1981 to 1989 it was 2.4 per cent, a figure that, if anything, underestimates the extent of the expansion given the size of the falls in output between 1981 and 1982.[29]

The ability of the system to carry on generating more wealth every year after 1983 suggested that it had been premature to conclude, as some Marxist commentators had, that the falling profitability, inflation and intensified class struggle within the advanced industrial countries during the 1970s heralded a profound crisis for the capitalist system.[30] As Hobsbawm has pointed out, the

TABLE 6.1: CHANGES IN WORLD COMMODITY TRADE, 1980–1992

	(Values) annual average rate of growth	Share in world merchandise exports (%)
Food	3.8	9.6
Fuels	−2.8	9.1
Iron and steel	2.5	2.8
Chemicals	7.2	9.0
Machinery and transport equipment	8.3	37.3
(of which automotive products)	8.8	9.9
Textiles, clothing	6.5	3.2

Source: Pollard, *The International Economy since 1945* (London: Routledge, 1997), 36, Table 3.1

TABLE 6.2: PROFIT RATES ON
CAPITAL, 1951–1983

1951–53	16.3%
1961–63	14.8%
1971–73	13.0%
1981–83	9.3%

Source: Pollard, *The International Economy since 1945* (London: Routledge, 1997), 106

growth of the collective GDP of the advanced economies was only interrupted twice up to 1991 – in 1974–5 and in 1981–3 – yet the criticisms could not be entirely dismissed. There were obvious strains, certainly not apparent during the golden age, in the prosperous western economies. Profit rates earned on capital in the six largest OECD economies did show a downward trend (Table 6.2) and unemployment in western Europe remained high even in the late 1980s, at the height of the recovery. In Britain the rate of youth unemployment between 1982 and 1988 was over 20 per cent; by the early 1990s New York was being haunted by large-scale homelessness, with over 20,000 sleeping on its streets or in its public shelters.[31] This was accompanied by a widening of inequality throughout much of the OECD, especially the USA, where the differential between the top 10 per cent of wage earners and the bottom 10 per cent widened by 34 per cent between 1979 and 1989.[32] Growth in much of Africa, western Asia and throughout Latin America virtually ceased for much of the decade.

What was wrong with the liberal capitalism of the 1980s? To begin with, the falling profit rates can be explained as a natural consequence of European and Japanese 'catch-up' of the United States in the postwar era (see Chapter 3). Maddison's figures show a general deceleration across the OECD during the period 1973 to 1989.[33] The internationalization of the consumer society, at least throughout the advanced industrial nations, had replaced scarcity with abundance in cars, electronics and domestic goods. Barring technological breakthrough it was inevitable that rates of return on investment would fall back from the levels of the 1950s and 1960s. At the same time, costs rose in response to the combined pressures arising from the need to undertake more innovation and investment in order to generate higher productivity, increasing outlays on raw materials (notably oil) and the success of organized labour in wage negotiations during the 1970s. Although both wages and raw material costs failed to sustain their increases into the 1980s, the impact of recession at the start of the decade kept the profit trend on the downward path. Thereafter there was a modest recovery but, even by 1987, business profits for the advanced industrial nations had failed to return to 1973 levels.[34] Given the existence, even in time of recovery, of mass unemployment in the largest European economies (Table 6.3), it is not surprising that the high and smooth growth levels of the golden age remained out of reach.

In addition it can be argued that the unemployment, inequality and social insecurity of the 1980s reflected the policy choices of the right-wing governments and their supporters during the years after 1979. There were powerful coalitions in the UK and the USA above all, but visible elsewhere in the OECD, that supported the rollback of the postwar mixed economy. The stabilizing impact of government investment programmes on cyclical fluctuations was lessened, leaving economies liable to perform sharp swings between recession or even slump on the one hand and rapid expansion on the other. This trend to instability was strengthened by financial liberalization, which left national economies vulnerable to speculative shocks and to disruption from international capital flows. Reaganomics did ensure that Keynesianism was not completely jettisoned and helped to sustain international economic growth in the 1980s, but the deregulation and regressive fiscal policies associated with it if anything contributed to the climate of macroeconomic insecurity. Meanwhile, the discernible increase in poverty at the bottom of the social scale was a function of cuts in welfare benefits; the widening gap between the richest and the poorest followed from tax reductions targeted at the middle class and the wealthy.

TABLE 6.3: Unemployment as a proportion of the workforce: selected countries, 1979–1989

	Belgium	France	Italy	Netherlands	UK	USA	W. Germany
1979	8.2	5.9	7.6	6.6	5.0	5.8	3.2
1980	8.8	6.3	7.5	6.0	6.4	7.0	3.0
1981	10.8	7.4	7.8	8.5	9.8	7.5	4.4
1982	12.6	8.1	8.4	11.4	11.3	9.5	6.1
1983	12.1	8.3	8.8	12.0	12.4	9.5	8.0
1984	12.1	9.7	9.4	11.8	11.7	7.4	7.1
1985	11.3	10.2	9.6	12.6	11.2	7.1	7.2
1986	11.2	10.4	10.5	9.9	11.2	6.9	6.4
1987	11.0	10.5	10.9	9.6	10.3	6.1	6.2
1988	9.7	10.0	11.0	9.2	8.5	5.4	6.2
1989	8.1	9.4	10.9	8.3	7.1	5.2	5.6

Source: derived from Maddison, *Dynamic Forces in Capitalist Development* (Oxford: Oxford University Press, 1991), 262–4, Table C.6

◆ From International Debt Crisis to International Debt Crisis, 1982–1985

The failure of growth to occur in much of Africa and in most of Latin America during the 1980s was a function of the increasing international indebtedness of countries throughout these regions and of the drastic measures, fully in tune with neo-liberal orthodoxy, taken by the IMF and the World Bank to correct the external imbalances.

By the end of the decade the development strategies of most debtor countries reflected what became known as the 'Washington consensus', reflecting conventional wisdom in the US Treasury, the IMF and the World Bank. This involved an enforced turn to the free market and the small state, integration into the world economy and, specifically, an opening to international capital flows. The debt crisis was therefore the catalyst for the extension of the new macroeconomics and deregulation to much of the Third World.

One of the main factors behind the debt crisis was the second major oil price rise within less than a decade, precipitated by the Iranian revolution of 1979. In the wake of this political upheaval, Saudi crude increased from $13 per barrel in 1978 to $32.50 a barrel in 1981. This put pressure on the balance of payments of the non-oil-producing LDCs, who found themselves devoting 21 per cent of all spending on imports to spending on oil by 1981 (in 1979 the figure had been just 5.9 per cent). Yet it remained possible for economic expansion to continue since, just as had happened after 1973–4, OPEC members saved the proceeds and placed them in western banks. The banks then lent the money to the non-oil LDCs, who were able to continue with their development programmes. As a result expansion continued and kept the average annual rate of growth of the non-oil Third World buoyant: it was 5.1 per cent between 1973 and 1981, only slightly down on the 5.8 per cent achieved from 1967–72.[35] It was a considerable achievement, given that most OECD economies were growing only erratically over this time.

In the mid- to late 1970s the strategy of 'growth through debt' had worked. Refusing to abandon expansionary policies the LDCs had been able to export their way out of a $46 billion debt generated by the first major oil price increase. They were unable to repeat this performance after 1979, however, since the international climate turned against them. High interest rates introduced by the industrialized nations in the wake of the oil shock put up the costs of debt service after 1979; UNCTAD estimated that the extra financial commitment could have been as much as $41 billion. These problems were compounded by the recession in the developed world, which hit proceeds from commodity exports. At the same time, given that most of the LDC debts were denominated in dollars, the rise of the dollar during the early 1980s was bound to increase the debt burden. It was a set of unfortunate circumstances that upset economic plans in both non-oil-producing and oil-producing developing countries. Indeed, by 1981–2 two of the most heavily indebted states were oil producers themselves: Mexico and Venezuela. Both countries stuck to their growth strategies (Mexico's target was an annual average rate of 8 per cent) and continued importing capital equipment. But revenue from oil was not enough to wipe out a growing external deficit, and both countries borrowed heavily as a result.

Why were developing countries with mounting debts and failing export markets able to continue with heavy borrowing after 1979? Perhaps the most powerful incentive to lending was provided by the availability and volume of funds, notably in the Eurodollar market. Between 1975 and 1984 Eurocurrency deposits, swollen by the oil price rises, grew from $650 billion to $2100 billion. As the money poured in, the banks recycled it in the form of loans, which could themselves be treated as deposits and platforms for further lending. The western financial authorities took the view that it would be a mistake to interfere in what was a flourishing trade. This attitude was especially marked in London, one of the main centres of Euromarket activity. Here, after 1979, a *laissez-faire* government, keen to encourage the expansion of the financial sector and the earnings related to it, stood back while net international bank credit exploded. By 1984 it had reached $1275 billion, having been $260 billion in 1975.[36]

Western governments enthusiastically encouraged this lending. They took the process as an example of the superior efficiency of the free market over intervention and official programmes of development aid. They felt themselves excused not only from establishing basic rules designed to regulate the volume of lending but also from the obligation of increasing aid and development budgets in line with the recommendations of the Brandt Report. Within the international financial community there was a consensus that all the lending was 'safe' – clients were not private businesses but governments, and these could not go bankrupt. If in one year a borrower happened to be short of money it would merely be a question of giving the country time to make economic policy adjustments, if necessary helped by the extension of additional finance.

In 1981–2 it became clear that this optimism was not justified. As LDCs ran up their deficits the banks began to increase short-term lending, with maturity dates of a year or less. It was an attempt to reduce the risks of further lending and therefore a sign that the banks were becoming concerned about the ability of the debtors to continue with repayment. With medium- and long-term loans becoming rare, borrowers were forced to redeem maturing credits by running down reserves and then by short-term funding. This bought time but only at the cost of increasing the volume of liabilities that needed to be paid off in the following year. Lever and Huhne point to the accelerating pace of lending in 1982, the most glaring example being Mexico, which borrowed $6.4 billion between February and August 1982, most of it from US banks.[37] This was a large sum of money, but it was surpassed by credits rapidly approaching maturity: these finally reached a volume so great that Mexico did not have and could not raise the funds to redeem them.

In August 1982 the Mexican government threatened to default. It was by now hardly in a position to repay the interest on its borrowing, let alone the principal. And it was not the only debtor in financial trouble. Brazil, Argentina and Venezuela were all approaching a point at which they might have to follow Mexico. With the proportion of total loans occupied by outstanding debt standing at 37.5 per cent (having risen from 11.6 per cent in 1973) this was a dangerous moment for many banks. The Managing Director of the IMF, Jacques de la Leroisière, warned that there was 'a real threat to the integrity of the international financial and trading system'.[38] It was a situation whose fragility underlined the risks of reliance on unregulated financial markets to take responsibility for international economic development.

In order to avoid defaults and widespread international bank failure it was necessary to organize a rescue package for the debtor states. This was known as 'rescheduling', and involved a rewriting of the debt so that interest payments continued to flow even if the principal was to be reduced or the due date for its full payment postponed. It suited both the borrowers (since they retained access to international credit) and the lenders (since they did not have to contemplate the loss of assets, and interest payments continued to flow to them). But since there were numerous lenders and many of these had their own terms and conditions for providing finance to borrowers, organized negotiations between creditors and debtors needed co-ordination by a public agency. Only the IMF could fulfil this task, and by intervening to manage the talks and rescue operations it both kept the banks afloat and acted as the guarantor of the international financial system.

The Fund's first intervention of many over the next few years was triggered by the Mexican crisis. The strategy followed in this case – a precedent to be followed regularly in the future – had three fundamental points: first, the commercial banks would agree to reschedule outstanding debt and make (modest) new lending available; second, IMF money would supplement this package; third, the provision of extra funding was to be conditional on the implementation of an austerity package by the debtor. This focused on cuts in public and private spending, to reduce demand for imports and release resources into production for the export market. Few of these 'adjustment programmes' were popular with the debtors, but they seemed preferable to default and were undertaken in the hope that they would lead to official relief of the debt, with further contributions from the IMF and the World Bank making it unnecessary to use a growing proportion of the export surplus to service it.

Although the rescheduling exercise successfully prevented any default, the hopes pinned to it by debtor governments were misplaced. The deflationary strategies imposed upon them led to a spectacular fall in output, notably in Latin America. Here GDP per head fell by 8.9 per cent between 1981 and 1984, the sharpest reductions occurring in Bolivia, Brazil, Chile, Mexico and Peru. Over this period 400,000 jobs were lost in São Paulo alone.[39] This certainly led to a fall in imports. Yet the fundamental problem of rising interest payments was not tackled by the IMF and the commercial banks and, as a result, these charges took a significantly larger share of export earnings after 1981–2 (Table 6.4), leaving domestic investment programmes languishing. Indeed, there was net flow of money out of the debtor states to their creditors in the advanced industrial world. In other words, a negative transfer of wealth from the poor to the wealthy started after 1983, the seven leading debtor nations losing $35 billion in 1984 alone.[40] The export of capital from developed to less developed economies had been one of the foundations of international economic growth over the preceding century; it had helped to account for economic growth in the USA, Canada, Australia and Latin America prior to 1914, and was currently assisting development in East Asia. Yet this process was now being reversed throughout Latin America and much of Africa in order to preserve international financial stability. In the circumstances it was not surprising that by 1984–5 some debtor countries were beginning to consider default a better alternative than continued rescheduling.

By 1985 the threat of default was serious. Debtor countries were in a better position to survive it without excessive disruption than they had been in 1982. They had accumulated reserves of foreign currency worth $422 billion since the onset of the debt crisis, while reserve cover for imports – essential if credit was unavailable – had grown from 17.3 per cent in 1981 to 31 per cent in 1984. At the same time there had been a turn to barter trade, estimated by UNCTAD

TABLE 6.4: EXPORTS AND INTEREST PAYMENTS OF 15
'HIGHLY INDEBTED' DEVELOPING COUNTRIES, 1979–1986

	Exports (f.o.b.) $ bn	Interest payments	
		$ bn	As % of exports
1979	94.2	17.1	18
1980	127.1	25.1	20
1981	126.1	37.0	29
1982	111.5	45.5	41
1983	111.1	41.5	37
1984	123.4	46.0	37
1985	119.2	44.0	37
1986	98.6	38.2	39

Source: Tew, *The Evolution of the International Monetary System, 1945–88*
(London: Hutchinson, 1988), 241, Table 32

to account for 30 per cent of all international trade in 1984.[41] All this allowed default to become a serious political issue in a way it had not three years before, and pressure in favour of it started to build in some debtor states.

Once again, the epicentre of the resurgent crisis was in Latin America: Argentina, Brazil, Mexico and Venezuela made up 60 per cent of the overall exposure of the nine leading US creditors (which included the Bank of America, Citibank, Chemical Bank, Chase Manhattan and Continental Illinois). But it was not just US banks that were threatened. British institutions were involved, notably the Midland Bank, whose exposure to the four main Latin American debtors accounted for 205 per cent of its capital. A default by the four major Latin American debtors would destroy the capital of seven out of the nine largest US and two out of the four largest British banks.[42] And the danger extended beyond the direct creditors of the LDCs. Much of the lending undertaken by the American banks had involved inter-bank credits deposited with them by institutions in other countries. Indeed, BIS statistics revealed that in 1985 66 per cent of the lending to Argentina, Brazil and Mexico had come from European and Japanese banks while 33 per cent of it was from US institutions. The results of a default would spread across the industrialized world, setting off a financial panic with banks calling in loans to domestic businesses. These, struggling to repay, would then save money on investment by running down inventories, closing plant and equipment and laying off workers.

◆ Baker, Brady and Structural Adjustment

What was to be done? An updated version of the Brandt Report, *Common Crisis*, appeared and proposed generosity to debtors on the part of the advanced world and multilateral institutions; its interventionism, however, was out of touch with the prevailing neo-liberal climate. The response of the creditor nations came with the Baker Plan, named after the US Treasury Secretary, James Baker. This plan, launched at the annual meeting of the IMF (in Seoul, October 1985), had three components. First, the debtor countries must commit themselves to the implementation of policies promoting 'adjustment, structural reform and freer markets'. Second, the commercial banks would continue with net lending to the LDCs; third, there would be an increase in the annual World Bank allocation to indebted developing nations. Baker promised $9 billion from the multilateral agencies and $20 billion from commercial banks in exchange for market-oriented reforms on the part of the receiving countries, or new lending based on 'market conditionality'.[43]

The first set of negotiations conducted under Baker's guidelines concerned Mexico (1986). A package that released $12.5 billion of further external finance was agreed in April 1987, half to be provided by official agencies (the World Bank, the IMF and the Group of Ten) and the rest to come from new lending on the part of the commercial banks. These would also reschedule their existing holdings of Mexican debt, writing down the principal without reducing interest payments in proportion. This deal was followed by a similar one for Argentina whereby rescheduling was agreed for part of the outstanding debt. At the same time the commercial banks, the IMF and the World Bank made $5.3 billion of new lending available. Agreements were also made with Chile, Venezuela and the Philippines during the course of 1987. All this was accompanied by emergency action on the part of some banks. Thus, in May 1987, the large New York bank Citicorp set aside the equivalent of 25 per cent of its exposure to LDCs as loan-loss provision. Its example was followed by other US and UK banks.

Yet the Baker Plan came under fire towards the end of the 1980s on the grounds that there had been no significant reduction of indebtedness, nor had the recipients demonstrated an ability to grow out of debt. The response came in the form of the Brady Plan (named after Baker's successor at the Treasury), the intention of which was to encourage the banks to write down the debts of their LDC clients and release new funds (from commercial banks and multilateral agencies) in exchange for continuing pro free-market reforms. The Latin American economies in particular responded very positively to the Brady Plan. Countries covered included Mexico and Costa Rica (1989), Venezuela (1990), Uruguay (1991), Argentina (1992) and Brazil (1992). By May 1994, 18 countries had signed up to Brady agreements, which now covered $60 billion worth of debt, and as a result of economic reforms signatories attracted a significant volume of capital from the international financial markets.

The exchange of assistance for free-market reform had in fact started several years earlier, under the World Bank's Structural Adjustment Loan (SAL) programme. By the start of 1986, SALs had become a familiar feature of loan rescheduling talks, but it was the Baker and then the Brady Plans that led to their spread throughout most of the indebted world. Following the Baker initiative the IMF established a formal Structural Adjustment Facility (in 1986), designed to promote closer co-operation between itself and the World Bank, particularly when it came to surveillance of debtor countries' economies and macroeconomic policies, and enforcement of 'market conditionality'. By the start of 1986, 12 of the 15 countries identified by the US State Department as 'top priority debtors'[44] had agreed to SALs. Structural adjustment credits rose from 3 per cent of World Bank lending in 1981 to 19 per cent in 1986 and, by 1992, there were 267 SALs in existence.

The free-market measures on which SALs were conditional boiled down to five essential reforms. First, cuts in public spending were required, even where this was on health, education and welfare, on the grounds that excess public spending was inflationary and had generated an unsustainable demand for imports of goods and capital. Second, there had to be wage reductions to reduce inflationary pressures and make exports cheaper. Third, debtors needed to open the domestic market to imports and remove restrictions on foreign investment in industry and financial services, on the grounds that this liberalization would encourage more competition and therefore more efficiency. Fourth, there had to be incentives for exports, which were seen as likely to be a more effective stimulus for growth than the expansion of the home market, partly through devaluation and partly through tax changes. Fifth, SAL recipients were required to set about privatizing state-owned enterprises on the grounds that free enterprise was better at allocating resources between producers and consumers than the public sector.[45] Acceptance of these conditions was a necessary but not a sufficient condition of assistance. Debtors had to accept that the aid would appear in tranches, and that they would be subject to continuous monitoring by the Fund and the Bank designed to ensure that they did not go back on their new commitments.

The philosophy behind the SAL programmes reflected the neo-liberalism of the Reagan and Thatcher administrations, which received some support after 1982 from the right-of-centre West German government led by the Christian Democrat Helmut Kohl. It was energetically promoted by the World Bank, even though this institution had previously been guided by an economic philosophy in tune with the post-1945 Keynesian consensus. But the Bank's most high-profile exponent of this consensus, Robert McNamara, its President since 1968, had retired in 1981. He was replaced by Alden ('Tom') Clausen, former head of the Bank of America, the world's largest commercial bank, and an ideological supporter of the Reagan administration. Under Clausen the SAL became more than a piece of technocratic tinkering designed to reverse a balance of payments problem with aid and create conditions conducive to export-led growth. It reflected the deeply held belief, which had surfaced in the US and

UK response to the Brandt Report and at the 1982 Cancun summit, that most LDCs were in the grip of socialism and that was why they were suffering from financial crises. The interventionist Third World state had to be dismantled so that growth would follow from a turn to *laissez-faire* capitalism. The SAL, as it spread throughout most of the heavily indebted developing countries under the Baker and Brady Plans, was central to the free-market counter-revolution intended to roll back all the advances made by the Left, whether in the newly industrialized countries or the less developed, since 1945.

The consensus in the worlds of international banks and corporations, as well as within mainstream financial journalism was that the SAL programme was a success. Vasquez noted how, after 1989, the Latin American states that were the plan's main targets introduced far-reaching free market reforms and attracted 'impressive levels of finance again from the international capital markets'. Yet there was a good deal of evidence to show that, in fact, SALs delivered sombre results when it came to living standards, social protection and growth. Greg Palast points out that under the ISI model of development between 1960 and 1980, per capita income grew by 73 per cent in Latin America and by 34 per cent in Africa. But between 1980 and 2000, with the turn to the free market, growth in Latin America virtually ceased, amounting to just 6 per cent over the period. During the same 20 years African incomes actually *declined* by 23 per cent, while between 1985 and the end of the century there was an increase in illiteracy and a fall in life expectancy in 15 African countries.[46] Cuts in public spending reduced demand, compounding the deflationary impact of a world recession at the start of the 1990s, and put pressure on pensions, health care and educational provision. Borrowers from the World Bank on the SAL programmes not only deregulated and privatized the economy but repealed legislation designed to protect workers and peasants in order to promote the maximum freedom for capital. Thus Argentina weakened its legal protection for trades unions, Ecuador eliminated communal land holdings, and India abolished laws that imposed a limit on how much land one person could own.[47] The 'adjustments' required by the SALs were generally accomplished at the expense of the middle class, the unions and the poor throughout the LDCs and, with increasing predictability, they frequently generated riots, strikes and social protest.[48]

The IMF and the Bank remained steadfast throughout all the upheavals created by their reforms, keen to argue that, whatever the short-term pain, the results for development and welfare would be beneficial. Yet the evidence did not support them. Mexico, often taken as the showpiece economy when it came to talking up the benefits of the SAL programme, enjoyed in fact only a modest annual average economic growth rate of 2.2 per cent between 1988 and 1994. It was hardly enough to compensate for the rise in population over the same period and was founded on continued borrowing, privatization and tax measures that turned the country into a safe haven for foreign investors.[49] There was no reduction in poverty and, in fact, by 1992 real wages were half of what they had been in 1982. Aid to the poor – for example, subsidies for milk, tortillas and school breakfasts – had either been stopped altogether or drastically reduced.[50]

Overall it appeared that the SALs had achieved largely negative results for the real economy of the LDC while punishing the inhabitants at the same time, all in order to sustain the western financial system. Indeed, most of the money lent to the LDCs in the 1980s went to service loans rather than finance development projects. Between 1984 and 1990, $178 billion drained from the developing countries to the private banks of the advanced industrial world.[51] Capital accumulation slowed across 20 states and, largely as a result, the share of manufacturing in GDP in 18 developing countries stagnated or contracted – a reversal of the trend between 1960 and the early 1980s. One survey found that out of 24 countries that had taken out SALs there were 13 whose exports fell up to 1992 and 11 whose exports rose – but, unfortunately, the impact of this increase on the external balance was usually negligible.[52] Yet SALs had achieved a wider macroeconomic objective: the integration of LDCs throughout Latin America and Africa into the deregulated, liberal international economy of the 1980s. By the end of the decade the Tiger economies and a disintegrating Soviet bloc (see Chapter 7) were the only significant obstacles on the road to a world without economic frontiers, one where goods and capital knew no home and where the concept of national economic sovereignty no longer existed.

◆ Notes

1. Also known in an increasing volume of literature as transnational corporations (TNCs), although strictly speaking the transnational corporation produces in one country while operating (selling and distributing) in many while the multinational produces, sells and distributes in many different countries.
2. Armstrong, Glyn and Harrison, *Capitalism since 1945*, 308–9.
3. Robert Solomon, *The Transformation of the World Economy, 1980–93* (New York: St Martin's Press, 1994), 68.
4. Ibid., 67.
5. Brenner, *The Economics of Global Turbulence*, 190–3.
6. Ibid., 219, 228.
7. Ibid., 189.
8. Investment excluding housing, inventories and land.
9. Brenner, *The Economics of Global Turbulence*, 211.
10. Ibid., 204–6.
11. Solomon, *The Transformation of the World Economy*, 33.
12. Ibid., 91.
13. Armstrong, Glyn and Harrison, *Capitalism since 1945*, 303.
14. Susan Strange, *Mad Money* (Manchester: Manchester University Press, 1998), 169.
15. Newton and Porter, *Modernization Frustrated*, Ch. 7.

16. Solomon, *The Transformation of the World Economy*, 80.
17. Armstrong, Glyn and Harrison, *Capitalism since 1945*, 260.
18. Strange, *Mad Money*, 69.
19. Walden Bello, *Dark Victory: The United States, Structural Adjustment and Global Poverty* (London: Pluto Press, 1994), 84.
20. Brenner, *The Economics of Global Turbulence*, 213.
21. Ibid., 216.
22. Ibid., 211.
23. Ibid., 218.
24. Solomon, *The Transformation of the World Economy*, 159–60.
25. Brenner, *The Economics of Global Turbulence*, 218.
26. Sidney Pollard, *The International Economy since 1945* (London: Routledge, 1997), 38.
27. Hobsbawm, *Age of Extremes*, 405.
28. Pollard, *The International Economy since 1945*, 37.
29. Angus Maddison, *Dynamic Forces in Capitalist Development*, 190–2.
30. This argument is made by Armstrong, Glyn and Harrison in *Capitalism since 1945*. See esp. Part III.
31. Hobsbawm, *Age of Extremes*, 405.
32. Pollard, *The International Economy since 1945*, 111.
33. Maddison, *Dynamic Forces in Capitalist Development*, 128–9.
34. Armstrong, Glyn and Harrison, *Capitalism since 1945*, 248–51.
35. Harold Lever and Christopher Huhne, *Debt and Danger: The World Financial Crisis* (London: Penguin, 1985), 61.
36. Ibid., 61.
37. Ibid., 60.
38. Quoted in Lever and Huhne, *Debt and Danger*, 64–5.
39. Lever and Huhne, *Debt and Danger*, 103.
40. Ibid., 35.
41. Ibid., 37.
42. Ibid., 28.
43. See Ian Vasquez, 'The Brady Plan and market-based solutions to debt crises', *The Cato Journal* 16(2) (1994).
44. Bello, *Dark Victory*, 30.
45. Ibid., 27.
46. Greg Palast, *The Best Democracy Money Can Buy* (London and Sterling, VA: Pluto Press, 2002), 48.
47. Catherine Caufield, *Masters of Illusion: The World Bank and the Poverty of Nations* (London: Pan Books, 1997), 145.
48. Ibid., 161.
49. Ibid., 153.
50. Ibid.
51. Wayne Ellwood, *The No-Nonsense Guide to Globalization* (Oxford and London: Verso, 2001), 48.
52. Bello, *Dark Victory*, 33.

7

GLOBALIZATION, 1990–2000

◆ Expansion

During the 1990s the aims outlined by the liberal planners who drafted Article VII of the Mutual Aid Agreement back in 1941 came closer to being achieved than at any stage in the postwar era. By the last years of the decade it had become a commonplace that the world was entering a new stage of development, characterized by the appearance of a single global market for goods and services ('globalization'). Yet this transformation was itself responsible for the generation of an economic instability and political opposition in the advanced and in the less developed economies that, by the start of the new century, threatened to derail the apparently triumphal progress towards an era of non-discrimination.

The move to globalization would not have occurred with such speed in the 1990s in the absence of steady if unspectacular international economic expansion. According to IMF statistics, world economic growth in the 1990s averaged 3 per cent, less than the 3.5 per cent of the 1980s and the 4.5 per cent of the 1970s.[1] World trade, however, enjoyed a boom period. There was no significant shift in the regional distribution of world merchandise trade during the 1990s (Table 7.1), but exports increased at an annual rate of 6.4 per cent, over twice as fast as the increase in income. Even more rapid than the growth of trade was the growth of foreign direct investment, at its most rapid between 1996 and 1999. During these years the annual percentage change in foreign direct investment averaged a remarkable 27.5 per cent.[2] As in the 1980s this was focused on the USA, western Europe and East Asia, these regions accounting for 90 per cent of outward and 79 per cent of inward foreign direct investment.

The expansions of trade and foreign direct investment were related. They stemmed partly from the activities of the multinational corporations, which continued to build international networks of production (by 2000 it was estimated that 33 per cent of all trade in the world economy was between different branches or affiliates of the same firm),[3] but they also increased in response to

TABLE 7.1: WORLD MERCHANDISE TRADE BY REGION AND
SELECTED ECONOMY, 1948–1999

Region	Exports: per cent of world total						
	1948	1953	1963	1973	1983	1993	1999
Western Europe	31.0	34.9	41.0	44.8	39.0	43.7	43.9
Eastern Europe	6.0	8.2	11.0	8.9	9.5	2.9	3.9
East Asia	4.3	5.5	7.2	10.5	15.0	22.2	21.3
North America	27.5	24.6	19.4	17.2	15.4	16.8	17.1
Latin America	12.3	10.5	7.0	4.7	5.8	4.4	4.4
Africa	7.4	6.5	5.7	4.8	4.4	2.5	2.0

Region	Imports: per cent of world total						
	1948	1953	1963	1973	1983	1993	1999
Western Europe	40.4	39.4	45.4	47.4	40.0	42.9	42.2
Eastern Europe	5.8	7.6	10.3	8.9	8.4	2.9	3.7
East Asia	5.1	8.0	8.1	11.1	13.9	19.1	16.8
North America	19.8	19.7	15.5	16.7	17.8	19.8	22.3
Latin America	10.6	9.3	6.8	5.1	4.5	5.2	5.8
Africa	7.6	7.0	5.5	4.0	4.6	2.6	2.3

Source: derived from WTO, *International Trade Statistics, 2000* (Geneva, 2001),
Table II.2

demand, and this was sustained throughout most of the 1990s by the US economy, which grew at an annual average rate of 3.7 per cent from 1991 to 1999[4] and at 4.5 per cent a year from 1996 to 2000.

The buoyancy of the US economy ensured a low rate of unemployment by the late 1990s (4 per cent). It acted as a magnet for foreign manufactures and helped to sustain growth in the rest of the industrialized world. This was particularly useful for the Japanese economy, which experienced stagnation and low growth in the 1990s following the collapse of the speculative boom governments had encouraged at the end of the 1980s. In July 1999 Honda's sales of motor vehicles in the USA expanded by 6.6 per cent, while Toyota enjoyed a 7 per cent increase. By 2000 the US trade deficit, rising from 0.76 per cent of GNP in 1992 to 4.17 per cent in 2000 (Figure 7.1), could in large part be accounted for by a rush of imported computers, telecommunications equipment, consumer goods and industrial supplies. It helped the EU economies to achieve a modest expansion

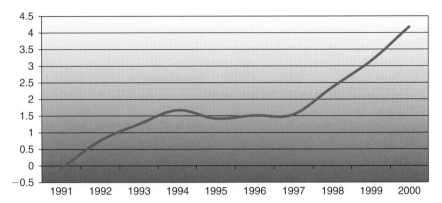

FIGURE 7.1: US BALANCE OF PAYMENTS DEFICIT, 1991–2000, AS A PERCENTAGE OF GNP
Source: derived from US Department of Commerce, Bureau of Economic Analysis: US National Income and Product Accounts and International Transactions Data

(rather limited by the determination of the European Central Bank to prioritize control of an already low inflation over more rapid growth) and to stave off the threat of a global recession. This had been a real prospect after the spread of economic crisis from East Asia to Russia and Latin America in 1997–8; the victims of this downturn were now able to export their way out of trouble thanks to the American expansion. At the same time a boom in the information technology sector stimulated demand for goods made in East Asia, with South Korean exports, especially of computer chips, rising by 25 per cent in 1999 and the first half of 2000.[5]

The sustained expansion of the 1990s led many commentators to assume that a 'new economy' had developed in the USA, which was now pioneering a new path for the world. This new economy comprised for the most part firms closely linked to the digital revolution and the growth of the Internet, in which the business cycle (so the argument went) no longer operated. One exponent of this theory was Alan Greenspan, Chairman of the Federal Reserve Board,[6] who argued that the information technology sector was responsible for what the economist J.A. Schumpeter (1883–1950) had called a process of 'creative destruction'; in other words, the replacement of old technology by new (just as the internal combustion engine had superseded steam power in the first half of the twentieth century). Advances in fibre optics, computing, software and in the sophistication of the World Wide Web, all coming together in the 1990s, had fundamentally altered the economic environment. Their ramifications extended to the whole economy and could be seen at work in higher productivity figures, low inflation, healthy growth and an uninterrupted stock market boom. Greenspan pointed out that computer modelling had 'dramatically reduced the time and cost' needed in the construction of items ranging from automobiles to commercial aircraft to skyscrapers. It had assisted the emergence of a more 'flexible' economy. Employers no longer needed to keep large inventories or surplus labour as a reserve against surges in demand: now the new technologies enabled them to operate systems of 'just in time' (JIT) production, which dramatically reduced costs per unit of output and allowed for high rates of return.

These were ambitious claims and were not based on firm foundations. To begin with, the strong growth experienced in the second term of President Clinton (1996–2000) was boosted by low interest rates and a significant rise in public spending. Federal, state and local infrastructure investment grew at an annual rate of 8.5 per cent, which compared well with an increase per annum of 10.5 per cent for business investment over the same period.[7] Second, the brisk (4.6 per cent) expansion in private spending, both on consumption and investment, which characterized the 1990s, was down to a rise in borrowing, with the level of debt reaching 165 per cent of private disposable income – a record – in the first quarter of 2001, while corporate debt also hit unprecedented heights at 74 per cent of corporate GDP.[8] The process was reflected in the international economic position of the United States, which by 2002 was the world's largest debtor country, with a net indebtedness to the rest of the world of $2.2 trillion. Third, from the end of 2000 there were distinct signs of overcapacity in the economy, with a last-quarter reduction in non-residential fixed investment, a decline in spending on software and sharp falls on Wall Street, the heaviest occurring in the 'dotcom' information technology firms that had been supposed to be at the forefront of the transformation to the new economy. It appeared that the expansion of the 1990s had after all ended in a speculative boom and bust; the business cycle lived on.

In the end it is arguable that the expansion of the 1990s could not be explained by reference to the 'new economy'. The period did see a real shift towards information technology, but this does not seem to have been the main factor in improving productivity: one survey concluded that between 1995 and 1999 it was responsible for just 0.07 per cent of a jump in productivity growth from an annual average of 1.42 per cent to one of 2.75 per cent.[9] Furthermore, the use of information technology was not spread evenly across the economy: the larger share continued to go, as in the previous decade, into the service sector; in the early 1990s as much as 76.6 per cent of computing input into business occurred within finance, insurance, real estate (FIRE) and trade.[10]

◆ Financialization

The evidence does not support the existence of a 'Schumpeterian gale of "creative" destruction' in the 1990s, but the information technology revolution did stimulate the expansion of the financial sector, both within the USA and globally. In doing so it played a crucial part in the development of globalization, a process that occurred on three levels. First of all, the Internet and email stimulated the creation of a single market for international financial transactions – they were easy to use and yet highly sophisticated. Players in the financial markets increasingly turned to the computer for their dealings and in so doing constructed one integrated, international system. Second, the web, email and the automated teller machine made it possible to arrange the movement of money across national boundaries at the press of a button. Third, as Susan Strange has remarked, innovation in computing encouraged innovation in finance,[11] all the way from the Eurodollar to the junk bonds that had facilitated the takeovers of the 1980s and the derivatives of the 1990s.

The IMF judged the growth of trading in derivatives to be the decade's most important innovation within the international financial system.[12] It involved dealing in the futures markets (this could cover foreign currencies and all kinds of commodities): deals were basically agreements, made well in advance of the actual time of the transaction, on the price of goods to be traded between buyer and seller. Their purpose was to protect participants in the market against losses arising from unpredictable movements in prices and exchange rates (especially important during the long era of floating). The opportunities afforded by the new technology and lax regulatory framework of the period led fund managers to invent increasingly complex financial instruments, so much so that by 2001 a 'Derivatives Dictionary' had appeared, appropriately enough, on the web.

Some of these instruments, known as hedge funds, revolved around bets on fluctuations in the market. Thus one form of hedge fund activity involved promises to deliver stock at a future date at an agreed price. For example, the owner of the fund might borrow stock from its owner and make a handsome profit by selling it 'short' – in other words, anticipating a fall in its price, and then repurchasing at the lower price. The transaction would leave the hedge fund with a handsome profit that could then be used to purchase assets whose values were rising in the expectation that these would deliver speculative gains (a 'long' position). Many of these deals were highly leveraged: funds used large volumes of borrowed stock, offering rather modest collateral to the owners, as the basis of their 'long' positions in the market – but the returns to be made from this activity were generally good enough to persuade the owners that the fund would always keep its promises. Krugman has noted that successful funds were able to take positions as much as 100 times larger than their owners' capital; in such cases a gain of 1 per cent in the price of their assets (or a fall of 1 per cent in the value of their liabilities) doubled the value of the original capital.[13] By the mid-1990s hedge funds such as Long Term Capital Management (LCTM) and George Soros's Quantum Fund were dealing in billions of dollars in financial markets throughout the world. Their activities were causes of concern to national governments that seemed unable to control these products of the globalized financial markets. Soros had been able to precipitate a sterling devaluation in 1992 when he sold the currency short on so grand a scale that the Bank of England did not have enough reserves to defend it. The Mexican peso's collapse in 1994–5 was also attributed to hedge fund activities.

The trade in derivatives and the expansion of the FIRE sector, a trend notice-able in the UK, the European Union and in East Asian markets, even if the USA led the way, was called 'financialization'.[14] The term reflected two develop-ments. First, there was the rapid expansion in volume of trade throughout the financial sector. Between 1986 and 1996 'bond issues tripled, securities issues increased tenfold and foreign exchange transactions quadrupled'. By 1995 the value of outstanding derivative contracts in 26 countries amounted to $47 tril-lion, double the world economic output at the time.[15] At the end of the twenti-eth century it was estimated that the *daily* value of foreign currency transactions was as much as $1.5 trillion, a figure that made the value of trade in goods and services seem puny: at an annual level of $6.5 trillion in 1998 it was equal to only four days of trading in the international currency markets.[16]

Second, financialization involved a pronounced tendency on the part of fund owners to search for short-term, speculative gain. Over 80 per cent of foreign exchange transactions were completed within a week and 40 per cent of them in less than two days.[17] At the same time, foreign direct investment was out-stripped by foreign portfolio investment, which was responsible for as much as one-third of all private investment in developing countries between 1990 and 1997. In Argentina, Brazil, Mexico, Thailand and South Korea this flow exceeded direct investment. These funds, invested in real estate and in the local stock markets, increased the vulnerability of the recipient economies to desta-bilizing capital outflows given that with the liberal financial markets of the day investors could sell their shares whenever they began to suspect that maximum profits had been made or that there were difficulties around the corner. Yet the capriciousness of portfolio managers, of hedge funds, and of corporate financial giants such as Citibank (whose business accounted for 7.75 per cent of the global market by 2000) and Morgan Stanley was not restricted to the developing world: in December 2002 an 'equity strategist' for the latter advised investors to 'look for the union label and run the other way'. The pension and health care plans for employees rendered unionized companies, even if they were rooted in the USA, 'toxic' to investors, who were advised to reward their non-unionized competitors accordingly.[18]

The financialization of the 1990s brought to a climax a process that had started some 30 years before, with the rise of the Eurodollar markets. These large funds had been responsible for starting an erosion of the controls that had supported the postwar social-democratic settlement. By the end of the century the nationally regulated financial systems of the 1960s had been transformed into a single global market characterized by minimal regulations and highly volatile capital movements.[19] Information technology, the mobility of money and the pressure for rapid returns on investment not only fed the development of an increasing short-termism but led governments to feel a growing anxiety about losing credibility with the capital markets. This fear, often reinforced by advice from the institutional pillars of the Washington consensus, the IMF, the World Bank and the US Treasury, led governments, especially those in the developing world, to continue offering international capital the concessions that had become common in the 1980s under the World Bank SAL programmes in order to secure and then retain investment. Favourable tax regimes (and tax havens) multiplied, state-owned enterprises were privatized and sold cheaply to foreign corporations, food and fuel subsidies were reduced or removed, and public investment programmes were cut.[20] Globalization was welcomed by professional economists and bankers convinced that the free market provided the only route to prosperity, but to many countries dependent on inflows of capital it set off 'a race to the bottom' in which the only chance of reward from what looked increasingly like a global casino came from policies that added to the social insecurity of their populations.[21]

◆ Multinational Firms and World Trade Liberalization

Globalization was also driven by the multinational firms, whose expansion in the period after 1960 was one of the most striking features of the world economy during the last decades of the twentieth century. By 2000, 50 of the largest 100 economies in the world were not countries but companies. Mitsubishi's product, for example, was larger than the output of the Saudi Arabian economy; General Motors' was greater than that of Greece, Norway, Denmark or South Africa; Royal Dutch Shell's exceeded that of Venezuela. By 2000 the combined sales of the world's leading 200 corporations had outrun those of all but the ten largest national economies, while from 1983 to 1999 their profits had risen by 362.4 per cent. Over the same period the number of employees in the top 200 multinationals had expanded by just 14.4 per cent.[22]

Two factors accounted for this remarkable progress. First, the market power of the corporation enabled it to ensure that there was generally an increasing margin of prices over production costs. This could be achieved by passing on higher costs to the consumer, by an intensification of the advertising effort to stimulate sales, by the employment of researchers to produce designs that would cut production costs and by the use of smart lawyers with a brief to protect the monopoly position of the firm. Prime production costs (labour and materials) fell as the proportion of this non-production staff grew relative to production staff. In 1997 Microsoft's prime production costs accounted for less than 10 per cent of sales revenue.[23] Nike, globally famous for its sportswear, contracted out production to factories in China, Indonesia and Vietnam, where wage rates were extraordinarily low. It directly employed a few thousand in management, advertising and sales promotion (8000 of these in 1992) and concentrated not on production but on promotion of its brand.[24] By 1996 the corporation was using 25,000 workers to produce 70 million shoes a year for $2.23 per worker per day, while the footwear sold in the USA for between $45 and $100 a pair.

The long-term trend to rising corporate profits became pronounced in the later 1990s. *Business Week* pointed out that in the second quarter of 1999 there was a 28 per cent rise in the profits of the 900 companies whose fortunes it followed on its Corporate Scoreboard.[25] It was a development that fuelled the euphoria about the 'new economy', but in fact it led to the intensification of a problem first identified by J.A. Hobson (1858–1940) and Thorstein Veblen (1857–1929) and taken further by Baran and Sweezy in the early 1960s with their analysis, *Monopoly Capital*. This revolved around the tendency of the corporation to generate what Baran and Sweezy called a 'rising surplus' – in other words, profits plus depreciation plus net interest, while wage levels were stagnant. This 'surplus' could be ploughed back into investment in the expansion of capacity; but there was no guarantee that there would be sufficient numbers of consumers to buy the product at prices that would ensure a continuing flow of profits. Less controversially perhaps, the problem can be viewed simply as 'How can the modern corporation sustain its profit margins given the tendency of effective demand (given prevailing wage rates) to fall below what is required to absorb all that it is capable of producing?' The Keynesian revolution had for a time resolved this problem within the boundaries of the nation state, but the failure to extend this *internationally*, with the rejection of the Clearing Union scheme in the 1940s and then of the Brandt Report in the 1980s, meant that there was no mechanism for sustaining global demand at a level that would ensure high or full levels of production and employment. As production became increasingly internationalized, the failure to create a mass global market combined with the increasing capacity of the large corporation to generate 'overproduction', particularly of the advanced industrial goods enjoyed by consumers in the developed world, such as automobiles, pharmaceuticals and telecommunications.[26]

How could the high profits of the 1990s be compatible with overproduction? One answer could be found in the ability of the multinational firm to build for itself a congenial international environment – in other words, one that would allow it to retain its market share. This dynamic was most obvious during the last years of the twentieth century in an unprecedented cross-border merger wave that took place mostly between corporations in the developed economies. In 1999, 70 per cent of these cross-border mergers and acquisitions were 'horizontal' – that is, they took place between different firms in the same industry (as opposed to 'vertical' – that is, between firms involved in different stages of the production process for one particular commodity).[27] Indeed during the first three quarters of 1999 the overall value of mergers and acquisitions reached $608 billion, a value never before achieved and one that was reflected in booming activity on the stock markets, especially in the USA and the UK.

Usually mergers were organized in the sectors most characterized by overproduction, although there were also horizontal deals in less advanced industries such as food and drink, and tobacco. Their purpose was to reduce competition through the simple strategy of joining with or swallowing a competitor. This would preserve competitiveness by eliminating excess capacity and spreading investments. There were some record-breaking examples.

America Online (AOL) purchased Time Warner in 2000 in a deal amounting to $183 billion, then the largest in history and only to be superseded by a merger between Vodafone and Mannesman costing $199 billion. In 1998, Daimler-Benz and Chrysler came together to create a car company worth $130 billion; this was 'the first car colossus', according to *Business Week*, and was created to rationalize production in an industry that had the capacity to build 15 million more automobiles a year than would be sold.[28] Firms in the pharmaceutical industry featured in the leading ten mergers and acquisitions every year throughout the 1990s, suggesting a major restructuring within this sector. By the start of the new millennium the ten largest firms in their sectors controlled 35 per cent of the pharmaceutical industry worldwide and 86 per cent of global telecommunications.[29]

The merger wave heralded an attempt by the large corporations to dominate the international economy and even write the rules governing international trade and investment flows. This was attempted on two levels. First, multinational banks and corporations co-operated with national governments throughout the advanced industrial world to push for continuing removal of barriers to trade: overproduction could only be relieved by market expansion. During the 1990s they campaigned for a Multilateral Agreement on Investment (MAI) and a General Agreement on Trade in Services (GATS). The MAI had been drafted by a corporate organization, the International Chamber of Commerce (ICC), and its US affiliate, the Council for International Business (CIB). The ICC's members included the world's largest companies, such as Bayer, BP, General Motors, Hyundai, Shell, Toshiba and Zeneca, in 130 countries. The CIB, founded in 1945 to promote what it called 'an open system of world trade, investment and finance', by the end of the century counted among its members over 300 leading corporations, law firms and banks.

The draft MAI agreement was approved by the OECD and taken to the new World Trade Organization, established at the conclusion of the Uruguay Round in 1994 to take over from the GATT. Talks between OECD members were continued in secret. The document gave multinational corporations the same rights in international law as national governments. Along with a sister treaty applicable to the less developed economies, the Multilateral Investment Agreement (MIA), it was designed to remove all discrimination from multinational firms and all discretion over the use of foreign investment by national governments. Governments intent on privatizing an industry would be forbidden from preferring domestic buyers. It would be illegal for nation states to require foreign investors to fulfil any criteria, such as local employment, domestic content or technology transfer.[30] Corporations would have been entitled to sue governments for taking actions that were deemed to have reduced profits, even if these actions related to environmental protection, health and safety at work or minimum wage legislation.

The MAI and MIA ran into opposition and failed to progress beyond the draft stage despite the support they received from the corporate world; but they both provided a clear signal of the intentions of the multinational firms. And the frustration of the two treaties did not stop the corporations from pushing ahead with their agenda, as the sequel to the Uruguay Round was to demonstrate. The Round had finished in 1994 not just with the creation of the WTO but with the establishment of the GATS, whose reach extends into banking and telecommunications as well as into public services. European, American and Japanese firms were especially keen to progress liberalization under the GATS, which covered the fastest-growing sectors in the advanced economies, and worked with their governments to this end. Within the European Union bankers and industrialists collaborated on a Liberalisation of Trade in Services (LOTIS) committee to produce an agenda for the removal of barriers to trade in services.[31] There was ongoing liaison on the GATS question between US and European corporations, conducted through the Transatlantic Business Dialogue (TABD), which presented joint industry demands to the EU Trade Commissioner and discussed with him how they could be implemented. The TABD was a major influence behind the radical demands of the EU that less developing countries open their public, financial, professional and business services, as well their telecommunications sectors, to foreign corporations on a basis of complete non-discrimination. Domestic regulations, it was argued, should only be permitted if they were not 'unnecessarily burdensome to trade'. The WTO, operating in closed session, would have the power to rule on this question.[32] The campaign to expand GATS was an extension of the unsuccessful quest for an MAI.

Second, there was a cultural campaign to universalize the values of the market place. This was led by the large media corporations, although large firms from all sectors (for example, Coca-Cola, Disney, Volkswagen and IBM) were keen to identify their product with the highest levels of taste and efficiency as well as with an entire lifestyle supposedly designed to bring relaxation and independence to consumers throughout the world. Indeed, consumer choice was identified with individual freedom while, throughout the advanced industrial world, shopping turned into a leisure pursuit as much as a means to an end – a development reflected in the construction of expensive shopping malls throughout North America, western Europe and parts of Asia. At the same time no field of human activity was left untouched by corporate sponsorship and brand advertising: by 2000 these even embraced all levels of education, especially in the USA, Canada and the UK.[33] Governments and corporations co-operated in the production of learning and training programmes for school pupils, which emphasized the positive values of 'enterprise' and 'free markets', and recruited pupils for campaigns to promote well-known products.[34] The project was a natural function of the corporate need for markets with consumers, its salience reinforced in much of the advanced industrial world by the long hegemony of liberal political economy, stretching back to the 1980s, and by the collapse of the USSR and the 'socialist' alternative to capitalism in 1989–91.

◆ 'The End of History'

The economic and political failure of the Soviet Union and its satellite states in eastern Europe during the 1980s, along with a turn to the market by China after the death of Mao Zedong in 1976, appeared to have left capitalism as the only workable model of political and economic development. The Cold War concluded with the dissolution of the USSR in 1991 but the long struggle was really over by 1989. At this point, with the Soviet leadership committed to internal democratic change and co-operation with the West in foreign policy, and the east European countries abandoning communist regimes in favour of liberal, reformist governments, an American commentator proclaimed 'the end of history'. By this he meant 'the end point of mankind's ideological evolution and the universalization of Western liberal democracy as the final form of human government'.[35] The disappearance of the ideological divide had its economic counterpart: the collapse of the 'socialist' bloc was another landmark on the road to globalization in the form of one integrated world market.

The Soviet bloc had not always been as decrepit as it appeared to have become in the 1980s. During the 1950s and 1960s the USSR had enjoyed respectable growth (5.7 per cent and 5.2 per cent respectively);[36] but problems had begun to develop during the 1970s. First of all, life expectancy stagnated and shrank. In 1969 Poles, Austrians and Finns could expect to live to just over 70, but by 1989 an Austrian or a Finn could anticipate four more years of life than a Pole. During the 1970s and 1980s the Soviet Union, its own plentiful resources notwithstanding, became dependent on imports of grain from the USA as growth slowed to just 2 per cent. Yet for a time the public were sheltered from the consequences of slow growth by oil exports: the USSR was a significant producer and enjoyed buoyant revenues after the price rises of 1973–4 and 1979. The money flowed in and major reforms to the country's economy were postponed.

One of the problems facing reformers was that a new approach to economic policy was not necessarily compatible with the existence of Communist Party rule. The developmental model that had generated good growth in the 1950s and 1960s had revolved around import substitution and state-led investment. It seemed to work as long as there were labour reserves that could be drawn from the land to the cities; this was an 'extensive' approach to growth, based on increasing the inputs of labour and capital. The strategy allowed the Party both to supervise and to conduct the economic planning exercise through the agency of its own technocrats, who would be responsible for meeting targets. It had been successful at building (indeed rebuilding after the destruction of the war) the infrastructure of a modern economy. By the late 1960s most of the Soviet bloc appeared to have efficient energy, transport, heavy industry, housing, health care and education sectors. The level of social provision compared well with that of western Europe, and full employment was maintained throughout the 1970s.

The drawback of this strategy was that it produced rather drab living standards, resulting from the high levels of investment being devoted to heavy industry and armaments. This was in marked contrast to the western states. Moreover, the loss of surplus labour by the end of the 1960s required a new policy for growth that would now have to be founded on 'intensive' development – in other words, on the improvement of productivity via the restructuring of existing technology and labour, and on innovation. In the USSR during the 1980s this was known as *perestroika*, a deliberate attempt at social and economic 'reconstruction' that included room for limited private ownership and profitability in industry. It aroused hostility within the Party where more conservative elements sought to retain the centralized and collectivist system of the post-Stalin era. The result was a political stalemate, not an economic transformation. The satellite governments sought to diversify through production for export markets in the hope that this would generate enough foreign exchange to drive new investment and lead to an industrial structure capable of producing more consumer goods for local as well as international markets.

The results were disappointing. The Party bureaucracies were suspicious of attempts at restructuring, especially those that devolved authority to local units and managers (only in Yugoslavia and Hungary was this achieved with any success). The export drives were, in consequence, often conducted with antiquated technology and were set back further by an adverse shift in the terms of trade after the first oil shock. By the early 1980s some Soviet bloc economies were having to increase exports by 33 per cent to finance the same level of imports they had enjoyed prior to 1973.[37] The way out of this without reducing living standards seemed to lie in foreign borrowing, and many east European states became large debtors on the international market. In the absence of genuine economic reform, the borrowing strategy could not generate significant growth, which failed to reach 1 per cent throughout most of the CMEA between 1985 and 1989, against an annual average of 3.6 per cent for the OECD in the same period. Indeed, only debt continued to rise, and by 1990 net debt in Poland had reached $41.8 billion and $9.8 billion in Bulgaria.[38] Neither country was in a position to make regular repayments, while Romania, a country rich in natural resources (including oil), was suffering from regular energy shortages.

The mounting economic failure of the Soviet bloc countries led to a popular crisis of confidence in the Communist Party itself. Throughout eastern Europe (East Germany and Romania excepted) and the USSR opposition to the old model of development continued to spread during the 1980s. By the early 1990s the Communist Party regimes had collapsed in favour of pluralist governments which had adopted free-market policies of varying intensity in an attempt to stimulate the economic reforms that had eluded the old order. Industries were privatized, many prices were decontrolled, foreign investment was welcomed (although in practice the inflow was limited, Czechoslovakia being the leading beneficiary), but the adoption of capitalism resulted in no economic miracles. By 2000 only Hungary, Poland, Slovakia (formerly part of Czechoslovakia but independent after 1993) and Slovenia had GDPs at or above 1989 levels;[39] the dismantling of the old state had undermined demand

and social protection but had failed to attract significant long-term capital from western governments, banks and multinationals, even though this was badly needed to regenerate a set of crumbling infrastructures. Exports continued to stagnate and imports fell so that, free markets notwithstanding, the former Soviet bloc traded less with the rest of the international economy in the 1990s than it had done a generation earlier.

Hungary apart, throughout the Soviet bloc market-oriented policies had only tended to follow from the loss of Party control over economy and society. In China, however, a dramatic economic reform was successfully accomplished while the Party kept its dominant role. China had followed a path of state-led development involving high investment in heavy industry and import substitution during the 1950s and 1960s. This permitted 'extensive' investment and increases in output, with growth per head running at an annual average of 3.6 per cent during 1960–76.[40] The government was determined to improve the performance given a fast-growing population and economic growth consistently twice or more as high in Japan, Singapore and South Korea. The shift away from reliance on the state started at this point on the initiative of the reformist Deng Xiao Ping, whose determination to modernize the country without too much attention to orthodox Communist Party teaching was summed up in his own saying: 'What does it matter whether a cat is black or white as long as it catches mice?'[41]

Reform started with a move away from the system of collective farming that had dominated Chinese agriculture since the 1949 revolution and the introduction of an 'individual responsibility' system. There were improvements in output and the scheme was well received on the land. This initiative was paralleled by the introduction of Town and Village Enterprises (TVEs), which operated outside the centrally planned sector of the economy. The TVEs were able to sell their produce at market prices and reinvest the profits. They grew in response to rising agricultural productivity, which performed two essential roles. First, it generated the accumulation of profits which could then be invested in the economy and, second, it liberated labour from the land, so providing the workforce needed for the growing industrial sector. By 1992 the TVEs were responsible for 33 per cent of all output[42] and employed 100 million people.

The move away from central planning and state ownership of industry was accelerated by inward investment on the part of foreign corporations. The process was encouraged and managed throughout by the Chinese state, which viewed inward investment as essential to the modernization of production. It introduced new equipment, technology transfer and managerial skill, and helped to establish a successful foreign trade sector, a process the Chinese government expected to deliver the same results in terms of growth as it had in the west European and then the East Asian economies during the decades since 1945.[43]

Foreign investment grew from $400 million in 1982 to $308 billion by 2000. Much of the capital came initially from Hong Kong and Taiwan, but during the 1990s it was joined by investment from multinationals based in the USA, Japan and South Korea. The corporations were attracted by the large market and the cheap labour costs, as well as by the government's concessions. China became one of the world's fastest-growing destinations for foreign direct investment, absorbing 1.4 per cent of the world total in 1990, but 6.4 per cent in 1999, by which time it lagged behind only the USA and the EU. To begin with, much of the investment was located in labour-intensive industries, especially textiles, but during the 1990s there was also a noticeable expansion in electrical machinery and electronic exports. Indeed, exports boomed throughout the 1990s, half of the increase being generated by enterprises partly or wholly consisting of foreign investment.[44] By 2000 such firms employed almost 20 million people, or 10 per cent of the non-agricultural labour force.

The result of Deng's revolution was the last great 'miracle' of the twentieth century. China went down the same road as the UK, the USA, western Europe, Japan and East Asia before it. Economic growth was rapid, running at an average rate of 10 per cent during the 1990s. The country's modernization was accompanied by a vast migration from the countryside to the towns, the inevitable by-product of industrialization. There was a steady and considerable reduction in poverty and, by 2000, real income in China and Russia was comparable.[45] The Chinese success was in sharp contrast to the record of the Soviet bloc. It saw the extension of the global market place into the world's most populous country (1.1 billion inhabitants by 2000). Was this the collapse of the last economic frontier?

◆ Globalization in Crisis I: The Consequences of Free Capital Markets

By the mid-1990s at the latest, the forces for globalization appeared to be in the ascendant. The growth of trade, 'financialization', the expansion of the multinationals, and the collapse or transformation of the old command economies was working to draw the world into a single market. These influences were supported by international agencies such as the IMF and the World Bank, which had long promoted liberalization of trade and capital markets; after 1995 their voices were amplified by the new WTO. At another level the process was supported by the advanced industrial nations, which had most to gain from the removal of barriers to the flow of goods, money and services. The US Treasury, historically committed to the goal of a world safe for non-discrimination, was in the vanguard of the struggle. Indeed, the interest of the Treasury and of organizations such as the IMF in the outcome was intensified as a result of their tendency to employ personnel from the global financial community. Individuals such as Robert Rubin, Treasury Secretary under President Clinton, were Chairs of the Executive Committee of Citigroup, the financial conglomerate that owned Citibank. Stan Fischer, Deputy Managing Director of the Fund left his post there to become Vice-Chairman at Citigroup. These were simultaneously public officials and corporate executives, who identified the interests of the global economy with those of the world from which they sprang – for them it was an article of faith that complete freedom of capital movements provided the key to rapid growth.[46]

There were, however, countervailing pressures and by the start of the new century the early emergence of a fully liberalized global economy appeared less certain than it had at the peak of the 1990s expansion. These pressures arose from the instabilities inherent in globalization itself, and from the political reactions it produced in the advanced as well as the developing nations. They all tended to undermine the legitimacy of the free-market ideology that had become so commonplace since the late 1970s.

The crisis of globalization itself operated on three levels. The first was dominated by a financial upheaval that led to widespread fears about the future stability of the international economy. This had its origins in the fashion for capital market liberalization, and started in East Asia. The Tiger economies, acting under advice from the IMF, the World Bank and the US Treasury, had freed their capital markets in 1992–3. Thailand, for example, dropped exchange controls, deregulated its financial system and opened up the economy to inflows of speculative foreign capital. The pattern was followed throughout the region (but not in China) and, by mid-1997, the combined debt to the foreign banks of Indonesia, Malaysia, Thailand, the Philippines and South Korea amounted to $274 billion. Almost two-thirds of this were short-term, and invested in property, especially in Thailand. This was where the trouble started. There was a property boom in Thailand that began to slow in the summer of 1997. Fund managers became anxious and began to withdraw money before the value of the assets held in their portfolios collapsed. These problems were intensified by setbacks in export markets: the currency, the baht, began to appear overvalued, especially against the yen. The baht came under pressure in the foreign exchange markets and the government attempted to support it with currency swaps, fearing that devaluation would ruin many who had borrowed in foreign currency (especially dollars and yen).

It proved impossible for the Thai government to hold the baht; it did not have the resources of the foreign exchange dealers who had bet on a devaluation and therefore sold the currency by the million. The measures undertaken to hold the baht merely intensified the crisis: high interest rates and spending cuts provoked business closures and unemployment, which left banks holding a growing volume of bad debts. This led the banks to curtail their lending and call in loans, steps that only exacerbated the difficulties facing Thai enterprise and added to the economy's downward spiral. The crash failed to assure foreign investors, who continued to pull their money out of Thailand; by the end of 1997 the baht had fallen 50 per cent against the dollar.

The panic withdrawal of capital from Thailand could not be contained. As the other Tiger economies had opened themselves up so they had borrowed and made themselves vulnerable to the fallout that results from loss of confidence.

Given the absence of exchange controls and the tendency of financial flows to be lumped into what were called 'emerging market funds' (and East Asia belonged to the category of 'emerging markets'), the crisis soon started to spread throughout the region, fed by rumours that the Indonesian and Malaysian currencies were about to collapse, while indebtedness was about to overwhelm the South Korean financial system.[47] The difficulties that had confronted the Thai economy became more general and provoked a massive IMF rescue package, worth $120 billion.

The money was used to bail out the creditors of the East Asian economies. A condition of the aid was that governments ensure that debt servicing continue while the Fund persuaded the creditors to roll over or restructure the debts.[48] The IMF sought to apply all the lessons of the conventional wisdom summarized in the 'Washington consensus'. Convinced that economic development could not be achieved in the absence of capital market liberalization it urged the victims of the crisis to balance their budgets through spending cuts, privatize sectors of the economy and ratchet up interest rates to attract foreign investors back to the region. The restoration of the 'confidence' that would generate a new inflow of capital required strict adherence to the neo-liberal orthodoxy that had reappeared after 1979.

The package may have insulated the creditors from the consequences of the financial crisis but the effects were devastating. Output collapsed and unemployment rose sharply; 25 per cent of the urban population of South Korea descended into poverty. In 1998 GDP shrank by 13.1 per cent in Indonesia, by 10.8 per cent in Thailand and by 6.7 per cent in South Korea. IMF insistence on the abolition of subsidies on food and kerosene (the cooking fuel most commonly used by the poor) in Indonesia led to a wave of rioting and protest, which threatened the social stability of the state itself.[49] The impact of the East Asian slowdown was not, however, confined to the region. It set back the growth of the world economy, causing a fall in commodity prices. Oil exporters suffered from falling revenues, the price dropping 40 per cent below the 1997 average in the first half of 1998.[50] This was especially bad for Russia, whose reliance on the raw material had increased as the economy failed to respond to post-Communist policies. Russian vulnerability was intensified by its exchange rate policy: on the advice of the IMF it had sought with some success to attract international capital by maintaining an overvalued rouble against the dollar. The high rate now combined with low oil prices to put a question mark against the profitability of Russian production. The international financial instability moved into Russia.

During the 1990s the Russian reformers, advised by the IMF, had embarked on a rapid privatization programme. At the same time, they had deregulated prices. It was a fatal combination of policies. Privatization of what had been state monopolies was not accompanied by a competition policy or by any restructuring of the companies. The new owners turned out to be political supporters of President Yeltsin – wealthy oligarchs, many of whom had hitherto occupied privileged positions in the old Party apparatus and within industry.

They were able to make a killing by allowing prices, especially in the energy sector, to rise. At the same time, this development fuelled a dramatic spurt in inflation that undermined the value of ordinary people's savings even as the oligarchs turned their profits into dollars and exported them out of the country into offshore bank accounts. There was a massive capital outflow. Even before the world slowdown and the fall in the price of oil, the Russian economy had been in trouble, with GDP shrinking most years after 1990. Now there was a crisis of confidence in the rouble. Once again the IMF stepped in with a bail-out programme, this time worth $22.6 billion (just over 50 per cent provided by the IMF itself). It called for the maintenance of the rouble's high value, arguing that this was a brake on inflation and made it cheap to borrow foreign currencies. Interest rates went up to 150 per cent but the capital flight continued. By 1999, the GDP was down 54 per cent on its 1990 level.

Just as they had in East Asia, the capital markets won. The rouble collapsed and was devalued so that in early 1999 it was 45 per cent lower against the dollar than it had been in the summer of 1998. The fall of the rouble sparked the extension of the crisis to Latin America. Investors, noting the slow growth of the Brazilian economy, began to speculate against its currency, the real. Among them were some hedge funds that had been burned by the Russian crisis and were now facing a growing number of margin calls; in other words, the funds' creditors were asking for larger deposits or for repayment from the operators. In these circumstances hedge fund managers needed to realize assets fast and even then some were unable to raise the money unless they sold stock heavily. One major fund, Long Term Capital Management (LTCM), required a rescue in case its failure sparked off a global wave of panic selling.[51] This loss of confidence was fed by Brazil's budget deficit and the markets became convinced that the country was a bad risk, the successor to the East Asian and Russian economies. In fact, the deficit was modest. The government had no difficulty in financing it and some European states had budget deficits that occupied larger shares of national income than Brazil's. But the free international financial environment allowed the investors and fund managers to make the rules. Objective indicators no longer mattered. As Krugman has noted, the belief of investors that Brazil would run into economic crisis because of its budget deficit became a self-fulfilling prophecy since their fears would lead them to precipitate this very crisis by causing them to withdraw their capital, which is exactly what happened in January 1999, when the real was devalued.[52]

Although the crisis of 1997–8 was not a function of irresponsible policies in East Asia and Latin America (Russia was slightly different), those who had long argued in favour of global freedom for capital sought to make it seem that way. The IMF, the US Treasury and Wall Street consensus was that the East Asian economies were in the grip of 'crony capitalism' – that is, corrupt interconnections between their finance, industry and politics. These had been responsible for foolish lending policies and an absence of transparency in commercial dealings, as a result of which foreign investors had lost confidence. Yet whatever the truth about 'crony capitalism', it had not prevented foreign portfolio managers and corporations from dealing with these countries over many years, nor had it been mentioned when the East Asian economic miracles had been in full swing in the period from the early 1980s to the mid-1990s. The real problem was the absence of controls over the movement of international money, a systemic flaw in the model of globalization favoured by the international financial community and by the advocates of liberal orthodoxy. This had been the destabilizing factor, something understood by a growing number of leading economists such as Paul Krugman and Joseph Stiglitz.

The economists' analysis was provided with empirical support by the experiences of Malaysia, China, South Korea and Russia during the 1997–8 crisis. Malaysia introduced capital controls and froze the repatriation of foreign capital for 12 months. These reforms allowed the country to cut interest rates, which made for many fewer bankruptcies here than elsewhere in the other East Asian economies, and for a steady recovery. China's move away from state socialism had not led its rulers to liberalize its capital controls. Its currency was not freely convertible and it had taken care to encourage the inflow of foreign direct, as opposed to the more volatile foreign portfolio, investment. It was therefore relatively insulated from the destabilizing exodus of money experienced by other developing East Asian economies, a position that allowed an independent national economic policy at the height of the crisis; the state undertook a $200 billion public spending programme on infrastructure, funded by national savings. China, like Malaysia following a Keynesian strategy (the political background of its leadership notwithstanding), was able to avoid a growth slowdown. South Korea, meanwhile, ignored IMF advice that banks with a low ratio of capital to outstanding loans should be allowed to close; the state itself moved in to recapitalize the overextended banking sector.[53] Meanwhile, Russia's fortunes started to improve after it had finally rejected IMF advice that it support the rouble and pay its debts. Having allowed devaluation and announced a default, the Russian government began to see real economic growth. This was stimulated partly by improved revenues from oil exports as the price started to rise again in 2000 and partly by the new-won economic independence that permitted a substantial reduction in interest rates. The combination of cheaper money with devaluation generated the expansion of production for the domestic market at the expense of imports.

The crisis of 1998–9 not only punctured the optimism of economists who believed that the world economy was on the verge of an era of unprecedented expansion driven by free-market policies, it also exposed the unsustainability of the liberal economic version of free-market globalization that had developed over the previous generation. A system based on non-intervention was not only inherently unstable but contained no mechanism that would prevent the globalization of one country's or one region's financial crisis, apart from drastic deflationary measures. These would bring to a grinding halt, and even reverse, the expansion such a system was supposed to guarantee. The nations that rode the storm most effectively were those that had either never accepted the free market or were prepared to curtail it – even in the USA the New York Federal Reserve had had to intervene to co-ordinate the rescue of LTCM.

The result was a shift away from the Washington consensus. It became respectable for economists to advocate intervention in the foreign exchange markets, either through controls (recommended by Krugman and Stiglitz) or via taxation (proposed by James Tobin). The IMF dropped its insistence that nations receiving assistance should take prompt and dramatic steps to balance their budgets[54] and began to consider a bankruptcy procedure for debtor nations. This would replace expensive bail-outs, more beneficial to creditors than debtors, with a code that would effectively allow default or 'standstill' on payments. The USA and the UK in particular began to introduce reforms designed to tighten offshore banking practices – though these measures were also reactions to the 11 September 2001 attack on the World Trade Center in New York, and some were therefore directed against terrorist organizations that had been able to shelter behind the liberal international financial regime. At a popular level, the Jubilee campaign for international debt forgiveness, led in the developed world by voluntary organizations and churches, succeeded in persuading governments and international agencies to write off $45 billion of debt. Its pressure helped to establish a $50 billion fund under the World Bank's Highly Indebted Poor Countries programme. There was an increase in official spending on overseas aid by developing nations, a turnaround from the orthodox faith in the private sector, which had marked the period since the Cancun summit of 1982. None of this pointed to an early move towards the kind of international monetary system envisaged in the Clearing Union scheme or in the Brandt Report, but it did signal a widening appreciation in governments and international agencies that globalization was bedevilled by its own contradictions and that these could not be resolved in the absence of interventionist policies.

◆ Globalization in Crisis II: Trade and Politics

The other two levels on which the crisis faced by globalization operated were political as much as economic. They derived from reactions to globalization on the part, first, of governments and, second, of popular protest in the developed and underdeveloped economies. These reactions were all stimulated by efforts to take the liberalization of the international trading system another stage beyond the Uruguay Round, which had been concluded in 1994.

The failure of the MAI and MIA treaties was evidence that governments could halt the momentum to globalization if they believed that doing so was in the national interest. Third World countries were vigorously opposed to both treaties, especially to the MIA which, they argued, would turn them into economic colonies. Early in 1996 the draft documents were subject to opposition in eight leading developing states, including India and Indonesia, which expressed their anxiety that the MIA would prevent their governments from managing flows of foreign investment in ways that would promote national development. Their opposition derailed the progress of the treaty. Talks proceeded within a working group established by the WTO, where they made little progress.

The difficulties facing the MIA treaty were paralleled by the history of the MAI talks. The success of these was critical to the joint undertaking. During the early stages (from 1995–7) the relevant parties co-operated efficiently. However, during 1997 the draft was leaked to politicians and the public, most of whom had never heard of the negotiations. There was a wave of protest. Public anxiety at what appeared to be the most severe erosion of economic sovereignty seen since 1945 became apparent throughout most of the OECD. This could not be ignored by governments, and national representatives at the MAI nego- tiations started to make difficulties. Those from the USA called for exemption for sub-federal law, providing states and localities with immunity from the treaty; the EU called for positive discrimination in favour of local investment in regional organizations such as itself, a concession that would have rendered the MAI meaningless in the world's second largest economic bloc; the French and the Canadians argued that culture should be entirely removed from the MAI. The talks made no headway and the deadline for ratification of the agreement (May 1998) was missed. It was the end of the road for the MAI and its sister treaty, a demonstration that globalization was not inevitable and that not just its own flaws, but politics, would impose a limit on how far it could go, just as they had with the US crusade for non-discrimination in the 1940s and 1950s.

The MAI talks turned globalization into an international political issue. They intensified the misgivings of the LDCs and generated a growing popular unease about it in the advanced industrial states. Third World leaders argued that the essential problem was that globalization was one-sided, a process run by the rich for the benefit of the rich. The OECD nations and the agencies they dominated, such as the IMF, the World Bank and the WTO, were accused of sponsoring pol- icies (such as the deflationary packages forced on the East Asian economies in 1998) that they would never have followed themselves. There was some justifi- cation in this given the history of Reaganomics in the 1980s and the increase in federal spending sanctioned by the Clinton administration after 1996.

The double standards were not limited to macroeconomic policies. They extended to trade. OECD members argued for freedom of trade in investment and services, where they had a comparative advantage. But they were not keen to apply a liberal regime to sectors of their own economies that were vulnerable to competition from developing nations. In 2002 the USA imposed tariffs on steel imports, citing cheap competition from South Korea and Brazil, as well as from OECD economies such as Japan.[55] As a result of lobbying from the US shipping industry little was done to liberalize the world's maritime transport industry. Under pressure from the pharmaceutical corporations OECD governments resisted a campaign on the part of the LDCs to override drug patents in the interests of public health. The large firms defended their intellectual property rights even though liberalization would allow LDC governments to develop cheap alternatives to the high-cost drugs produced in the developed world and so combat the many and various epidemics, of which AIDS was the most serious, that were killing millions.[56] At the same time the industrialized states would not open up their agricultural sectors to competition from Third World producers. It followed that developing states were denied export markets while their own agricultural sectors were undermined by subsidized competition. Thus Jamaican dairy producers were having to dump their own produce because they could not compete with cheap imports from the EU (whose dairy industry received £1.1 billion a year in subsidies). The tomato processing industry in West Africa was undercut by low-cost competition from Italy. Maize farmers in the Philippines endured falling incomes because they could not compete with US imports.[57]

Frustration with the process of globalization erupted at the WTO conference in Seattle at the end of 1999. This was meant to prepare the ground for a new round of trade liberalization, but the meeting was a fiasco. LDC governments made it clear that they would refuse to sign any text that failed to include substantial concessions on the part of the wealthy countries. But so little progress was made with agricultural protectionism, patents or even with the reduction of barriers to the export of textiles that the talks were abandoned without reaching any consensus on the agenda for a new round.

OECD countries found that it was not politically feasible to promote globalization where this would endanger sectors of the economy that were regarded as strategic and that were also traditionally capable of mobilizing considerable political support. Willingness to bend to market forces here was not shared by governments or by corporations. It was arguable that liberal rhetoric notwithstanding, the attitude to trade policy was redolent of mercantilism – that is, national power was to be used to open up markets in foreign countries and protect those at home *at the same time*. The exercise was in reality motivated by the corporate priority of extending or at least retaining *market share*. Meanwhile, the LDCs refused to progress globalization because they could see no benefits for themselves: they were being asked to exchange the ability to manage a domestic and foreign investment policy designed to nurture economic growth and the health of their populations for virtually no offsetting benefits in terms of access to markets in the developed world. The evidence tended to support their lack of enthusiasm: during the 1990s the number of people (according to the World Bank definition of income at a level of $2 per day) actually living in poverty increased by almost 100 million.[58] In these circumstances it was not surprising that the drive for trade liberalization ran into the sands early in the new century. There was a new WTO conference at Doha in late 2001, which agreed on the need for a 'development round' whereby OECD nations agreed to reduce agricultural protectionism and act over patent rights, but by the time of writing (May 2003) the results had been modest indeed.

Just as the financial crisis of 1998–9 undermined confidence in the goal of international freedom for capital, so Seattle and its aftermath revealed that few governments genuinely supported the ongoing reduction of barriers to trade. Whatever governments said about the desirability of globalization as a means of stimulating trade and expansion, the process had run into crisis because there was no consensus on how the institutions that had been sponsoring it – notably the IMF and the WTO – were to proceed. The lack of faith in these institutions shown at an official level, in deeds if not always in words, was reinforced by a growing popular movement whose strength became apparent at Seattle. The conference took place amid a volatile atmosphere generated by mass demonstrations and some rioting on the part of protesters given the blanket description of 'anti-globalization movement', a pattern repeated at a series of economic summits held thereafter.

The term was an oversimplification. The anti-globalization movement was itself a product of globalization. International economic injustice and instability generated a popular reaction against economic liberalism. This became internationalized via the use of information technology. Just as this had accelerated the movement towards a global market place, so it drew together a loose worldwide coalition of democratic socialists and trades unionists, farmers, peasants, green activists, intellectuals, religious organizations such as CAFOD (the Catholic Fund for Overseas Development) and Christian Aid, charities such as OXFAM, environmentalists and anti-capitalist revolutionary groups. These forces came from both the Third World and from advanced industrial states. Similar groups within the framework of the nation state had created the first socialist and social-democratic organizations in Europe, the Americas and Australasia a century before. Now the expansion of capitalism was generating the beginnings of an international alliance opposed to neo-liberalism and its consequences. Members of this growing political movement built their own networks of resistance against the consequences of corporate globalization. These functioned at a local level, but the campaigns tended to have common themes that jumped national boundaries – multinational capital bred multinational protest. Thus Bangladeshi women garment workers fought against sweatshop conditions, while in San Francisco demonstrations against the same conditions took place outside Gap shops; protests in Madrid and London targeted the cities' stock exchanges; a G8 (the world's eight largest economies) economic summit in Cologne was an occasion for a counter-summit that was joined by 500 farmers who had travelled from India.[59] Few within this growing political movement were advocates of rolling back globalization in the sense of taking steps to reduce the volume of world trade, although what were seen as the engines of globalization, namely the multinationals and the Bretton Woods organizations, were the subject of radical criticism.

The size as well as the diversity of this coalition became obvious with the emergence of the World Social Forum (WSF), which held its first meeting in Porto Alegre, Brazil, late in 2001. Over the next two years, attendance at the WSF increased to over 100,000 and by 2003 it was at the heart of an international network, all of whose members campaigned to promote alternatives to neo-liberalism and the globalization of the 1990s. The WSF argued that 'another world is possible' – at a minimum this meant a new international financial regime, debt forgiveness, basic labour, income and education stand-ards, fair trading rules and the prioritization of environmental protection over corporate profit. But many in the WSF and anti-globalization movement sought a new relationship between the rich and the poor countries, and an international economic and political order that would place economic exchange at the service of social justice and democracy.[60]

The new century had opened paradoxically. The world economy was more integrated than at any time since the start of the Great Depression. The long struggle to make the world safe for liberal capitalism, which the USA had started during the Second World War, appeared to be nearing final success. Yet at no time in the past 20 years had capitalism's instabilities and injustices been more obvious or its international reputation lower. Political developments throughout the world reflected its unpopularity. In Latin America electorates voted in radical left and populist administrations, notably in Venezuela in 1998 and in Brazil in 2002. Reformed communist parties remained influential in eastern Europe. The Indians exchanged the socialist aspirations of the Congress for the economic and political nationalism of the Bharatiya Janata Party. The Chinese and Malaysian administrations ignored the orthodox advice of the IMF, while the South Koreans, having tried it, returned to interventionism. The kernel of an alternative international political economy, with popular support, had begun to emerge in movements such as the WSF. Meanwhile, even governments in the developed world showed themselves unwilling to accept the full implications of the free market gospel they preached to the Third World. Had neo-liberalism and corporate globalization already passed their high-water mark?

◆ Notes

1. International Monetary Fund, *World Economic Outlook*, October 2001 (Washington).
2. Henry Wai-chung Yeung, Peter Dicken, Jeffrey Henderson, Martin Hess and Neil Coe, 'Foreign direct investment, trade, and global production networks in East Asia', presented at the Third Annual Development Conference on 'Blending Local and Global Knowledge', Rio de Janeiro, 9–12 December 2001, Table 4.
3. Ellwood, *The No-Nonsense Guide to Globalization*, 54.
4. Wynne Godley, 'What if they start saving again?', *London Review of Books* 22(13), 6 July 2000.
5. Carnegie Hill Partners, *US Trade Balance, 1990–1999* and Larry Elliott, 'When Uncle Sam sneezes, watch out Asia', *Guardian*, 4 December 2000.
6. In a speech on 'Structural Change in the New Economy' delivered to the National Governors' Association on 11 July 2000.

7. *Business Week*, 6 August 2001.
8. Godley, 'What if they start saving again?'
9. Survey by Robert Gordon (North Western University), quoted by John Bellamy Foster, Harry Magdoff and Paul Sweezy, 'The new economy: myth and reality', *Monthly Review*, volume 52, no. 11 (2001), 5–6.
10. Ibid.
11. Strange, *Mad Money*, 17–18.
12. Ibid., 26.
13. Paul Krugman, *The Return of Depression Economics* (London: Penguin, 2000), 120.
14. Kevin Phillips, 'The cycles of financial scandal', *New York Times*, 17 July 2002.
15. Strange, *Mad Money*, 19, 29.
16. Ellwood, *The No-Nonsense Guide to Globalization*, 72.
17. Ibid., 74.
18. Advice reproduced on the website of the International Union of Food, Agricultural, Hotel, Restaurant, Catering, Tobacco and Allied Workers' Associations (IUF), 12 December 2002.
19. Strange, *Mad Money*, 16.
20. Palast, *The Best Democracy Money Can Buy* and Joseph Stiglitz, *Globalization and its Discontents* (London: Allen Lane, 2002), 97–8 ff.
21. Ellwood, *The No-Nonsense Guide to Globalization*, 100.
22. Sarah Anderson and John Cavanagh, *The Rise of Corporate Global Power* (London: Institute for Policy Studies, 2000).
23. John Bellamy Foster, 'Monopoly capital at the turn of the millennium', *Monthly Review* 51(11) (2000), 8.
24. See Naomi Klein, *No Logo* (London: Flamingo, 2002), Ch. 1.
25. *Business Week*, 2 August 1999, 28–31; 16 August 1999, 88–90; 27 December 1999, 52–5; quoted in Foster, 'Monopoly capital at the turn of the millennium'.
26. The tendency of the advanced industrial state to overproduce also forms the kernel of Robert Brenner's thesis in 'The economics of global turbulence', *New Left Review* 229 (1998). However, unlike Baran and Sweezy, he sees this as a recipe for ongoing competition between national economies likely to put downward pressure on costs and prices.
27. United Nations Conference on Trade and Development, *World Investment Report, 2000* (New York and Geneva, 2001) and Eva Cheng, 'What's driving the wave of corporate mergers?', *Weekly Green Left* 438 (2001).
28. Foster, 'Monopoly capital at the turn of the millennium', 11.
29. Ellwood, *The No-Nonsense Guide to Globalization*, 56.
30. Ibid., 65.
31. Palast, *The Best Democracy Money Can Buy*, quote from minutes of a LOTIS meeting held on 22 February 2001, 71.

32. The demands were leaked early in 2002 and can be found on the Internet at www.GATSwatch.org.
33. See Klein, *No Logo*, Ch. 4.
34. Ibid., 94–5.
35. Francis Fukuyama, 'The end of history?', *The National Interest*, summer 1989.
36. Hobsbawm, *Age of Extremes*, 400.
37. Ivan T. Berend, 'The collapse of state socialism', in David F. Good (ed.), *Economic Transformations in East and Central Europe* (London: Routledge, 1994), 78 ff.
38. Berend, 'The collapse of state socialism', 79.
39. Stiglitz, *Globalization and its Discontents*, 153.
40. Solomon, *The Transformation of the World Economy*, 145.
41. Stiglitz, *Globalization and its Discontents*, 184.
42. Solomon, *The Transformation of the World Economy*, 147.
43. Lee Bransletter and Robert Feensta, 'Trade and foreign direct investment in China: a political economy approach', *National Bureau of Economic Research Working Paper* 7100 (Cambridge, MA., 1999), 7.
44. Solomon, *The Transformation of the World Economy*, 150–1.
45. Stiglitz, *Globalization and its Discontents*, 182.
46. Ibid., 207.
47. Krugman, *The Return of Depression Economics*, 97.
48. Ellwood, *The No-Nonsense Guide to Globalization*, 81.
49. Stiglitz, *Globalization and its Discontents*, 77, 97.
50. Ibid., 146.
51. Krugman, *The Return of Depression Economics*, 134.
52. Ibid., 103.
53. Stiglitz, *Globalization and its Discontents*, 116 ff., 126.
54. Ibid., 250.
55. 'Trade war looms over steel dispute', BBC News, 6 March 2002.
56. Naomi Klein, 'Doha, the economic frontline', *Guardian*, 8 November 2001.
57. Larry Elliott, 'It's about putting food in mouths', *Guardian*, 26 November 1999.
58. Stiglitz, *Globalization and its Discontents*, 5.
59. Klein, *No Logo*, 444.
60. See the World Social Forum Charter of Principles, notably paragraphs 4 and 10–12 inclusive.

CONCLUSION

What was the upshot of the period from the 1940s to 2000 in international economic history? In truth, there was not one outcome but several. The first and most obvious was the creation of a worldwide market. This had resulted from the encouragement given by the advanced industrial powers, in particular to the expansion of trade. Trade had helped to sustain the growth that had been generated by the Keynesian and social-democratic approach to postwar reconstruction in western Europe. It became central to the Japanese economic miracle of the 1960s and 1970s, and to the successes of the Tiger economies of the 1980s. In the 1990s Chinese development was accelerated by the accessibility of the US market: the gradual integration of China, with one-fifth of the world's population, into the global economy, and the rapid modernization of what had been a largely peasant, agrarian society not only helped to forge this world market but was unprecedented in world history. This relationship between trade and growth led the nation states that had derived advantages from it to use the GATT and then the WTO to support measures designed to reduce barriers to the flow of goods and capital between them. It was a process backed by the multinational firms and financial corporations whose increasing wealth and power was characteristic of the era and dependent on the expansion of free markets.

Second, the interconnected world that had developed by the end of the twentieth century was one in which hundreds of millions throughout Europe, North America, Australasia and East Asia were able to enjoy material wealth, in terms of access to abundant food and consumer goods, pensions, employment prospects, education and health care, far in excess of anything their predecessors could have envisaged in the first half of the twentieth century. Yet this prosperity existed alongside widening inequality between the world's richest and poorest citizens, a gap measurable not just in terms of income but also in terms of life expectancy and vulnerability to disease. By 2002 European men could expect to live until they were 74.9 years old and European women could anticipate 81.2 years. But in Africa the average life span for both sexes was 48, a figure that represented a fall of 15 years in two decades, caused by poverty and war, and by the spread of AIDS. This epidemic had infected over 28 million Africans and was advancing at the rate of 9,000 cases per day.[1] In the worst-hit countries, in sub-Saharan Africa, life expectancy was already less than 40.[2] Africa as a continent had not shared in the spread of prosperity – an experience it had in common with large parts of Latin America, although here the setbacks to living standards were by no means so catastrophic.

This tragic situation was a function of the third fundamental feature of the international economic system: the rules governing trade and financial transactions were unfair. They had been devised by the wealthy nations and the institutions they dominated – the GATT, the WTO and the IMF in particular. During the last 20 years of the century these agencies had been more responsive to the call of western governments and multinational capital than they had to the less developing countries. The result had been a financial regime that subordinated national development programmes to the whims of the international financial markets and a set of rules governing trade and investment that denied export markets and cheap drugs to Third World countries while opening up their markets to foreign ownership.

The fourth significant attribute of the global economy by the end of the twentieth century was its instability. The catastrophic potential of liberalized capital markets had been revealed in the 1998–9 financial crisis. This systemic flaw became the subject of much discussion thereafter, but action was slow in coming, and the vulnerability of the world to a major economic shock began to rise after 2000, a function of the growing US deficit with the rest of the world, which by 2002 was not far from running at 5 per cent of the GDP. The imbalance meant that the USA was sucking in imports from other industrialized nations and therefore sustaining international economic growth. But there were two problems. First, the dollars earned by the countries in surplus with the USA were deposited in banks. Some of these were within the domestic banking systems of the surplus countries and they used the dollars as the basis for credit creation. The credit drove investment in those industries whose output (cars, consumer goods, electronics, telecommunications) sold well in the American market, but in so doing it contributed to the overproduction of these commodities, which had helped to drive the merger wave of the 1990s. The dollars could also be placed in international banks and funds, so contributing to the potential for volatile capital flows that already existed as a result of financial liberalization.

The next difficulty stemmed from the size of the US deficit, running at a rate of $1 million per minute. This could only be sustained by vigorous consumer spending which, however, slowed in 2001 in response to the collapse of the dotcom bubble and a series of high-profile financial scandals involving leading corporations. Stock market values fell sharply as the economy entered a cyclical downturn. Lost or depreciated savings checked the rise in private spending and in 2001 imports actually fell by $79 billion (6.3 per cent), setting off a decline in economic growth in all the major trading partners of the USA.[3] A return to Reaganomics – increases in military spending and tax cuts – helped to stimulate more robust expansion in 2002 but the need for some adjustment (in other words, for consumer spending to fall more in line with income) remained. Its arrival would export deflation to the rest of the world and in so doing would compound the problems of spare capacity arising from overproduction. Could the US Treasury and Federal Reserve postpone the reckoning long enough for growth in other nations to become so buoyant that the contribution to it of the US market would shrink, relative to the contribution of European or Asian markets, without causing a downturn?

The fifth key feature of the world economy at the turn of the century was the collapse of consensus about the rules by which it was supposed to operate. The key events were the demise of the MAI negotiations and the international financial crisis of 1998–9. The former sparked off a crisis for the campaign for world trade liberalization, exposing it as far as many less developing countries were concerned as an exercise in hypocrisy by the industrialized powers. The latter undermined the hegemony of neo-liberal economics; it was impossible to argue that *laissez-faire* generated growth, development, efficiency, stability and just-ice after a roll-call of disaster that included Thailand, South Korea, Indonesia, Russia and Brazil. The IMF accepted that it had made mistakes in dealing with these countries – notably in its advocacy of contractionary economic policies – however, it did not repudiate its support for freedom of capital flows, the advice of economists and the successful interventionism of Malaysia and China notwithstanding. On the other hand the Fund did support a campaign in the United Nations and in the G7 in favour of a new mechanism for debt relief and national bankruptcy.

Unfortunately, efforts to introduce a bankruptcy procedure for debtor countries ran into opposition on the part of US banks. These had lobbied the US Treasury for 'collective action clauses', which prevented creditors from holding out for full repayment of debts when others had settled for a writing down of the original loan's value. It was a strategy that would allow for the continuation of the bail-out packages of the past. What one commentator called 'welfare on Wall Street' was preferable to a restructuring exercise likely to involve substantial reductions in the debt owed to private creditors. In mid-April 2003 it was reported that the US government had decided to go with the banks, in the face of opinion throughout the G7 and the LDCs.[4] Although the neo-liberal synthesis had collapsed, an agreement on an agenda for international financial reform that stood some chance of implementation seemed distant given the tendency of the USA, the IMF, the G7 and the less developed economies to pull in different directions.

It was difficult to see where the international economy was heading. There were three scenarios. One involved the revival of neo-liberalism. On the face of it, this appears an unlikely turn given what has happened in the world economy since 1998. But the reaction of the USA to the events of 11 September 2001 involved a reassertion of American military power on an international scale not seen since the height of the Cold War. Operations in Afghanistan and Iraq established a US presence in Central Asia and gave what was now the world's only superpower the opportunity to dominate the Middle East. This was all done in the name of the 'war against terror' in general and against Islamic fundamentalism in particular. But ideology and economics followed the expansion of US influence: the reconstruction of Iraq was to revolve around 'free markets' and good business for American corporations; there was a liberal component to the 'Plan Colombia', designed to fight the revolutionary FARC (Revolutionary Armed Forces of Colombia). The war against terror inevitably became a struggle for capitalism against groups and in countries where its presence was weak or challenged. At Doha in November 2001 Washington explicitly identified success in the WTO's drive for open markets as 'an antidote to the terrorists' "violent rejectionism"'.[5] Since the US government envisaged no end to the fight and since, unlike in the Cold War, there was no politico-economic bloc capable of resisting its expansion, it was possible that the neo-liberal revolution would be given a new lease of life with the backing of US state power.

The second scenario involved the persistence of the trend away from neo-liberalism, but no alternative politico-economic project to replace it. Instead, with the trade negotiations for a new round of liberalization at stalemate it was likely that the world would drift slowly towards an era of unplanned protectionism. There was already considerable evidence for such a movement in the policies of the EU and the USA (free-market rhetoric notwithstanding). It was a prospect that meant the poorest nations would continue to struggle to find export markets while the wealthier countries would continue to press for open markets in the Third World and start to draw themselves into regional groupings at the same time. The seeds of such a development were present in the North Atlantic Free Trade Area, the EU, now with its own single currency, the euro, and in the 1997 creation of an Asian Monetary Fund to provide Asian economies in financial difficulty with rescue packages designed to generate reflation rather than contraction. The existence of these organizations remained compatible with liberal capitalism, given the scale of international co-operation between governments and corporations in the developed world, but it also pointed to the possibility of globalization fragmenting into powerful economic blocs.

Finally, there was the possibility that the global economy might embrace rules that promoted justice in relations between the rich and the poor nations. A start had been made with the achievements of the Jubilee campaign. Moreover, following the United Nations millennium summit in 2000 there was international agreement on a set of targets: the Millennium Development Goals (MDGs). These covered a wide field, including poverty eradication, the establishment of universal primary education, gender equality, reduction of child mortality, the improvement of maternal health, the campaign against AIDS, malaria and other diseases, and environmental stability. They included the creation of a 'global partnership for development' involving open trade, technology transfer, debt reduction and access to essential drugs at prices affordable in developing countries.

The British government identified a funding gap of $100 billion a year; without this money it was unlikely that the MDGs would be reached by the target date of 2015. To this end, London launched its International Finance Facility (IFF) initiative, which was intended to lever the dollars out of the rich countries through the issue of bonds. The IFF would then distribute the proceeds to the poor countries through grants and concessional loans. Negotiations started early in 2003.[6] Other proposals for the redistribution of the world's wealth included reform of the IMF and the World Bank. The former should become what Keynes had originally intended it to be – a mechanism that allowed countries to sustain expansionary policies even when they were in debt. The latter should support more egalitarian social policies in developing countries and at the same time encourage the creation of export-oriented enterprise rather than the opening of their economies to imports. Both should drop 'conditionality' – in reality, a vehicle for neo-liberalism.[7]

The possibility that justice may come cannot be dismissed. There is much intergovernmental support for the proposed reforms, especially the IFF. The World Bank has started to follow some of the recommendations made by informed critics such as Stiglitz. The size of the 'anti-globalization movements' and the genuinely international popular backing for organizations such as the World Social Forum all make it clear that the creation of an international economic order based on equity had a higher profile at the start of the new century than at any time since the launching of the Brandt Report. Will this latest enthusiasm go the same way as the Report? Given the latest turn in US policy and the strength of the forces supporting mercantilist trade policies in the advanced industrial nations, such a fate must be a real possibility. If so, the gap between the world's rich and poor will continue to widen.

◆ Notes

1. 'Life expectancy still falling in Africa', BBC News, 11 February 2002.
2. 'Aids sets life expectancy in Africa back 15 years', *The Advocate*, 13 February 2002.
3. Interview with Richard Duncan on *The Dollar Crisis: Causes Consequences Cures*, at www.business-in-asia.com/dollar_crisis.html.
4. 'US leaves Brown's aid plan in doubt', *Guardian*, 14 April 2003.
5. Naomi Klein, 'Doha, the economic frontline', *Guardian*, 8 November 2001.
6. HM Treasury and Department for International Development, *International Finance Facility* (London: HMSO, 2003).
7. Stiglitz, *Globalization and its Discontents*, 241–2.

SELECT BIBLIOGRAPHY

◆ Unpublished Sources

National Archives (Public Record Office, Kew, London)
Cabinet (Cab)
Economic Policy Committee (EPC)
Foreign Office (FO)
Treasury (T)

◆ Published Official Papers

HM Treasury, *Proposals for an International Clearing Union*, Cmd. 6437 (London: HMSO, 1943)

HM Treasury and Department for International Development, *International Finance Facility* (London: HMSO, 2003)

United Nations, Economic Commission for Europe, *Survey of the Economic Situation and Prospects of Europe* (United Nations: Geneva, 1948)

United Nations, Economic Commission for Europe, *Economic Survey of Europe since the War* (United Nations: Geneva, 1953)

United Nations, Economic Commission for Europe, *Economic Survey of Europe in 1954* (United Nations: Geneva, 1955)

United Nations, Economic Commission for Europe, *Economic Survey of Europe in 1960* (United Nations: Geneva, 1961)

United Nations, Economic Commission for Asia, *Economic Survey of Asia and the Far East in 1957* (United Nations: Geneva, 1958)

United States Department of State, *Foreign Relations of the United States* (Washington: United States Government Printing Office)

◆ Newspapers, Journals and Periodicals

Business Week
Economist
Guardian
London Review of Books
The Times
Washington Post

◆ Books and Articles

Anderson, Sarah and Cavanagh, John, *The Rise of Corporate Global Power* (London: Institute for Policy Studies, 2000)

Armstrong, Philip, Glyn, Andrew and Harrison, John, *Capitalism since 1945* (Oxford: Basil Blackwell, 1991)

Baran, Paul, *The Political Economy of Growth* (London: Penguin, 1978)

Baran, Paul and Sweezy, Paul, *Monopoly Capital: An Essay on the American Economic and Social Order* (London: Penguin, 1966)

Bello, Walden, *Dark Victory: The United States, Structural Adjustment and Global Poverty* (London: Pluto Press, 1994)

Berend, Ivan T., 'The collapse of state socialism', in David F. Good (ed.), *Economic Transformations in East and Central Europe* (London: Routledge, 1994), 75–92

Berghahn, Volker R., *Modern Germany: Society, Economy and Politics in the Twentieth Century*, 2nd edn. (Cambridge: Cambridge University Press, 1988)

Black, Stanley W. *A Levite among the Priests: Edward M. Bernstein and the Origins of the Bretton Woods Monetary System* (Boulder CO: Westview Press, 1991)

Block, Fred, *The Origins of International Monetary Disorder: A Study of United States International Monetary Policy from World War Two to the Present Day* (Berkeley: University of California Press, 1977)

Brandt Commission, *North–South: A Programme for Survival: The Report of the Independent Commission on International Development Issues Under the Chairmanship of Willy Brandt* (London: Pan Books, 1980)

Brenner, Robert, 'The economics of global turbulence', *New Left Review* 229 (1998)

Brett, E.A., *The World Economy since the War: The Politics of Uneven Development* (London: Macmillan, 1985)

Caufield, Catherine, *Masters of Illusion: The World Bank and the Poverty of Nations* (London: Pan Books, 1997)

Clarke, Sir Richard, *Anglo-American Economic Collaboration in War and Peace, 1942–49*, ed. Sir Alec Cairncross (Oxford: Clarendon Press, 1982)

Coakley, Jerry and Harris, Laurence, *The City of Capital: London's Role as an International Financial Centre* (Oxford: Basil Blackwell, 1983)

Dalton, Hugh, *High Tide and After* (London: Muller, 1962)

Diebold, William, *Trade and Payments in Western Europe: A Study in Economic Co-operation, 1947–1951* (New York: Harper & Rowe, 1952)

Ellwood, Wayne, *The No-Nonsense Guide to Globalization* (London and Oxford: Verso, 2001)

Etherington, Norman, *Theories of Imperialism: War, Conquest and Capital* (London and Canberra: Croom Helm, 1984)

Fairbank, J.K., Reischauer, Edwin O. and Craig, Albert M., *East Asia: The Modern Transformation* (London: George Allen & Unwin, 1965)

Foreman-Peck, James, *A History of the World Economy International Economic Relations since 1850* (Brighton: Harvester, 1983)

Foster, John Bellamy, 'Monopoly capital at the turn of the millennium', *Monthly Review* 51(11) (2000), 1–20

Foster, John Bellamy, Magdoff, Harry and Sweezy, Paul, 'The new economy: myth and reality', *Monthly Review* 52(11) (2001), 1–12

Galbraith, John Kenneth, *Economics and the Public Purpose* (London: Penguin, 1975)

Galbraith, John Kenneth, *The Affluent Society*, 2nd edn. (London: Penguin, 1977)

Gardner, Richard N., *Sterling–Dollar Diplomacy: Anglo-American Collaboration in the Reconstruction of Multilateral Trade* (New York: Columbia University Press, 1980)

Grosser, Alfred, *The Western Alliance* (London: Macmillan, 1980)

Harrod, R.F., *The Life of John Maynard Keynes* (London: Penguin, 1975)

Holland, Stuart, *The Socialist Challenge* (London: Quartet Books, 1975)

Hoogvelt, Ankie M.M., *The Third World in Global Development* (London: Macmillan, 1982)

Horsefield, J.K. (ed.), *The International Monetary Fund, 1945–66. I: Chronicle II: Analysis* (Washington DC: International Monetary Fund, 1969)

Kaldor, Mary, *The Disintegrating West* (London: Penguin, 1979)

Kaplan, Jacob J. and Schleiminger, Gunther, *The European Payments Union: Financial Diplomacy in the 1950s* (Oxford: Oxford University Press, 1989)

Kemp, Tom, *Industrialization in the Non-Western World* (London: Longman, 1983)

Keynes, John Maynard, *Collected Works of J.M. Keynes*, ed. D.E. Moggridge (London: Macmillan, 1971–89)

Keynes, John Maynard, *The General Theory of Employment, Interest and Money* (London: Macmillan, 1973 edn.; first published 1936)

Klein, Naomi, *No Logo* (London: Flamingo, 2002)

Kolko, Gabriel and Joyce, *The Limits of Power: The World and United States Foreign Policy, 1945–54* (New York: Harper & Rowe, 1972)

Krugman, Paul, *The Return of Depression Economics* (London: Penguin, 2000)

Kuznets, Simon, *Modern Economic Growth – Rate, Structure and Spread* (New Haven: Yale University Press, 1966)

Lebra, Joyce C. (ed.), *Japan's Greater East Asia Co-Prosperity Sphere in World War II* (Kuala Lumpur: Oxford University Press, 1975)

Lever, Harold and Huhne, Christopher, *Debt and Danger: The World Financial Crisis* (London: Penguin, 1985)

Lippgens, Walter, *A History of European Integration, 1945–47: The Formation of the European Unity Movement* (Oxford: Clarendon Press, 1982)

Little, I.M.D., *Economic Development* (New York: Basic Books, 1982)

Macdougall, G.D.A., *The World Dollar Problem: A Study in International Economics* (New York: St Martin's Press, 1957)

Maddison, Angus, *Dynamic Forces in Capitalist Development* (Oxford: Oxford University Press, 1991)

Magdoff, Harry, *The Age of Imperialism* (New York and London: Monthly Review Press, 1969)

Magdoff, Harry and Sweezy, Paul, *The Deepening Crisis of US Capitalism* (New York and London: Monthly Review Press, 1981)

Mazower, Mark, *Dark Continent: Europe's Twentieth Century* (London: Penguin, 1999)

Mikesell, Raymond F., *The Bretton Woods Debates: A Memoir* (Princeton: Princeton Essays in International Finance, No. 192, March 1994)

Mills, C. Wright, *The Power Elite* (New York: Oxford University Press, 1956)

Milward, Alan S., 'French labour and the German economy, 1942–45: an essay on the nature of the fascist new order', *Economic History Review*, 2nd series, XXIII(2) (1970), 336–51

Milward, Alan S., *The New Order and the French Economy* (Oxford: Oxford University Press, 1970)

Milward, Alan S., *The Reconstruction of Western Europe, 1945–51* (London: Methuen, 1984)

Milward, Alan S., *War, Economy and Society, 1939–1945* (London: Penguin, 1987)

Milward, Alan S., *The European Rescue of the Nation-State*, 2nd edn. (London: Routledge, 2000)

Moggridge, D.E., *Maynard Keynes: An Economist's Biography* (London: Routledge, 1992)

Newton, Scott, 'The sterling crisis of 1947 and the British response to the Marshall Plan', *Economic History Review*, 2nd series, XXXVII (1984), 391–408

Newton, Scott, 'A "visionary hope" frustrated: J.M. Keynes and the origins of the postwar international monetary order', *Diplomacy and Statecraft*, Vol. 11 (2000), 189–210

Newton, Scott, 'Deconstructing Harrod: some reflections on the life of John Maynard Keynes, *Contemporary British History* 15 (2001)

Newton, Scott and Porter, Dilwyn, *Modernization Frustrated: The Politics of Industrial Decline in Britain since 1900* (London: Unwin Hyman, 1988)

Palast, Greg, *The Best Democracy Money Can Buy* (London and Sterling, VA: Pluto Press, 2002)

Pollard, Sidney, *The Development of the British Economy, 1914–1990* (London: Edward Arnold, 1992)

Pollard, Sidney, *The International Economy since 1945* (London: Routledge, 1997)

Raghavan, Chakravarthi, *Recolonisation: GATT, the Uruguay Round and the Third World* (London and New Jersey: Zed Books, 1990)

Rowthorne, Bob, 'Imperialism in the 1970s – unity or rivalry', in Hugo Radice (ed.), *International Firms and Modern Imperialism* (London: Penguin, 1975), 158–80.

Scammell, W.M., *The International Economy since 1945* (London: Macmillan, 1983)

Shonfield, Andrew, *British Economic Policy Since the War* (London: Penguin, 1958)

Shonfield, Andrew (ed.), *International Economic Relations of the Western World, 1959–1971. I: Politics and Trade* (London: Oxford University Press for the RIIA, 1976)

Siracusa, Joseph M. (ed.), *The American Diplomatic Revolution: A Documentary History of the Cold War 1941–1947* (Milton Keynes: Open University Press, 1978)

Solomon, Robert, *The International Monetary System, 1945–1976* (New York: Harper & Rowe, 1977)

Solomon, Robert, *The Transformation of the World Economy, 1980–93* (New York: St Martin's Press, 1994)

Stewart, Michael, *Keynes and After*, 2nd edn. (London: Penguin, 1975)

Stiglitz, Joseph, *Globalization and its Discontents* (London: Allen Lane, 2002)

Strange, Susan, *Casino Capitalism*, 2nd edn. (Manchester: Manchester University Press, 1997)

Strange, Susan, *International Economic Relations of the Western World, 1959–1971. II: International Monetary Relations*, ed. Andrew Shonfield (London: Oxford University Press for the RIIA, 1976)

Strange, Susan, *Mad Money* (Manchester: Manchester University Press, 1998)

Tew, Brian, *The Evolution of the International Monetary System, 1945–88* (London: Hutchinson, 1988)

Van der Pijl, Kees, *The Making of an Atlantic Ruling Class* (London: Verso, 1984)

Van der Wee, Herman, *Prosperity and Upheaval: The World Economy, 1945–1980* (London: Penguin, 1987)

Vasquez, Ian, 'The Brady Plan and market-based solutions to debt crises', *Cato Journal* 16(2) (1994)

Williams, William Appleman, *The Tragedy of American Diplomacy* (New York: W.W. Norton, 1988)

INDEX